T0279009

PRAISE FOR *AMERICAN CASTLE*

"An enthralling narrative of extreme American opulence and unforgettable characters set within Marjorie Merriweather Post's Mar-a-Lago. *American Castle* is the brilliantly detailed, must-read prologue to the estate's current chapter of excess and scandal."

—GILBERT KING, Pulitzer Prize–winning author of
*Devil in the Grove: Thurgood Marshall, the Groveland
Boys, and the Dawn of a New America*

"A history of a grand mansion and its numerous occupants. . . . A well-told story that's full of surprises, its storied subject generating headlines for a century."

—KIRKUS REVIEWS

"If you think Mar-a-Lago is just the site of corruption, espionage, and the attempted hiding of top-secret materials, think again. Mary Shanklin's riveting book is a thrilling deep dive into the property and its astounding history."

—DANIEL M. FREED, coauthor of *Call Me Commander:
A Former Intelligence Officer and the Journalists
Who Uncovered His Scheme to Fleece America*

"An entirely new perspective of the now world-famous Mar-a-Lago. The public tends to look at Mar-a-Lago as the residence of Donald Trump, without realizing that it once belonged to them as part of the National Park Service—and before that to one of the wealthiest and most compelling socialites in American history, Marjorie Merriweather Post. Bookended by the FBI search and Trump's arrest, *American Castle* is an opulent, lively history of Post's grand estate."

—TIM FRANKLIN, senior associate dean
of Northwestern University Medill School,
former president of the Poynter Institute

AMERICAN CASTLE

The Notorious Legacy of Mar-a-Lago

MARY C. SHANKLIN

DIVERSION
BOOKS

To my dear husband, Chris

Diversion Books
A division of Diversion Publishing Corp.
www.diversionbooks.com

For more information, email info@diversionbooks.com.

Originally published in hardcover by Diversion Books, September 2023
First trade paperback edition, October 2024
Hardcover ISBN: 978-1-63576-896-1
Trade Paperback ISBN: 978-1-63576-986-9
e-ISBN: 978-1-63576-963-0

Book design by Neuwirth & Associates, Inc.

Printed in The United States of America
1 3 5 7 9 10 8 6 4 2

Diversion books are available at special discounts for bulk purchases in
the US by corporations, institutions, and other organizations. For more
information, please contact admin@diversionbooks.com.

"Extinction is the rule. Survival is the exception."

—Carl Sagan

CONTENTS

PREFACE TO THE 2024 EDITION

In the spring of 2018, I stumbled upon a National Park Service forum about Donald Trump's Mar-a-Lago winter retreat in Palm Beach, Florida. At the time, it wasn't quite yet a household name, but it was quickly becoming one. News feeds were populated by images of heads of state shaking hands with President Trump and the First Lady amidst the opulence. Mar-a-Lago was gaining a reputation as a place where club members and guests could enjoy unfettered access to the top power of the Free World.

As a journalist who had long reported on Florida's real estate deals, I was interested in what the park service insiders had to say. The forum went on to mention an out-of-print book with a chapter detailing Mar-a-Lago's years in the National Park Service from the perspective of a high-level service administrator. The little thread of posts entreated: ". . . for a good read . . ." Hooked, I got a copy of *Our National Park System* by Dwight F. Rettie and realized the public was largely clueless about the fact that Americans once owned this place of privilege and exclusivity. The few who were aware seemed happy to write off the historic twist as fate intervening so that Mar-a-Lago could serve as a presidential residence.

The more I dug, the more stories I realized this palatial house could tell.

Combing through videos, diaries, and news stories, I learned about the six years of back-breaking construction work endured by hundreds of laborers who brought Mar-a-Lago to life—even in the shadow of devastating hurricanes. All of this happened in the Roaring Twenties.

Photographs and newspaper pages detailed a Palm Beach life-style gilded with parties, royalty, orchestras, and costume balls. With little humility, New and Old Money paraded their wealth for all to see in newspapers and magazines in a way that largely died with the Great Depression.

For four years, I picked through the records of four presidents. My research took me through Palm Beach's debut as a presidential winter retreat starting in 1960 with President Kennedy and an assassination attempt against him there. I listened to audio diaries of Lady Bird Johnson recounting her pivotal visit with an aging Marjorie Post. I examined the logs of Richard Nixon's helicopter touchdown on site with his friend Charles "Bebe" Rebozo during the final weeks of his presidency. Missives from the Gerald Ford and Jimmy Carter administrations further told a story of Mar-a-Lago's demise in the National Park Service. Sadly, even during Carter's last months, his Center was unable to convey the former president's thoughts on his role in purging the mansion from the federal government.

During all this period of research, I was fortunate my husband never asked me how much of a return I might get on this invest-ment of my time.

More than anything, I wanted to unearth the truth behind two popular notions:

1. The park service dropped Mar-a-Lago because it was too costly to maintain.
2. Mar-a-Lago was now serving the purpose that Marjorie Merriweather Post intended.

So many investigative trails stopped with knowledgeable sources who had died a few years earlier. But an interview with former Palm Beach congressman Dan Mica proved pivotal in casting the forces at work during the estate's final years in the park service.

Of all the research I did over the years, nothing could compare to my tour of this period of history. In my travels to places including the Biltmore in Asheville, North Carolina, and Catherine Palace near St. Petersburg, Russia, I have never seen anything like Mar-a-Lago's Thousand Wing Ceiling and lanterned reception hall. As Mrs. Johnson described after her visit there with Ms. Post: ". . . the last of the queens in a setting that probably will not continue or be duplicated in this country in the lifetime of my children."

While still in polished condition, the estate is not the same place as it was when Ms. Post held court there. A spa and other quarters sit where the carriage house had been. Seemingly endless planes fly overhead. The glittering ballroom and helipad are new. A bar area is decorated with an airbrushed-looking painting of a younger Donald Trump, wearing tennis garb. Next to that, a museum-quality portrait shows Mar-a-Lago's original owner wanly looking on.

In the years since I first spotted that chat in the National Park Service forum, I suppose my most interesting find was a 1995 National Trust for Historic Places easement signed by Mr. Trump. It called for limited public access to a few people who would not otherwise be allowed there. I saw it as a tiny crack in a monolithic door locked to most people. It's uncertain whether it will ever lead to any further public appreciation in years to come.

The one certainty is that all things change.

PROLOGUE

PILLORIED
AND PLUNDERED

I f there was anyone on the continent who hadn't yet heard of Mar-a-Lago in the summer of 2022, they would soon be educated. What would happen at this historic Florida estate would ignite Donald Trump loyalists and stoke the flames of civil unrest across the country.

But for now, a "serious situation" pressed Palm Beach.

Against the town's ardent pleas, the state of Florida plowed ahead with plans to paint the Royal Park Bridge later that year, during the height of South Florida's winter season.

Certainly no one of note remained at this latitude in August. But by January they would all be there—Sylvester Stallone, Rod Stewart, Howard Stern—driving their Range Rovers and Tesla Roadsters around Palm Beach only to hit a cardiac arrest of traffic. Appallingly, this painting project would intermittently block one of the two westbound lanes for months. If a hurricane targeted the island, off-season residents would be forced either to wait their turn to cross the bridge or drive a few extra miles to one of the other bridges connecting the island to the real world.

The mayor had a word for the state's timing—*untenable*. Wildfires were ravaging the West. Dozens had just died in Kentucky flash floods. Other towns contended with not just paint-chipped bridges but compromised ones. In most cities across the country, entire regional highway systems choked daily at rush hour. But, here in Palm Beach, make no mistake: Wealthy winter residents faced the prospect of a major inconvenience due to this poorly timed bridge painting.

The town's reputation was on the line. One official said the Town Council could be "ridden out of town on a rail if we don't do our utmost against this." Even though some might dismiss the brouhaha as minutiae, was anything more important than appearances—well, anything other than family trust funds?

Just a few years earlier, the town might have sidestepped a political fight of this nature. But everything changed when part-time Palm Beacher Donald Trump became president of the United States. Since then, the exclusive enclave too often woke to congestion and the glare of the national spotlight. Perspiring correspondents from all the media outlets, mainstream to fringe, descended upon the town at every turn. Local news that used to interest only the "Shiny Sheet"—officially known as the *Palm Beach Daily News*—was national news. The world now read about everything from Palm Beach's "Impeachment Now" billboards to its club memberships and celebrity galas.

With the impending shutdown of a lane of the Royal Park Bridge, townspeople girded themselves for the inevitable headlines—"Golden Gridlock," "Parked in Palm Beach," and "Billionaires Blocked."

When Trump became president in 2016 and turned his Mar-a-Lago Club into the unofficial Winter White House, the town navigated the fishbowl effect. Eyes from around the world watched local police pull over vehicles along South Ocean Boulevard, spied

Coast Guard boats patrol Lake Worth, and leered at camera crews setting up near the presidential retreat.

Even the very embodiment of Palm Beach grandeur—Mar-a-Lago—had changed its personality during its presidential era. Outside the estate's arched coquina walls, American-branded pickup trucks paraded past with Trump flags flapping in homage. Trump disciples wearing MAGA baseball hats starred as protagonists against a backdrop of protesters brandishing signs like: "Keep your tiny hands off my rights." Inside its iron-grill front door, the Mar-a-Lago Club became a jackpot for the Trump Organization, doubling fees and charging a quarter of a million dollars for the chance to party in a Trump-era ballroom decorated with a glitzy wall relief the color of a gold tooth.

At galas, the staid ranks of Palm Beach now bumped up against the red, white, and yellowed socialite cheerleaders known as the Trumpettes. Mar-a-Lago's lavish halls, envisioned a century earlier by American philanthropist Marjorie Merriweather Post, had now been transformed into a "gliterati" parlor for backroom deals. The Mar-a-Lago Trio, a group of three businessmen plotting to profit off the Department of Veterans Affairs, patronized the commander in chief as members of his home-turf club and then attempted to take over the department, according to the House Committee on Oversight. The dinners once dominated by old money now revolved around dealmakers and opportunists.

How did this hamlet so lacquered in grace and elegance come to find itself rooted in controversy? How, in fact, did Palm Beach's most famous manse become the chew toy for headline writers at New York tabloids: "Nobody wants to host events at Trump's resort," "Japanese prime minister lucky he didn't get sick eating at Mar-a-Lago," "Trump's Mar-a-Lago club to partially reopen—with social distancing in the Jacuzzi." They wrote of Chinese spies, a child pornographer, and would-be bombers all drawn to this manse where royals had dined.

But those embarrassments were just the mere opening lines of what would become an unimaginable drama in this nation's history. What unfolded next for Mar-a-Lago's chief resident was a series of events that would divide the entire country. Midway into the nation's forty-fifth presidential administration, New York prosecutors bore down on the business dealings of that state's most famous resident. The Queens native turned his back on his lifelong Big Apple home. More than a year before he was banned from Twitter, then-president Trump announced on the social media platform:

> My family and I will be making Palm Beach, Florida, our permanent residence. I cherish New York, and the people of New York and always will, but unfortunately, despite the fact that I pay millions of dollars in city, state and local taxes each year, I have been treated very badly by the political leaders of both the city and state.

Air Force One flew the Trumps to their adopted Sunshine State home, staking their identity to this monster of a house stubbornly surviving atop a bed of coral. Trump declared it as his new primary residence. It was a king's castle with more rooms than New York has museums. It was his rightful place to hold court. There was no mention of Florida's lack of income tax in this change of address. It was simply that Floridians appreciated his leadership, intelligence, and even the very magnetism he exuded. The people of this Republican-controlled state clearly championed him.

Of course, there are always a few malcontents. One neighbor filed a complaint protesting Trump's permanent residency on the grounds that it would devalue property. And the Town Council had to review whether he could even live there, as the Mar-a-Lago Club wasn't intended for permanent residents.

Admittedly, Trump had butted heads with locals before—erecting an oversized flag and flagpole that violated codes and suing the town for allowing airport traffic so excessive that it harmed the very roof tiles over his head. But those matters were all in the past. Things seemed to have settled down in the oppressively hot days of late summer 2022. Palm Beach's presidential resident wasn't president anymore. The council could direct its attention to things of real import, like the anticipated traffic fiasco during the paint job on Royal Park Bridge.

As officials stewed over the bridge contract, something else began to stir on the island. What was quietly taking shape on South Ocean Boulevard in the midmorning hours of August 8, 2022, would overshadow any headlines Palm Beachers had seen about their town and its flagship residence. This place that had survived untold pressures over the decades was now about to become a crime scene the likes of which this country had never seen.

AMERICAN CASTLE

CHAPTER 1

A CAPITOL DAY

The air in Washington, DC, was the kind of January chill that numbs your nostrils and punches a cold blow to your throat. Fogged breath spewed from the mouths of the few people outside. Some seemed to bounce up the stairs of the Capitol that sixteenth day of January, 1969, as though carried by the wind. On the other side of groaning entry doors, polished floors echoed with the thuds of dress shoes on the tile. The etched walls of the Rotunda hummed with indistinct conversations that drifted between idle chatter about the upcoming weekend to a host of new environmental policies to next week's inauguration of a new president.

Behind the doors of congressional offices, phones rang on staffers' desks, and aides sliced open letters from mothers, fathers, and others demanding answers. Why was the Vietnam War continuing to claim American lives? Why was there no resolution after almost four years of conflict? Why were we making the ultimate sacrifice for a seemingly insignificant country?

The Paris peace talks had been dragging on for eight months with no end in sight. Stress from the war bore down on politicians and bureaucrats. Every night, television fueled Americans' anger as Walter Cronkite ticked off the daily tally of casualties. The starched collars of the nation's political elite, meanwhile, tightened just a little more.

Compounding tensions, the country seemed wavering in its space battle after the Soviet Union had just docked two manned spacecraft in orbit. Race relations combusted as Olympic sprinters Tommie Smith and John Carlos raised fists in a Black Power salute during their Mexico City awards ceremony. And months after Bobby Kennedy had been gunned down at a rally in California, Richard Nixon launched a divisive campaign that played to White, working-class Americans.

"And that's the way it is," Cronkite summed it up.

But just a few miles from the mounting anxieties that permeated the Capitol, sunlight glanced into the offices of the Department of the Interior. Deep inside, a thick-browed, buzz-cut lawyer was wrapping up his eight-year command of the nation's prized assets—its public lands. Stewart Udall had only days left of an eight-year stint running the Interior.

On that January afternoon in 1969, Udall saw no new initiatives or emerging battles. First appointed by President John F. Kennedy to serve in 1961 and then again by President Lyndon Johnson, the Interior secretary, who was sometimes called "Stu," had built a legacy by preserving millions of acres with the Wilderness Act of 1964. He contributed to natural resource protections with the Land and Water Conservation Fund Act of 1965. He helped establish the Water Quality Act of 1965, the Endangered Species Preservation Act of 1966, and the Wild and Scenic Rivers Act of 1968. Even the first federal bicycle paths and pedestrian trails emerged under his watch.

The architect of those preservation efforts was about to depart the courtyard-view offices that were just a two-minute stroll to the National Mall. While the rest of Washington wrung its collective hands over the nation's heightening unrest, the former Arizona congressman packed up to make way for President Nixon's appointee replacing him as head of the Department of the Interior. It was time to get out of the way.

One of Udall's last remaining tasks contrasted with his record of preserving mountains, rivers, and seashores. The vanguard of the National Historic Preservation Act of 1966 was about to sign an order aimed at salvaging an aging icon of America's industrial wealth.

A South Florida oceanfront estate teetered on the brink of extinction. Owned by longtime Democratic patroness Marjorie Merriweather Post, this relic of the 1920s faced a bleak future. Post's heirs didn't want it. A new class of social elite preferred jets, yachts, and racehorses over high-maintenance albatrosses filled with their parents' rococo trimmings.

Mar-a-Lago, as it was called, wasn't the only grand residence built with the audacity of pre-Depression wealth. But many of the estate's peers had been crushed out of existence by New Yorkers who pined for new seaside villas, even when it meant destroying the storied mansions that were there first. Developers eyed Mar-a-Lago and its seventeen acres as a prime candidate for demolition, dissection, and redevelopment.

Grab, chop up, and build anew was the mantra for prized pieces of property across the country and particularly on a tropical peninsula that drew monied Northerners like human flesh draws mosquitoes.

Reflecting on his time overseeing the Interior Department, Udall knew a statement of wealth like Mar-a-Lago could never be replicated. What did the name mean? Oh, yes—"sea to lake," because it banked the Atlantic Ocean on one side and part of the Intracoastal Waterway called Lake Worth on the other.

Not only was the land unique, but the residential monument built atop it was also an endangered species. Constructed on a coral reef forty years earlier, Mar-a-Lago was built by the calloused, scarred hands of an estimated six hundred workers who suffered through South Florida's dripping humidity for three years. At the time, cheap manpower was the construction model of the day. Hard labor muscled Mar-a-Lago and a handful of other American castles into existence in a way that was no longer cost-effective. Architects and craftsmen assembled a residential showcase befitting the royals who would visit there. The talents behind the manse's famed tiles and elegant carvings were long gone.

Unlike other sites that had won national landmark status, this ode to Roaring Twenties excess stood primarily as a memorial to the bygone lifestyles of American opulence.

Secretary Udall was also keenly aware that Mar-a-Lago wasn't mentioned in the pages of American history books as a place where Revolutionary War generals strategized or presidents convened. And with interiors by former Ziegfeld Follies designer Joseph Urban, the architecture drew mixed reviews. But Mar-a-Lago begged salvation in a different way.

The landmark stood as a symbol of the country's self-made hubris. It was forged by something as homespun as cereal sales.

Mar-a-Lago's backstory was rooted in a start-up breakfast food company: An invalid father experimented with oats and barley recipes until he struck upon the Postum energy beverage. C. W. Post then embraced marketing and his sole child helped him with his production efforts. His daughter would later leverage the Postum Cereal Company into General Foods.

At the end of the sixties, as the nation reeled from a war on the opposite side of the globe, was there a better story to rally its citizens? Were there many other places in the country that so captured the spirit of all America could be?

Bankrolled by cereal profits, Mar-a-Lago stood as a testament to the American spirit of triumph and success. The architectural wonder was an antidote to a bleak international landscape. If any story could spark some patriotism during this time of national discord, this was it.

Okay, so it wasn't the purple mountain majesties of the West, but the Mar-a-Lago acquisition into the National Park Service made logistical sense. The bulk of America lived in the East and could drive their children to a prime example of what ingenuity and hard work can accomplish.

Really, Udall and Johnson were only salvaging the place after Florida had bungled the job. Post heirs shunned the idea of taking on the sixty-thousand-square-foot winter residence. So, six years earlier, the queen of the Post family had lobbied Florida politicians to preserve her residential icon and use it for educational seminars and high-level meetings of state officials.

The deal had legs. Governor Farris Bryant appointed an advisory committee headed by Florida State University president Emeritus Doak Campbell "to plan to acquire the mansion." Also on the powerhouse acquisition team: Tampa attorney Cody Fowler, known for his work desegregating White-only lunch counters, and Circuit Judge James R. Knott, who advocated public access to the halls and grounds of Mar-a-Lago.

They even had a name—the Mar-a-Lago Center for Advanced Scholars.

Publicly, Florida officials rejected the treasure due to the high costs of keeping up the behemoth. When Governor Bryant inquired about Mar-a-Lago's maintenance bills, Post cited the annual upkeep costs, but a quarter-million-dollar expense was probably a little pricey for a sleepy state just starting to awaken from its agrarian roots. Citrus still ruled the economy there. Walt Disney had not waved his magic wand to transform citrus groves and swamps into theme park attractions. Even Florida's space industry was in its infancy, with Floridians gushing about the 1962 launching of *Friendship 7* from Cape Canaveral, propelling John Glenn around the earth.

Certainly, maintenance costs were a consideration, but the state was no stranger to them. Florida had just a year earlier acquired a ten-acre estate near the Gulf Coast of the state's Panhandle. And it had long ago acquired other properties laden with overhead.

Pressures other than upkeep were at play, according to the state's leading political newspaper. The *Tallahassee Democrat* reported in the summer of 1965 that the elite residents of Palm Beach derailed the idea over concerns that their island would become, well, a little less special with the prospect of buses, events, and crowds.

Negotiations fell through when Mrs. Post's Palm Beach neighbors vigorously opposed her plans, which they said would threaten the exclusivity of the resort.

In the end, the aging cereal baroness walked away from Tallahassee, Florida, with an honorary state citizenship. Instead of accepting the gift of Mar-a-Lago, the governor bestowed an empty title on Post and thanked her for her "warm-hearted generosity and sympathetic dedication to human needs and human betterment."

Sitting at his desk in the Interior Department headquarters that cool January afternoon, Udall knew Mar-a-Lago's history. As caretaker of America's treasures, he recognized the government channels the rich navigated to get their way. Why, even he had frequented Post's place in the Adirondacks.

Marjorie Merriweather Post, the premier hostess of Palm Beach social circles, had invited Lady Bird Johnson and National Park Service Director George Hartzog Jr. for a tour. The First Lady, her secretary, and seven others relaxed as Post entertained them for several days just last year.

"The last of the queens." That's how Lady Bird described her hostess, showing grace and charm as she oversaw an "exquisite" meal on the terrace. The only thing lacking, the First Lady said, was conversation with Post, who couldn't hear well.

Lady Bird called it "that beautiful never-never land." She stayed in Deenie's house—the fairy-tale suite where Post's youngest daughter spent much of her childhood. Post walked the First Lady and her entourage through every inch of the house, reciting the origin of every piece, collectible object, and artifact.

The grande dame couldn't afford a repeat of the Florida fiasco. In hopes of wooing Congress to consummate a Mar-a-Lago deal, a Post protégé invited members of the House Interior Committee— and their wives—to stay at the historic oceanfront casa. The party enjoyed a dinner given in their honor by Post. She toured them through the mansion and encouraged them to play the nine-hole golf course and climb the stairs leading to the seventy-five-foot-tall tower.

The plan worked. Representative Wayne Aspinall, chairman of the House Committee on Interior and Insular Affairs, was smitten.

Now, as the Johnson administration neared its end, mounting uncertainties loomed for Mar-a-Lago. A former real estate developer was about to take Udall's place at the Interior Department. Nixon had appointed Walter Joseph "Wally" Hickel to take over stewardship of federal lands and resources. The self-made entrepreneur had earned a reputation for building subdivisions, apartments, hotels, and shopping centers in his adopted state of Alaska. How the construction magnate would view Mar-a-Lago's waterfront acreage, one could only guess.

With bulging files marking the end of the administration, it was apparent that no one else would rescue this throwback to another era. Without the Interior Department stepping in, gone would be this American castle known for entertaining royalty and heads of state.

Udall determined that the last vestiges of the Kennedy-Johnson era would finalize the job that Florida could not. Udall would cap off his federal service by securing for the country a national park property like no other. The public would now come to understand the makings and the perseverance of this monumental estate. Florida, with its growing population, would get a gem in the National Park Service's collection. And Mar-a-Lago itself could serve for generations to enlighten the public with a fast-vanishing chapter of American history that would otherwise be bulldozed for underlying land that stood fertile enough to sprout developers' plans.

Udall penned the agreement on that warming January 16, 1969, morning: Mar-a-Lago would forever be saved for all of America to enjoy and learn from.

In that moment of sealing Mar-a-Lago's fate, Udall and his staff understood how they came to this place. What they could not know were the personal tragedies that had shaped one of the most celebrated estates in the country. Neither could they grasp the full bore of pressures and near misses that 1100 South Ocean Boulevard had somehow endured.

All they could know was that now, at last, this landmark would be protected in perpetuity. Indeed, even with the rest of the nation gripped by unrest, this was a fine January morning in at least one corner of the capital.

CHAPTER 2

DEATH'S DOOR

US intelligence knew about the deaths. Overseas, tens of thousands of American soldiers had been dying near the end of World War I, not from gunshots or explosives, but from a strain of the flu.

Spanish influenza led to a quick but punishing death when patients turned blue and suffocated from a lack of oxygen as their lungs filled with a bloody substance.

Scientists at the time were vexed by the world of viral transmissions and treatments. With limited vaccines to protect against flu-virus infections, no effective antiviral drugs to treat the illness, and no antibiotics to combat secondary bacterial infections like pneumonia, Spanish influenza usually meant the death sentence.

Leading into the Christmas season of 1917, health officials downplayed news of the deadly influenza strain. Better to pump up wartime morale. Communications about the severity and spread of the disease had been hushed.

In New York City in those early days of winter, a rainstorm engulfed city streets and sidewalks that soon hid under sheeting ice. It was the kind of winter that old-timers liked to talk about (at least, in past tense).

Just months before, thousands of New Yorkers stood in the streets waving flags and applauding a parade of soldiers and National Guardsmen before they shipped off to France. Patriotism, sacrifice, and austerity defined the shape of the days after the United States declared war on the German Empire. Flags were the gift of the year, and families shipped every manner of parcels to any soldier for whom they had an address. Americans sent so many books, magazines, and foodstuffs to the troops that Adjutant General of the Army Henry Pinckney McCain called for a stop. Soldiers wrote home saying: Send no more. "One corner of our barracks is piled up with magazines from all over the United States," Army soldier Salvator Cillis, an Italian immigrant, wrote in one letter. "All over the camp have shelves filled with books of every description, newspapers and more magazines. So you see we have plenty of reading matter."

In her stylish home just a few blocks from the iced-over ponds in Central Park, Blanche Hutton had just celebrated the last birthday of her thirties. It would be a festive yuletide for her and her family. Her husband's banking business was prospering, and their teenage son was showing the kind of academics and athletics to get into a top university—if he kept up his studies. Perhaps during the holidays, they would spend a few days at their retreat just two hours away in Bay Shore, Long Island. The boys could hunt pheasant, and she could enjoy the countryside.

Things had turned out well for them. Her father had first introduced her to Edward Francis "E. F." Hutton at the turn of the century. Both were investment bankers; her father and Hutton had worked next door to each other on Broadway. The young man lacked quite the pedigree of some of her New York courtiers, but he showed tenacity by parlaying mechanic work and mailroom duties at a stock company into a finance career.

Life really took off for them when her husband joined forces with his brother, Franklyn, to forge their own investment group. Now they ran in the same circles with J. P. Morgan and Ned Stotesbury. Of course, when Blanche's own father died two years earlier, he left them an entire block of prime real estate next to Carnegie Hall. The collection of two-story buildings was fat with tenants, including the acclaimed Yellow Aster Tea Room. Well, that helped too.

Yes, even though so many young American men—boys, really—were fighting overseas, this Christmas could still be special. A little flu bug might set her back, but it wouldn't derail their celebration of the holiday season.

Then, a week before Christmas, Blanche Horton Hutton died. One day contemplating the upcoming holiday, the next in a fast and irreversible death spiral. A short notice in the *San Francisco Chronicle* attributed her seemingly instantaneous demise to pneumonia, a sickness that usually clears up in a few weeks for people in their thirties.

"Mrs. Hutton had been ill only a few days," the piece read.

During the ensuing months, hundreds of thousands of otherwise healthy Americans would suddenly die a similar death as the influenza pandemic spread to a public that had been left in the dark.

Unlike the more common strains, the Spanish flu claimed an unusually high mortality rate among healthy people even in their twenties and thirties. By the time it was over, Americans' life expectancy dropped by a dozen years, to less than thirty-seven years for men and forty-two years for women.

For the Huttons, the once-promising holiday season had blackened overnight. With Blanche's death, a Wall Street rising star stood widowed and with full responsibility for his fifteen-year-old son. While Hutton might have found solace in his brother / business partner, the elder sibling had his own problems.

Franklyn Hutton had been at the family summer home on the south shore of Long Island when he got the call. His wife of a decade, Edna Woolworth Hutton, was found dead at age thirty-three in her apartment at the Plaza Hotel. Early reports cited suffocation due to chronic ear disease. There was no autopsy. Researchers and family members later reported the heir to the Woolworth fortune had been distraught over her husband's infidelity and committed suicide, only to be found by the couple's six-year-old daughter, Barbara.

Guilt, mourning, and depression all lay in the wake of a spouse's suicide. For the Hutton brothers, this was not their first encounter with the darkness of loss. They had barely sprouted chest hairs when they lost their dad. Hoping for a better life, James Laws Hutton had moved from an Ohio farm to New York, but died at age thirty-seven, leaving behind three young children and a widow.

There were bills, groceries, and rent demanding attention, but their main breadwinner was gone. As teens, the Hutton boys worked manual labor jobs to help out at home. They learned early how to prevail even as the world turned upside down.

The sudden loss of both their wives left them, once again, sorting out their lives. By this time, though, they had assets. While E. F. Hutton would get the prime New York properties that had belonged to his wife, Frank's trove from Edna included a marquise diamond ring and an emerald ring encrusted in diamonds. In addition to leaving behind hundreds of thousands of dollars and no will, she also left valuables including a Louis XVI parlor set, silver, and a pair of Chinese vases.

And despite the crippling personal losses, the Hutton brothers continued building their business into the dawn of the 1920s.

The war was over. Opportunities abounded for enrichment, if you were smart. The Hutton brothers pioneered some of the first stock-trading offices on the West Coast. In the summers, the two widowers rolled into the tony New York town of Saratoga

Springs, where thousands of gamblers gathered to bet on horse races.

Winter brought them to Palm Beach, which was becoming fat with speculators mining the profits of buying and quickly reselling property. As the Hutton duo could see, the beach-lined island town hugging Florida's southeast coast was a magnet for monied winter vacationers who could benefit from their advice. Even with their studied approach to this new enclave, they could not have foreseen how it would change their lives and eventually reorder the axis of political power for the entire country.

The very existence of Mar-a-Lago—and everything it would come to signify—could be traced back in part to E. F. Hutton's decision to explore Palm Beach and all that the budding enclave for the elite had to offer.

Shortly after Valentine's Day 1920, the widower rented the houseboat *Dorinda* in Palm Beach for the rest of the winter social season.

Meanwhile, in town to escape the freezing temperatures of Manhattan and Greenwich, Connecticut, divorcée Marjorie Merriweather Post accepted an invitation to a party aboard a vessel that had been anchored off the shore of Palm Beach. Not much is known about the night but, when she stepped aboard, she could have no way of knowing that the next few hours of her life would set the course for new family, riches, and one of the grandest estates the country had ever seen. That moment would undoubtedly be charged by the electricity of reacquainting with a dashing, dynamic, and newly widowed man. That first touch of skin could not foretell the parties, revelry, and also the heartbreak to follow.

How had this union first sparked—and on a houseboat in Palm Beach, of all places? In at least some ways, it made sense.

Her father had taken her to the Florida shore from an early age. The once-desolate landscape of Palm Beach became a winter haven for wealthy families. Railroading pioneer Henry M. Flagler opened what would become the world's largest resort, the Royal Poinciana Hotel, with three miles of corridors and accommodations for thousands of guests. Visitors delighted in the private train cars that ran from a mainland hotel across a bridge spanning the Intracoastal Waterway to the barrier island of Palm Beach. Monied New Yorkers found a budding winter playground where they partied, swam, golfed, lobbed tennis balls, boated, and fished.

Even her ex-husband had indulged her with Palm Beach winter trips. When she was in her early twenties, they rented a seaside cottage in the town. Far from the icy winters of the Northeast, the beach area blossomed with fanning silver palm trees, fruity sea grapes, and passionflower vines. For the young power couple from Greenwich, the balm of Palm Beach winters would entice them back to the resort island half a dozen times, staying at the Royal Poinciana Hotel and The Breakers.

So, for Marjorie Merriweather Post, it was perfectly logical that Palm Beach would be the backdrop for a post-divorce romance.

That meeting on the houseboat wasn't the first encounter she'd had with this Hutton man. They had met two years earlier at a party on Long Island. At the time, they were both married. The strapping New Yorker was in his early forties and building a reputation as a bicoastal investment funds manager. As they reacquainted themselves this time around, there seemed to be an ever-so-slight hint of a tan line from the missing wedding rings they used to wear. This encounter differed in more ways than that.

The investment advisor smoked cigars, played golf, and had the ear of the monied class. His advice on stock trades and sell-offs ran in newspapers across the country. In many ways, this newly widowed entrepreneur was impressive simply on the grounds that he differed so completely from her ex.

If single men and women veer toward partners who are completely different from their last relationship, then Post must have been drawn to Edward Francis Hutton like tides and waves to the moon.

Her ex had been a product of bygone times, staid and steeped in Greenwich society. The Columbia Law School grad was descended from the Knickerbockers—the Greenwich Knickerbockers, that is. In contrast, Hutton had overcome a lack of pedigree with attributes her first husband sorely lacked—financial acumen and ambition.

She could explain away her freshly failed marriage, which had ended just months before. After all, she had been barely sixteen when she met Edward Bennett Close at a dance in Greenwich.

At the time, she was being groomed to be a wife, albeit an astute one. Her father had toured her through Europe, brought her to his board meetings, and enrolled her in the Mount Vernon Seminary and College in Washington, DC. With women virtually invisible at the upper echelons of corporate America, C. W. Post's message to his daughter was clear: Guide the Post company from the side chair as a wife.

When she was just eighteen, the couple wed at Grace Church, which was built on land donated by Close's family. Within four years, they had two daughters. Even Hutton, who married in his mid-twenties, would have seen that she had been too young the first time around.

She tried to balance between New York during the week and Greenwich on the weekends. Her father worked to mold his new son-in-law into a formidable corporate leader, at least until the old man died a decade later. Close tried to bring his young bride into the conservative ways of New England's "polite society."

No one won those battles.

In the heat of a late July day in 1917, Close sailed off with his brother and other Greenwich men on the USAT *Saratoga* bound for France. They would deliver to US troops medical supplies that had been purchased by his wife. Since the death of her father and her husband's deployment, Marjorie Post Close supported whatever causes pleased her. Without anyone trying to meld her into the customs of Greenwich society, Post began to embrace the world at large.

Cohosts of the *History Chicks* podcast said Marjorie Merriweather Post may have first started to really command her own life when her first husband deployed.

"Not only is she funding hospitals, she's like, 'I'm going to go see the president because we need to get women the right to vote,'" said hosts Beckett Graham and Susan Vollenweider during a June 2021 show about Post. Her husband's trip was a turning point, the history buffs said.

"She became so independent while Ed [Close] was deployed, so accustomed to taking complete control of her days, her fortune, her life, that when Ed got back from war after the Allied victory, Marjorie asked Ed for a divorce."

Gone was any trace of the relatively meek, naïve, and obedient wife.

"She'd grown up and grown away from him," they said.

Now, at the dawn of the new decade, she stood before a different type of man, one who seemed to have her father's business sense. As water slapped the bottom of the houseboat, Hutton and Post assessed each other. He embodied all that her ex-husband did not, and the thirty-two-year-old beauty wore the newly minted mantle of being perhaps the wealthiest young woman in America. With a blood right to a multinational conglomerate, she was worth an estimated $27 million, or more than $400 million today.

Even beyond what was happening on the houseboat, they would continue their budding relationship amid a Palm Beach atmosphere that was supercharged in its own way. Merchants and restaurateurs launched shops and dining experiences catering to winter residents. Kettler's Bijou Theatre enticed with its big screen. The streets hummed with visitors, and the architecture was anything but parochial. Railroad entrepreneur Henry Flagler, a Standard Oil magnate, had imported New York architects to design his winter residence, Whitehall, which the *New York Herald* described as "the Taj Mahal of North America." Flagler's ever-expanding Florida East Coast Railway drew development along the country's southern Atlantic coastline as industrial growth quickly transformed the country.

A new flirtation in exciting environs seemed the perfect elixir to the starched collars of Greenwich. Beyond the intoxications of South Florida, the entire country bubbled into the 1920s like bottles of New Year's Eve champagne.

Throughout America, a rising class of industrialists quickly amassed fortunes by tapping a new workforce. Millions of newly arrived immigrants and migrants from rural areas moved to manufacturing towns. They provided the affordable muscle that drove a new age of wealth. Nouveau riche entrepreneurs behind such brands as International Harvester, Metropolitan Life, and Ford Motor Company watched their empires grow during a period known as the Progressive Era (1896–1917). Dynasty fortunes of the Rockefellers, du Ponts, and Vanderbilts multiplied. Much of the newfound riches bankrolled elaborate overseas vacations and US mansions that were modeled off the castles of Europe. The residential status symbols lined Palm Beach's shore in a collective salute to capital riches.

It was a heady atmosphere swirling with excess, opportunity, and fast fortunes. The world moved so quickly. Slow-evolving friendships and patient courtships seemed such a dated notion for a world coming out of war. The budding romance could usher in new promise for Post's two girls, Adelaide and Eleanor. And then there was Hutton's son, Halcourt, to consider. If a relationship with Post bloomed, the motherless boy might regain a sense of family with Post and her two preteen daughters.

Within months of kindling a relationship, the country's wealthiest bachelorette was engaged to one of its savviest investors. Weeks later, they married. For a couple who would come to shake the financial world and reshape the skylines of Manhattan, the Adirondacks, Long Island's Gold Coast, and Palm Beach, it was a quiet ceremony. The pair each took their second set of wedding vows in Post's Upper East Side Manhattan home, known as the Burden Mansion.

Marjorie Merriweather Post Close Hutton ventured into the Roaring Twenties by moving E. F. Hutton's suits and casual attire into the chambers where Ed Close's wardrobe had hung barely six months before.

Hutton and his bride had a honeymoon summer in the Adirondacks. When they were in Manhattan, the Burden Mansion afforded plenty of room for family, guests, and its eighteen servants. Wall Street and Hutton's offices on Broadway were just a half hour's drive to the south, although he shifted his attention to the Postum Cereal Company.

Even as the nation reeled from relatively high jobless rates and fast-rising prices, the granite exteriors of the Stock Exchange, J.P. Morgan bank, and surrounding buildings had the calming effect of familiarity. Hutton's life had been upheaved during the previous two years, but a sense of permanence permeated these buildings, even as the country came out of a pandemic and war.

• • •

Clang.

The busiest corner of America's financial district was brimming with stockbrokers, secretaries, and messengers as the lunch hour neared midday on that mid-September day. A few metal-black

Buicks and Model T Fords rumbled down Wall Street amid streams of people dressed in fedoras and suits.

Clang.

The steady clop of horse hooves in the late morning likely drew little attention as a wagon driver eased his load and parked across the street from the headquarters of J.P. Morgan & Co. In the wagon bed lay one hundred pounds of dynamite and shrapnel.

Clang.

At 12:01 p.m., as the last notes of Wall Street's Trinity Church bell died away, there came a tremendous, ear-shattering explosion. A newspaper reporter walking down Wall Street from Broadway felt the concussion of the explosion before he heard it. The sound of the blast, which seemed to shake the mighty buildings all around him to their foundations, was followed by flames and smoke a hundred feet high.

The thunderous crash of concrete, twisting metal, and people's screams were so loud that the president of the stock exchange suspended trading within one minute.

Author Lona Manning described the scene as a narrow passage flanked by tall buildings with hundreds of fallen victims "trapped in the carnage." Strewn about the streets were overturned vehicles unable to withstand the power of the explosion. Deafening sounds multiplied as nine stories of windows shattered instantly, spewing shards of glass onto every exposed patch of skin. Worse yet were the chunks of hot metal spraying the scene like the firefighter hoses that would come later. The velocity of the projectiles was so intense that they bit holes into the once-smooth face of the J.P. Morgan building.

Building awnings disappeared in flames. The smell of burnt hair and clothing hung in the air and pools of blood lined the sidewalks where Wall Street had bustled moments before.

"Flying glass injured Ulysses S. Grant, grandson of the civil war general and president, who worked in the Treasury building," Manning wrote. "A secretary who had just stood up from her chair to answer the telephone turned and saw glass shards all over her desk and chair."

Emergency responders raced to a dust-choked scene strewn with debris, glass, mangled cars, and too many lifeless bodies. Men began lining up a row of corpses, covering them with blankets, awnings, or anything else they could find.

Fears mounted of an attack on the sub-Treasury Building, which now stood with doors and windows blasted. A policeman called for all veterans to help guard the buildings and, within minutes, hundreds of men gathered. Soldiers from nearby Governors Island quickly cordoned off the financial district.

Killing dozens, the explosion marked the worst act of terrorism in the United States at the time. Perhaps aimed at what anarchists considered to be the big banks and oppressors of society, it instead killed wage-earning chauffeurs, couriers, secretaries, and bank tellers.

At the time, the newly formed Hutton family had been at E. F.'s longtime Mill Creek Lodge retreat in Bay Shore, Long Island, but the explosion had destroyed the very streets, buildings, and offices he frequented. The center of his professional world now lay in wreckage. As news of the mounting death toll reached them, all the family could do was mourn, await updates, and be thankful they were safe. They could also distract themselves with hunts, horses, walks, and boating around the bays of north Long Island.

Marjorie Post Hutton had full custody of her adolescent daughters, Adelaide and Eleanor. This was their opportunity to bond with their new stepfather and his handsome nineteen-year-old son, Halcourt. The rolling hills of Bay Shore were Halcourt's domain. He knew its paddocks, paths, and trails. When his mother was alive, the two had competed in equestrian events sponsored by the Islip Polo Club at Oakwood Park. The young Hutton earned ribbons riding his bay gelding at the club's signature summer show, "the most important fixture of the summer social season, and one that draws together the entire summer colony of the South Shore," according to the *Brooklyn Daily Eagle*.

This would be the blended family's last days together before Halcourt left for New Haven, Connecticut, for his freshman year at Yale University. E. F. Hutton had built one of the largest investment firms in the United States, and he had an heiress like no other sitting at his side. But perhaps most significant, the self-made icon and former student at something called Packer's Business School watched as his only child prepared for his freshman year at Yale. Yale was not just another elite school; rather, it had shown its force by completing construction on perhaps the tallest structure of its kind in the United States—Harkness Tower. The university had recently expanded the campus with its Yale Bowl, the largest amphitheater completed since the Roman Colosseum. It was a fast-growing force in the Ivy League.

Even with so much to anticipate, it was hard to avoid talk of the Wall Street explosion for days afterward. Still, escaping from the chatter and the confines of their country house was easy enough. As he had done so many times, Halcourt donned his riding gear and headed to the familiar aroma of hay emanating from the stables. His saddled horse awaited him for a ride through the gentle terrain. Stepping up into the stirrups must have felt like second nature for the horseman. But as Halcourt began to trot his steed, something was wrong. The horse stumbled and the saddle dropped. Its rider could not free himself. An instant of panic would disappear all too quickly for Halcourt. For those who knew him, it would haunt the rest of their lives. The saddle had slipped below the animal's abdomen and took the young athlete with it. As he lost control of his mount, Hutton's only child suffered severe blows to his head as it pounded the cobblestones.

It seemed impossible. By coming to the family hunting lodge, Hutton had steered his family away from the calamity of Wall

Street. But if he had gone back to the city and taken Halcourt with him, could this have been avoided? Had he contributed to his son's death by not watching more closely? Had Halcourt needed more oversight in the stables?

The family rushed the young man to the Bay Shore, Long Island, hospital of Dr. George S. King, who performed emergency surgery along with two other physicians. The attempt to repair the fractured skull failed. Halcourt Horton Hutton was dead at the age of nineteen.

CHAPTER 3

BORN ON
A BED OF CORAL

B lack Model Ts and an occasional Rolls-Royce filled parking spaces on both sides of Clematis Street in West Palm Beach as mornings stretched into afternoons during the winter of 1920. With royal palms towering overhead, an occasional bike rider cruised down the town's main drag. Visiting winter residents and vacationers wore suits, ties, and brimmed straw hats, chatting on sidewalks in front of real estate offices, Western Union, and clothiers.

To help newcomers navigate the town, railroad tycoon Henry Flagler named the streets of West Palm Beach in alphabetical order. He envisioned the grid-street system as a bustle of workers and activity supporting the exclusive island of Palm Beach, which jutted eastward from the mainland past part of the Intracoastal Waterway known as Lake Worth. Running east and west, Clematis Street drew commerce. Real estate—land, to be specific—was the hot commodity quickly trading hands.

As early as 1920, one West Palm Beach real estate company compared the fast-money deals to the kind of profits that scammer

Charles Ponzi promised: "Real estate has increased more than 40 percent each year and is still climbing higher."

FORTY PERCENT A YEAR

CAN YOU BEAT IT?

ALMOST AS GOOD AS PONZI

—J. R. Marshall real estate firm newspaper ad

On the mainland in West Palm Beach, Clematis Street became a hotbed of property flipping. Northerners did not even have to make the trip south to get into the game. They traded Florida properties using "binder boys" often on sidewalks hawking properties like newspapers and sometimes reselling the same lot eight times over in one day.

Across the Sunshine State, the steamy lure of tropical weather, flour-colored beaches, queen palms, orange trees, cheap land, and more cheap land drew hundreds of speculators. As buyers came from Ohio, New York, Pennsylvania, Michigan, Maine, and elsewhere, property prices defied gravity.

The road to Florida's ballooning real estate prices was paved partly by mass-produced cars. The new, assembly-line mobility eliminated economic barriers and empowered a growing middle class to travel. New north–south highways funneled Americans to warmer winter environs. The Spanish flu had taught this young nation the importance of fresh air and sunshine. And Florida's relatively affordable land enabled them to own it. The fact that some of the land was too wet to be buildable was a mere detail.

Hundreds of thousands of Americans from varied financial backgrounds poured into the beach-ringed state. In what would become a buying frenzy, lots for houses were bought and sold for double their prices in a matter of weeks. Options on the properties were traded, sold, and repurchased.

As is usual during a boom, money for loans was easy to come by. Securities companies packaged the financing, backing it up with office buildings, shops, restaurants, and even newly built homes.

"But here is where the fun comes in," wrote Harvard economics PhD Homer B. Vanderblue in his 1927 research paper on Florida's land boom. Buyers paid 10 percent down—also known as a "binder"—and quickly resold the lot. New subdivisions usually sold out overnight. A lot would be resold before the second payment was due in a month.

This qualified as a pyramid scheme when the second buyer of a lot paid an inflated price. The price on the second sale of the same lot was high enough to repay the first buyer and give him some profit. The poor second buyer also had to immediately make the second and third payments on the mortgage. Cash was king, and buyers gambled on the risk that the pool of cash buyers would vanish—leaving them stuck with worthless property.

The "art" of those deals was in reselling the same property multiple times before the first sale was recorded at the county courthouse.

Not since the days of pioneers and gold rushes had investors flipped so much property. Vanderblue said the cheap, easy loans fueling the Florida frenzy created "probably the wildest speculation in vacant real estate, both above water and below it, which has occurred since the thirties and forties when the West was being opened to settlement."

From 1920 until 1925, land values in Palm Beach County quintupled. Of course, that was just on paper. What the cheap land and road-trip fever didn't do, Florida lawmakers made up for. Inheritance taxes shrinking your family's wealth? Florida legislators outlawed those taxes. Need more excitement? Government officials in the state allowed dog- and horse-racing tracks. Income taxes cutting into finances? Lawmakers prohibited such a tax. The state had enacted an income tax long before, in 1845, but it failed so miserably that the state abolished it within a decade, and pro-business leaders weren't about to resurrect it.

The man whose company doled out investment advice regularly to newspapers across the country must have seen it staring him right in the face: Buy now or regret later. Less than a year after their houseboat reacquaintance, Edward and Marjorie returned to Palm Beach as husband and wife. They rented a two-story apartment at the exclusive Everglades Club, which had actually been reinvented from a World War I hospital by an heir to the fortune of the Singer Manufacturing Company, maker of the Singer sewing machine.

Then the inevitable happened. The power couple from New York started looking for land. The prices surely would only go up, right? Their search for a lot didn't take them far from the club. They purchased a half acre with views of the club's golf greens and immediately hired New York transplant Marion Sims Wyeth to design a Mediterranean-style house. They called it Hogarcito, "little house." The building permit showed a value of $28,000, modest by any measure in the couple's portfolio of real estate holdings. Within five months of construction commencing, they moved from the Everglades Club to their diminutive, new winter home.

In those early days of the 1920s, Florida real estate wasn't the only thing booming. Postum Cereal Company rode the rising economic tides as well. Hutton traded on his wife's position and landed the spot of chairman of the company's board of directors. His ascension to that role would spin the cereal company in a new direction. He raised cash to acquire sister companies that could share production, marketing, and distribution chains.

In 1922, Hutton gambled on issuing two hundred thousand shares of common stock to bring the company public. At the time, such a move was considered highly speculative. By the following year, though, the risk began to pay off with a stock split and a 20 percent boost in dividends. It was not the last time Post stock and fortunes would multiply. As the company moved to embrace advertising and finances, its headquarters moved from Michigan to New York City.

On a personal level, the family's hope for a legacy emerged. Post became pregnant. As 1923 neared an end, the heiress delivered what would become the couple's only biological child—Nedenia Marjorie Hutton. With Nedenia, Adelaide, and Eleanor in tow, Hogarcito may have translated into the "too little house." The Huttons expanded it in 1923 to make more room for a nursery and Marjorie's growing parties, but the quaint house on Golf View Drive was still, well, quaint. It wasn't just bedroom space they needed but something more substantial—something affording the kind of entertainment lounges, decks, dining halls, and reception areas where they could throw parties and galas befitting their station in life. Something with a view of the Atlantic was necessary for this next generation of Palm Beach royalty, wasn't it?

The wealthy were not building mere beach houses. On the northern end of the eighteen-mile-long barrier island that is Palm Beach, J.P. Morgan partner Edward Stotesbury and his wife had just completed building their oceanfront estate, El Mirasol. The forty-one-room mansion was appointed with a forty-car garage, a tea house, and an auditorium. Monkeys and parrots inhabited the forty-two acres of oceanfront property.

Three years after commissioning Hogarcito, Hutton sold it to his brother. It was time to make a statement. As the lady of the house commented to the *Palm Beach Post* in 1922: The golf course, winter getaway just didn't compete with the larger mansions of the established hostesses. Her next creation budded as more of a village than a mere villa.

When one of the wealthiest women in America scoured the coastal hammocks of southeast Florida in 1922 looking for a place to build her winter trophy estate, she could have seen the coral reef lying underground below her more easily than the political battles that eventually would be waged over the estate—battles that might not have been fought if she had selected a different location.

Later in life, Post recounted for historians the thoroughness of her search.

"It had to be unoccupied land, from the ocean to the lake and well wooded," she said almost four decades afterward, describing the bug-infested jungles. "We became quite used to following the animal paths, sometimes on our hands and knees."

As she studied topographic maps and visited properties with her real estate agent and a contractor, one prospect emerged as a possible site. Overgrown with lush native plants, the seventeen-acre property sat on a coral reef between the Atlantic Ocean and Lake Worth. The land was on Palm Beach's southern end, where the island winnowed down to about a half-mile width. Of course, it was a fraction the size of the Stotesburys' El Mirasol acreage, but it afforded ample views and had a slight rise, which could help buffer a massive house from hurricane-force winds.

• • •

Decades later, Interior Secretary Stewart Udall could have told her that the location would be revered by her guests, coveted by developers, and controlled by neighboring islanders. The very attributes that would make it a celebrated stop for royalty, power brokers, and socialites would ultimately make it impossible to save for the enrichment of society, as Post had worked for during much of her adult life.

Less than a half-century after the matriarch of what would become General Foods crawled on that jungle floor, federal efforts to protect her property would incite powerful forces fighting to keep her land—together with the entire island resort—off limits to the public. For them, the environs were best left to the monied elite with family connections.

If Mar-a-Lago had been built elsewhere—the same house but not on billionaire row—the Mar-a-Lago National Historic Site would be unnecessary. Udall had the background to understand that. But the property was so valuable that the mansion would never survive free-market appetites for development.

What started as Post's hunt for property embraced by two water bodies would lead to construction of an estate almost too well placed and too frequently teetering on the brink of demolition.

• • •

The prize of Marjorie Hutton's search was the seventeen-acre expanse with five hundred feet of oceanfront. Sieges of herons and coveys of other waterfowl nested in palmettos and cabbage palms, which would soon be removed. The site promised beachside sunrises and lakeside sunsets that crept southward until the vernal equinox. The ecosystem baked in summers as oceanic temperatures swirled with the potion for hurricanes. In the winters, warm winds drew grebes, warblers, and loons as well as New Yorkers intent on building vacation villas.

"We finally decided on the property. And we are anchored on a coral reef and have a lovely stance of lawns and gardens from the oceans to the lake," Post would say years later.

News of the Huttons' plans for the southern end of Palm Beach stoked civic pride in a region getting a reputation for ballooning land deals. A column in the *Palm Beach Post* on May 2, 1925, conveyed that this family had the kind of pedigree the island needed in order to distance it from the hoi polloi:

Palm Beach is fortunate indeed in having people with great fortunes, like the Huttons, who will uphold its traditions and, despite the southward trend of building, still retain their love for Palm Beach and their loyalty to the resort. Mrs. Hutton, who was Miss Margaret Post, is principal owner in his great business of manufacturing Postum cereal and other health foods, while Mr. Hutton, who is a member of an old New Jersey family, is regarded as one of New York's most important and successful brokers. His offices in Palm Beach were the rendezvous of many millionaires and many affairs. Mr. Hutton has large financial interests in Florida, and is one of the firm believers in its great development and prosperity and, like so many others who are investing their fortunes here, believes that it has a future unequaled by any other state in the union.

Deciding what to build atop such a unique site would pit two adverse personalities against one another, each with a completely different vision. So toxic was the relationship between Mar-a-Lago's architect and its inventive interior designer that one would later disavow working on the project.

After getting comfortable with the steady hand of architect Marion Sims Wyeth at Hogarcito, the Huttons hired him again to design something on a much different scale. There would be nothing diminutive about this next project.

Wyeth may have lacked the cache of the more popular Addison Mizner, who crafted Palm Beach's architectural backbone with a résumé of noteworthy buildings and residences. Wyeth, though, had graduated from Princeton University and had studied at the esteemed École nationale supérieure des Beaux-Arts in Paris.

"Many, many hours of the day I would be in his office on one of the high stools at the drafting table," Post would later say, adding that they discarded dozens of schematics.

The Huttons came to the table with a heightened sense of good living. They were making their mark not just on Palm Beach but also with residences in Manhattan, Long Island, and the Adirondacks.

Back in Manhattan, developer George A. Fuller was redeveloping the Burden Mansion, where the Huttons had married less than five years earlier and lived when they were in the city. Fuller replaced the mansion with fourteen floors of Central Park apartments and what may have been Manhattan's first multistory penthouse, which would now belong to E. F. and his wife.

Hundreds of A-list guests partied at the pre-demolition send-off for the Big Apple manse on a Tuesday night just before Thanksgiving 1924. William K. Vanderbilt, media giant Condé Montrose Nast, and Countess Schönborn di Frasso were among the guests. Comedian Fanny Brice, musicians, and dancers entertained in rooms laden with red roses and white chrysanthemums.

What was to come next for 1107 Fifth Avenue would top all that Manhattan's upper crust had seen. In a nod to the site's roots, Post used valuable paneling, fittings, and fixtures stripped from the mansion before demolition. Including a wood-paneled dining hall that easily accommodated more than one hundred guests, the signature features were a twelfth-floor entry, marble staircase, ballroom, and skylight. The afternoon sun angled over Central Park and pierced the penthouse's Palladian windows. Upstairs, tiled terraces wrapped the fourteenth floor and offered some of the best views in the city.

With an escalator and porte cochére entrance, Hutton could easily commute a few miles south to the new Postum headquarters in the company's own building on Park Avenue.

The Huttons were also in the throes of creating a luxury compound in the Adirondacks named Camp Hutridge (later renamed Camp Topridge).

Dotted with rustic lodges and guest cabins that could be reached only by water, the place was named in honor of Hutton.

They poured hundreds of thousands of dollars into expansions, new accommodations, and Native American artifacts. Animal skins, stuffed owls and foxes, Eskimo kayaks, Native American rugs and tapestries, and deer-antler chandeliers decorated the sixty-eight-building compound.

In this alter ego to Mar-a-Lago, guests flew to a small airport near Lake Clear and found a limousine waiting to whisk them two miles to the lake. From there, a yacht ferried them to the other side of the lake. They then boarded a funicular that climbed to the top of the ridge. The final leg of their journey was to their own private cabin, attended by a footman and maid.

Cabins were appointed with fireplaces, telephones, and fully stocked bars. Camp Hutridge became an Adirondack hideaway for a select guest list. Stewart Udall frequented the camp. Other Washington politicians, diplomats, and ranking military officers congregated there, as did businessmen riding the surging economic cycle of the 1920s boom market. Prince Felix of Luxembourg and India's Kamala Kaul Nehru visited. It was a place where high-level friendships warmed and financial deals firmed. Later renamed Topridge and sold, it would become an undisclosed and controversial get-away for Supreme Court Justice Clarence Thomas and his wife, as guests of Texas billionaire Harlan Crow.

For now, the celebrated couple also turned their attention to Long Island, purchasing the old Warburton Hall estate that had been designed by Addison Mizner. They were not buying it for the architecture. They demolished much of the original house and set about building a Tudor-style estate that would emerge slowly throughout the 1920s, with artisans and craftsmen painstakingly carving details in wooden relief throughout. The 177-acre estate was largely self-sustaining with greenhouses, nurseries, stables, and a racetrack to indulge Hutton.

In comparison to these sister properties, perhaps their Palm Beach estate would even be understated.

• • •

As the hydrangeas and tulip trees bloomed on the island resort leading into winter 1925, Palm Beach's high season got underway. The *thwack* of tennis balls and *thud* of golf balls resounded like a metronome of the rich. Seaside buffet picnics preceded costume balls and jazz parties that began at 11:00 p.m.

But the air seemed different than in previous years when speculators and investors shuffled cards at the club and promenaded in their suits along Worth Avenue. In past winters, so many new residents descended on South Florida that the state's land boom forged entire cities. Coral Gables, Hialeah, and Miami Shores all sprang into existence seemingly overnight.

Heading into this winter season, investors' appetites for a piece of the Sunshine State had softened. *Forbes* and other publications reported that Florida land prices reflected the abundance of buyers more than any intrinsic value in the property itself. As news of shaky Florida real estate deals resonated northward, buyers began canceling purchase contracts.

Post's own financial advisors cautioned her against undertaking a monumental winter home just as the economy was turning. Plans, though, continued for a residence that would cost millions and take years to build.

As a passing reminder of life's blind corners, a fire sparked on the fourth floor of The Breakers, where Marjorie Hutton was a guest during Mar-a-Lago's construction. Faulty wiring started the fire in the room of Mrs. William Hale Thompson, the wife of a former Chicago mayor who was renowned for his friendship with gangster Al Capone. As alarms sounded and flames spread, guests panicked. Furs and jewels were tossed from windows to the lawn below before the National Guard arrived. If a structural skeleton of milled timber had ever been considered for Mar-a-Lago, it was no longer.

Fires, competing properties, Florida's land bust—nothing would dissuade the Huttons from this project.

As first sketched by Marion Sims Wyeth, the estate would have a primary residence, a house for the children, and another for guests. It was all quite stately with Wyeth's reputation for "quiet, subdued, and rational" interpretations of both the Spanish and Italian styles.

About a month after site work started, Hutton treated his Broadway celebrity friend Florenz Edward Ziegfeld to sail Palm Beach's coastal waters with him aboard his yacht. The two had opened Montmartre nightclub on Royal Palm Way, and Ziegfeld had his own interest in construction. Flush with financing from William Randolph Hearst, he was about to build a Manhattan theater showcasing musical comedy acts—an idea that would morph into the Ziegfeld Follies. His boy wonder of design was Viennese impresario Joseph Urban. Unlike Wyeth, Urban commanded flair and drama with a knack for surprise. He had worked with Ziegfeld on theater projects for a decade, designed residences in Europe and America, and worked for Hearst as art director for Cosmopolitan Productions.

With Wyeth toiling over the floor plan, Urban could dazzle high society by creating a venue for parties, balls, and concerts. He could give it panache. The set designer was soon at work drawing each room like a new canvas, varying themes with eclectic abandon. Motorists on South Ocean Boulevard would be able to see a crescent-shaped, seventy-five-foot tower that framed the centerpiece of the 118-room house—a circular patio overlooking sweeping sunset views of the Intracoastal Waterway.

Post made sure that visiting Mar-a-Lago would be a signature experience completely different than the Manhattan reality of guests relegated to the indoors.

CHAPTER 4

THE TRUTH
ABOUT FLORIDA

As the 1920s wound down, the sea spray and tangerine-colored sunrises could no longer hide an undercurrent that was fast eroding South Florida. News of con artists' real estate scams reached the North. Panicked investors canceled their long-distance real estate contracts. The Internal Revenue Service spent so much time unraveling the transfers in sham sales that it created a new division specifically for Florida.

Florida officials fought back against the stinging news stories. Governor John W. Martin helped organize a seminar—"The Truth about Florida"—at the Waldorf-Astoria Hotel in New York City. His appeal to the public, of course, could not reverse what was fast becoming the great Florida land bust.

Collapses seldom occur from just one thing going wrong. Layers of safety nets are supposed to protect buyers' investments. The next round of buyers, though, had disappeared. Hadn't the Sunshine State opened opportunities for everyone—even the middle class—to own a piece of paradise? How could tropical land so near the ocean do anything but climb in value? What peril could there be?

South of Palm Beach, in Miami, the population by 1926 had more than doubled in six years, and most of the transplanted Northerners were ignorant about Florida's most potent natural disasters. Even seasoned Florida natives were caught off guard by what would soon hit them.

In mid-September 1926, a tropical system formed in the Central Atlantic. The fast-forming system passed north of Puerto Rico, skirting normal routes of weather intelligence. Long before the days of reconnaissance aircraft and satellite imagery, a budding hurricane remained "somewhat of a mystery, with only a few ship reports to tell of its existence," according to the National Weather Service.

With storm communications centralized in Washington, DC, no warnings had been issued even twenty-four hours before the massive system made landfall. At noon on September 17, the weather service was authorized to issue storm warnings for the Florida coast from just north of Palm Beach southward to Key West. Weather officials hoisted the hurricane-warning flag at 11:00 p.m.—barely an hour before hurricane-force winds hit. The system's pelting outer bands introduced the Great Miami Hurricane to thousands of Florida newcomers. Warnings were so inadequate and residents so naïve that crowds of people took to the streets about 6:30 a.m. on September 18 as the winds died down. Far from over, it was the eye of the hurricane. For about a half hour, people emerged and headed onto the roads, not knowing a fourteen-foot storm surge would soon claim many lives.

"They were suddenly trapped and exposed to the eastern half of the hurricane shortly thereafter," Robert Ferguson, longtime president of the Science and Public Policy Institute, wrote in a 2007 report on Florida hurricanes. "Every building in the downtown district of Miami was damaged or destroyed. The town of Moore Haven on the south side of Lake Okeechobee was completely flooded by a lake surge from the hurricane. Hundreds of people in Moore Haven alone were killed by this surge, which left behind floodwaters in the town for weeks afterward."

Despite deaths and utter devastation, Miami promoters attempted to spread the word that the city was still in business. A makeshift radio station echoed national headlines that "Miami was down but not 'wiped out.'" Ultimately, the Great Miami Hurricane death toll surpassed 370. It damaged more property than Hurricanes Katrina and Andrew combined, experts found. Even closer to Palm Beach, in Fort Lauderdale, seventeen victims died and almost five thousand people were injured.

Despite Palm Beach being so nearby, the Great Miami Hurricane of 1926 merely swatted at it. Mar-a-Lago's reinforced concrete walls protected the villa as it was nearing completion. This, though, was just a warm-up to what was soon to come for the estate emerging on South Ocean Boulevard.

What his 1926 storm did not do to the mansions of Palm Beach, it did to the slim labor pool saddled with building more of them. Workers headed south for cleanup and rebuilding opportunities. Some were conscripted for burial duties.

Of course, having the town mayor as your general contractor does come in handy when it comes to finding workers. Like the Stotesburys and others, the Huttons hired Palm Beach mayor Cooper C. Lightbown to see the mighty residence to completion. Starting in 1923, the town's chief elected official used his connections to help manage an estimated six hundred workers heaving Mar-a-Lago into existence over the course of four years. As much as basic muscle, Lightbown also needed craftsmen who could meld masonry, pottery, tile, and iron. Workers unloaded boatloads of Doria stone from Genoa, Italy. Craftsmen carved the earthen material for wall facings, archways, and sculptures.

Austrian sculptor Franz Barwig carved and molded figures of gulls, griffins, monkeys, eagles, and rams, tucking them into the folds of Mar-a-Lago. The sculptor had first become acquainted with Joseph Urban at the Hagenbund collective of Austrian artists in Vienna. Barwig's signature contribution to Mar-a-Lago would be lasting. Even almost a century later, his sculpted forms help define the architectural work. His artistry would later come to stand as one of the reasons the United States should preserve the famous house.

Decades later, just nine months before Interior Secretary Udall helped bring about the public's stake in Mar-a-Lago, Post flew Lady Bird Johnson to the manse in her private jet, the *Merriweather*, for a lobbying effort to save the gem of her real estate collection. The First Lady was particularly impressed with sculpted figures carved into doorways, mantels, and corbels throughout the enormous house. "The stone looked like four centuries instead of four decades, so mellowed it was," Johnson would say years later. She marveled "that Viennese sculptor, Franz Barwick and his son, Walter, spent two years designing and carving the Doria stone from Genoa into the infinite pattern of grapes, pelicans, parrots, scrolls, and flowers."

Elsewhere on the construction project, roofers installed twenty thousand barrel tiles. Crews painstakingly transferred truckloads of weather-beaten river stones from Post's Long Island hunting preserve and laid them across the patio floor in a pattern the matriarch had seen at the Alhambra in Spain.

Then there was the collection of thirty-six thousand Spanish tiles, some of which may have dated back to the Moors' fifteenth-century occupation of Spain. Post acquired them from the Horace Havermeyer family, who had collected them in the 1880s. Artisans installed the collection in the entrance hall, patio, and cloisters in what may be the largest such display in the world.

Decades later, the wife of the thirty-sixth president of the United States would describe the setting as unparalleled: "We went out on the terrace and were seated at round tables, in a setting whose elegance and grace and opulence I shall probably never see repeated."

More than a half-century later, when it was nominated for the National Register of Historic Places, Mar-a-Lago stood recognized for artistry, architecture, and unique appeal. When Cecil McKithan, head of the Southeastern Regional Office of the National Park Service, saw the spread in the early 1980s, he recognized craftsmanship rarely found.

"From the lakeside, when looking back to the house, it becomes apparent that the intricate stone sculpture, the wonderful old tiles, the general workmanship, the whole artistry could not be duplicated in the foreseeable future," McKithan reported after his visit. "It is truly one of America's Treasures."

Intricate details defined seemingly every square foot and begged visitors to study walls, windows, doorways, lighting, and the main hall ceiling, which closely copies the Thousand-Wing Ceiling in the Accademia in Venice. It is decorated with a bas-relief sunburst surrounded by pairs of feathered wings in gold leaf.

Recounting her 1968 visit, Lady Bird Johnson said her eyes devoured the room: "And like a crab, my eyes tried to look in all directions at once—to the unbelievably magnificent ceiling that looked like gold sunbursts, coats of arms of the doges of Venice."

Golden ceilings, sculpted beasts, and a cache of historic items—those were the ingredients of Mar-a-Lago's stew. With hints of Spanish, Portuguese, and Venetian architecture, the villa was described as having a Hispano-Moresque style popular in South Florida for decades.

Both the exterior and interior of the house displayed elaborate rows of Egyptian ram heads under the eaves, a two-story living room with a gold-leaf ceiling, and a dining room that was adapted from the Chigi Palace in Rome.

Expense seemed not to be an issue. The ultimate cost doubled from early estimates to create this residence that seemed intolerant of anything less than perfection. Although Mar-a-Lago would be impossible to re-create in any era, the final tab equated to at least $30 million a century later.

It arrived, though, to some mixed reviews.

"It is understood that the ultimate cost of the mansion will, with landscaping and furnishings, cost in the neighborhood of a million dollars and will be one of the most pretentious dwellings in Palm Beach," read a front-page story in the *Palm Beach Post* on January 14, 1926.

Underneath the historic tiles and sculpted images, Mar-a-Lago paid homage to modern amenities. Gates and exterior doorways operated electrically, timed to open and close at specific hours. Clocks ran on electricity and wall outlets empowered a new age of cleaning.

By mid-January, completion of the nearby Bath & Tennis Club was delayed so that workers could finish the Huttons' million-dollar baby in time for the couple's usual arrival for the season. On their arrival, they found a Mediterranean version of a European castle equipped to host parties, concerts, weddings, balls, galas, dinners, fundraisers, and royalty.

The *Palm Beach Post* painted it as a "veritable fairyland at night, with a 'moon' shining down from the tower and wrought-iron lanterns dangling from the limbs of banyan trees." Post played up the tropical setting for guests by lavishing rooms with bougainvillea, oleander, snapdragons, and orange blossoms.

Historians would come to describe Mar-a-Lago as one of the most extravagant of the mansions built in Florida during the early twentieth century when the country's wealthiest and most prominent families wintered there. Once it was in the hands of the National Park Service, the federal government said the house and grounds best portrayed winter resort life in Palm Beach prior to the Depression.

Others, though, saw it as a mishmash of excess. *Miami Herald* reporter Pat Bellew wrote that "Mar-A-Lago's freewheeling architecture style leaps from the most garish periods of Italian, Spanish, Dutch, Moorish, French and Portuguese architecture to the most severe periods of English and Early American design."

Bellew wrote that it reminded her of "an impressionable tourist who, having made her way doggedly through Europe's cathedrals and castles, wants to display all the geegaws she'd collected on one shelf."

The Epcot-style whiplash was an international tour de force with Grecian busts, Ming vases, Persian rugs, a Roman-style dining room, a Dutch bedroom suite, and an Arabian nights theater.

Decades later, the official architect disavowed his role in setting the vision.

"It isn't my taste. It's the taste of Joe Urban. I don't want anyone to think I was the architect in charge," Wyeth told a reporter for the *Palm Beach Daily News* in 1981.

Whether revered or reviled, Mar-a-Lago and its celebrity owners enthralled Palm Beach's social cliques during the Roaring Twenties. The Huttons proudly brandished their wealth with lavish parties that were detailed in the newspaper society pages. Industrialists, film stars, and aristocrats dined, drank, and danced at the newest "villa" on South Ocean Boulevard.

The pinnacle of the Palm Beach season was the costumed revelry of the Everglades Club Ball, thrown in late February with about five hundred guests toasting their good fortune to be far from the bone-chilling claws of another Northeastern winter. Of all the Palm Beach dinner parties on the night of the ball, the Huttons' was the grandest.

Post, the budding philanthropist, also hosted the first of dozens and dozens of fundraisers at her new winter estate. During Mar-a-Lago's first spring, Post opened its doors to friends for a musical tea she hosted in support of the Animal Rescue League of the Palm Beaches, as it was called at the time. They hosted a recital and benefit for the Women's Guild at the Episcopal

Church of Bethesda-by-the-Sea. Under her watch, Mar-a-Lago's doors opened to charities that didn't pay to lease the space. After all, the ranks of disadvantaged men, women, and children were mounting.

Mar-a-Lago was conceived at the apex of an era when the rich guiltlessly indulged themselves and their friends, throwing lavish parties for the sake of their own enjoyment. Wealth was celebrated openly with newspaper society pages filled with costumed guests photographed at masquerade balls. With just spare change, the working class could escape its low-wage realities and read news of high-society parties with imported entertainment and royal guests. Stories noted the strands of pearls and rare jewels worn by Marjorie Hutton and others. They were rich, and they were proud to show it. The heightened state of conspicuous consumption created an appetite for material possessions and drove a spirit of consumerism throughout a country clinging to its self-made identity.

Such was Mar-a-Lago's timing. Had it been conceived even a few years later, the coming economic collapse likely would have undone the idea of such an ostentatious display of riches. The concept of building an ode to status soon fell out of favor as education and occupational achievements became the badge of honor over flamboyance. Bill Gates's Xanadu in 1995 in Medina, Washington, could not compare to Mar-a-Lago's girth or crafted details. Of the hundred largest homes built in the United States, two-thirds were completed prior to the Great Depression. Of those, eleven have been demolished as of the publication of this book, including one home that was once the center of Palm Beach society.

The grand estate being erected on the south end of Palm Beach would become one of the last residential statements of the monied class openly and ambitiously flaunting its wealth outside the confines of gated communities. It would be one of the last examples of an Old World castle built in a New World country.

But while bands serenaded guests at Palm Beach's newest elite hub, the party ended suddenly on the mainland.

On March 15, 1927, three banks in Palm Beach County bolted their doors. Fears mounted and sparked a run on the two financial institutions that remained open. Thousands of newcomers suddenly lost the money they had sunk into buying land in and around Palm Beach. The crash had officially arrived in South Florida, and it would prove to be a harbinger for the country as a whole.

How much collateral damage the Huttons and their peers endured from the Palm Beach banking collapse is unknown. Even though the value of Mar-a-Lago undoubtedly sank, their overall fortunes were insulated from the Florida land bust.

In the spirit of sporting a good face, Palm Beach officials reported the town's "best ever" winter season and actually hinted at prospects for a Florida oil boom. Under the headline "Palm Beach Showing Signs of Life as Many Homes Open," a local story reported that architects and builders had a busy summer while there was no end to sales and leases for real estate operators.

The story was more bleak just a half-mile away on the mainland with families facing hunger, joblessness, and westward migration for a country still hungover from the Roaring Twenties. Across the brackish waters of the Intracoastal Waterway, those troubles must have seemed a continent away. Years later, a *New York Times* correspondent would sum up the townspeople's panache in this way: "In financial Palm Beach, recessions and depressions happen to other people."

By the time orange tree blossoms puddled on the ground in late spring, seasonal Palm Beachers departed the tony tropical town. In summers, year-round residents had the beaches, roads, and grocery stores to themselves. As red mercury climbed up glass thermometers, life's pace slowed. The population of Palm Beach shriveled. The month of May introduced the wet season and thunderous afternoon rains that cleared the humid air for a dusk deluge of mosquitoes. Sweat became the glistening accessory that freckled brows and cooled skins. Despite breezes blowing inland from the sea, temperatures pushed into the nineties by day and eased too little at night.

The air wasn't the only thing getting warmer. Looking eastward from the grand, round-arch windows of Mar-a-Lago, the waters of the Atlantic collected the sun's warmth. Full-time Floridians and summer vacationers luxuriated in churning bathtub conditions. With temperatures in the mid-eighties, shallower spots of Atlantic waters were barely cooler than body temperature. The salt water grew its own energy, with sea liquids evaporating into swirls of wind.

Those warm Atlantic waters weren't confined to Florida's offshore waters. Thousands of miles to the east, off the coast of Africa, ocean waters warmed similarly to the Western Atlantic in the dog days of that summer of 1928. Warmer waters generated more energy. As the salty evaporation rose, winds began to generate speed, and soon, a storm formed. The high-energy conditions had the makings of a tropical storm.

Palm Beach residents could recall the Great Miami Hurricane just two years earlier. Certainly, it had maimed entire towns to the south, but they had been safe on those shores due west of Grand Bahama Island. Precautions they took during the last hurricane had served them well.

Two years after Miami's encounter, South Floridians listened to radios and watched newspapers for updates as the latest tropical storm morphed into a hurricane. On Wednesday, September 12, the bowling ball of a system smashed into Guadeloupe, killing twelve hundred people. Next, it crushed Puerto Rico, leaving half a million residents homeless. It was no typical tropical system and, now, the boom-bust peninsula was more vulnerable than ever. During the previous two years, thousands of new residents had built homes and relocated there; entire new towns had emerged. And palatial estates had risen on the precipice of the ocean.

By early Saturday, September 15, the year-round crowd of Palm Beachers took some comfort in the forecast from the head of the National Weather Service that the storm would bypass Florida. Still, it was massive enough to monitor. Telephones were few in the coastal locale, but word of the storm's mass spread quickly. Some reported the eyewall was thirty-five miles wide.

By Saturday night, the National Weather Service advised storm warnings up and down the coast of Florida with hurricane-force winds offshore. Wary residents began to realize that even the Palm Beach area could feel the effects. Just to play it safe, homeowners secured awnings with ropes and reinforced garage doors.

As the storm approached in the Atlantic, an officer aboard the steamer *August Leonhardt* told the weather service that it was a beast that sounded like "the New York subway going full speed passing switches." As it ripped through Nassau, Bahamas, at 3:30 a.m., the weather bureau's wind-recording anemometer cups blew away. They were later found a third of a mile away.

When they awoke Sunday morning, Palm Beach County residents felt winds picking up. Gusts pelted windows, slashed palm fronds, and slammed bands of rain into homes. At 10:30 a.m.— less than nine hours before it would hit the mainland—weather officials hoisted hurricane flags from Miami 250 miles north to Daytona Beach. Advisories warned of hurricane-force winds hitting in Jupiter just north of Palm Beach by that evening.

The Huttons and other elite Palm Beach winter residents watched the unfolding news from their perches in the Northeast, far from danger's path. Their substantial investment in ocean-front property now seemed risky at best. Eighteen-month-old Mar-a-Lago would face winds and storm surge the likes of which few structures could survive. Its sunrise-view windows, seventy-five-foot tower, and stone walls now lay prone as this system became one of the most severe acts of nature ever to slam into the United States. Not only were southeast Florida's architectural legacies facing possible damage or even destruction, but the staffs who cared for them during the off-season were also in peril.

By the time revised forecasts reached those families, there was no time to pack bags and head inland. Even if they had left, inland areas offered little sanctuary.

As clocks ticked past noon, winds strengthened, and deluges began dumping eighteen inches of rain onto ground that was already saturated. Water choked canals and ditches. Windows, doors, and roofs proved no match for the onslaught. Families tried in vain to mop up puddles that collected on floors. Soon, though, those floors disappeared under a black soup of water.

Winds estimated at more than 150 miles per hour began lifting houses from foundations. They severed garages, rolled cars, and chopped telephone poles in half. Projectile debris assailed anything in its way.

Usually, hurricane forces weaken as they exit open Atlantic waters. The muscle of this system, though, only grew as its front wall reached the shallow warmth of Lake Okeechobee—a water body large enough to earn the nickname of Florida's Inland Sea. The combined rains and wind ripped apart hand-built earthen levees meant to protect farms from floodwaters that now surged twenty feet high.

Migrants and laborers in the Palm Beach County town of Belle Glade climbed to rooftops in hopes of a savior. They could only pray as water moccasins and rattlesnakes slithered through the churning current. Roofs, lumber, metal framing, dogs, and cows floated past in the dark waters.

Ultimately, the human strength powering an entire region of the United States would be decimated that day. An estimated 2,500 victims—mostly migrant laborers of African American descent—drowned. Bodies floated away and then disappeared into the Florida Everglades.

Survival was a weak thread. Several hundred people swam to a barge and clung to life there. About one hundred farmworkers walked six miles through four feet of water, dropping exhausted in West Palm Beach. Even then, they faced dim odds against impending waves of typhoid and other diseases.

Destruction knifed through coastal resort towns that had so recently beckoned both wealth and workers. Beyond the muck farms of Lake Okeechobee, three-quarters of the businesses in Boynton Beach had been destroyed. In the nearby community of Lake Worth, half of the houses were decimated. Evacuation shelters proved no match for the wind. Fifteen evacuees died when the roof of a Boynton high school auditorium collapsed.

News of the devastation traveled quickly. Reports cited hundreds of hurricane victims stranded atop a small ridge of land next to the Everglades. Stories about damage at hospitals ran next to articles about military units encamped in West Palm Beach to prevent looting.

Details about Palm Beach emerged slowly because downed bridges limited island access.

A headline in the *New York Daily News* cautioned "Palace Dwellers Fix Worried Eyes on Florida." A columnist for the newspaper consternated about losing some of the country's most significant residences: "There's no place in this hemisphere to compare with it as a winter playground and only Newport can rival it in the number and magnificence of mansions." The families of Henry Carnegie Phipps, A. J. Drexel Biddle Jr., Otto Kahn, Harold Vanderbilt, John Sanford, and John S. Phipps must be resting none too easily, the story continued.

The writer cast the potential damage at Mar-a-Lago by noting that money had been no object in its recent construction. Even the grounds had been planted with costly, eight-ton tropical trees meant to make the new residence look mature, the newspaper reported.

The hurricane had indeed taken a toll on the winter resort island. The Breakers and Royal Poinciana hotels, both just a few miles north of Mar-a-Lago, suffered damages. The system had also damaged a Palm Beach estate that would later become a winter home for President John F. Kennedy.

In the days following the hurricane, building inspectors wearing straw-brimmed fedoras, ties, and short-sleeved collared shirts walked the island. Bare trunks of palm trees, stripped of their palm fronds, listed sideways. Telephone poles leaned westward with no electrical lines in sight. Balconies and concrete-balustrade railings lie in rubble. Glass skylights became open-air circles studded around the edges with pointed shards.

The wind patterns had been so erratic—and buffered in spots— that some courtyard urns still stood upright with their plantings in place.

Within days, the Huttons would learn their residential jewel had somehow weathered what would be its mightiest blow. Against the bomb-blast backdrop of Palm Beach County, the mighty residence had survived in an almost surreal way. Some of its trees had fallen and a large, Roman-style window was shattered, but its stone walls and tile roof had remained largely intact.

Post described the damage that may have seemed costly and serious to her but could not compare with the devastation elsewhere.

"The very first year after the house was completed, the most dreadful storm came and it killed most of the trees, took off their tops," she said years later in an interview at Mar-a-Lago. "We had put in seventy-five wonderful old royal palms on a walkway from the ocean to the lake—we lost thirty-five of those."

Longtime Mar-a-Lago superintendent James Griffin said two mules that got loose from a nearby construction site wandered the grounds of the estate. Even the tower topping the estate stood as though it were ready to greet the next round of winter guests. While other estates on Palm Beach had been crushed, the grandest testament to the Huttons' wealth and power had dismissed the potentially devastating blow. Once again, the parties, balls, and elaborate dinners could go on as the next social season awaited just a few months away.

But the hurricane of 1928 had levied the ultimate regressive tax on its victims. While wealthy owners of Mar-a-Lago and other elaborate winter estates had to repair damages during those upcoming autumn months, thousands of poor, Black laborers living in shacks died by drowning.

Weather service officials reported that salvation rested on sturdy construction and storm shutters:

"One of the noteworthy features in connection with the storm was the absence of serious structural damage to substantial buildings. This was also particularly noticeable after the Miami hurricane of September 18, 1926. These two hurricanes, both of major intensity, have shown that buildings properly constructed will not suffer serious damage from hurricanes and that the use of storm shutters will prevent practically any damage to such buildings. This statement applies to frame buildings as well as those constructed of steel, concrete, brick or stone."

The disparate worlds of rich and poor became more evident in those days after the storm when the sea breeze gave way to the stench of inland death. Vultures circled overhead, signaling the location of drowned workers floating in hyacinth-choked canals. Belle Glade physician W. J. Buck worked for eighty-two hours trying to save lives.

"Nowhere for nobody to stay and nobody couldn't put nobody up in their own house 'cause nobody had one to stay in," said survivor Ethel Williams. "So the people just living out in the street, taking hand-me-downs, whatever they could use.

People would give it to them, [people] that did have something to give away."

The bodies of hundreds of laborers were dumped into mass burial graves six miles northwest of Mar-a-Lago in West Palm Beach. While 68 White victims were buried in Woodlawn Cemetery, 647 "colored" bodies filled the City Cemetery. A week later, the death toll became so high that recovery teams no longer hauled the corpses to cemeteries. On September 26, fifty-five more White victims were buried while 212 "negroes," as the newspapers identified them, were buried or burned. One funeral pyre had 87 bodies.

"Well, I remember trucks that were loaded down with bodies," survivor Lucille Salvatore Herron recalls. "It's amazing to me that I even remember that, 'cause when my brother said, 'Do you know what that is?' I think I said it's dump trucks . . . and he said, 'They're full of dead bodies.'"

Whether buried, burned, or drowned, the dead warranted relatively little ceremony during those long summer days. Attention quickly turned to reclamation and restoration of the resort village's economic engine.

In the weeks following the hurricane, workers stoked trash fires and burned wrecked wood framing, trashed boats, and other debris. They repaired houses and rebuilt roads, erasing reminders of the barrier island's wreckage. Most important, the show must go on.

CHAPTER 5

THE CIRCUS

If the "old money" ways of Palm Beach shied from notoriety and spotlights, Mar-a-Lago would always veer off the track of discretion. It would become the beacon where pop idols Michael Jackson and Lisa Marie Presley honeymooned, a place where *Lifestyles of the Rich and Famous* host Marvin Leach enthralled television viewers, and the backdrop where rhinestone-bejeweled boxing promoter Don King chanted, "We're going to make American great again." Not to mention the disco-ball parties cast with NFL cheerleaders cavorting about, beauty-pageant vixens vying for their own talent competitions, and a cavalcade of pickup-truck patriots sometimes backlit by police-car lights out front.

And even from the beginning, exhibitionism had its place there.

The heartbeat of the winter showplace regained its rhythm in late 1928, months after the massive storm that slayed South Florida that year. The country's second-deadliest hurricane became a mere memory.

North of Mar-a-Lago, Palm Beach icons Ned and Eva Stotesbury hefted their political clout to get hurricane-damaged North Ocean Boulevard rerouted westward, better preserving their forty-two-acre estate's ocean view.

Hutton family members began to arrive at their island getaway three months after the storm. Within about a week of the Huttons' return to Mar-a-Lago in January, the deadly hurricane seemed so distant that the Huttons hosted royalty.

A writer for the *New York Daily News* cast that post-hurricane, winter season as a balm to all harsh realities:

> My dears, just to see lovely peach trees in blossom, and scarlet hibiscus everywhere and green grass and smooth sea, and white yachts on Lake Worth and everyone in summer clothes, and the miles and miles of houses of pink, yellow, red, and blue stucco makes one feel simply swell. February, the gayest month in this winter colony, is arriving to find a very large reception committee waiting for her.

In that same society column, correspondent Nancy Randolph reported that Lady Wavertree and Duchess Di Simonetti were staying at the Huttons' magnificent home on South Ocean Boulevard.

The list of royal visitors ran long for the Huttons' mid-February dinner party, where a Hawaiian band serenaded and dancers performed to a Hungarian orchestra. A society publication in Brooklyn, New York, reported that the most celebrated afternoon event of the season was a Mar-a-Lago tea for hundreds of guests.

The couple threw benefits too—a card party for the Animal Rescue League of the Palm Beaches. At two benefits, Mar-a-Lago's grounds showcased acrobats, trapeze artists, rodeo performers, tightrope walkers, and a trick mule named Spark Plug. A carnival barker enticed guests to see a circus freak show featuring French and Belgian midgets, a "living" skeleton, monkey man, an armless wonder, a sword dancer, a magician, and a seven-hundred-pound woman.

In its early days as a kind of amusement park, not even the dark hangover of a hurricane could cloud Palm Beach's perennial parade of wealth, which grew with the ranks of newly minted millionaires.

Riches mounted from the manufacturing and sale of cars. Fortunes multiplied for businesses selling electrical household appliances. Americans craved radios, electric iceboxes, powered irons, fans, electric lighting, vacuum cleaners, and other labor-saving devices. Utility icons built empires by transporting wattage. The electrical boom of the 1920s did more than light up Mar-a-Lago; it rapidly fueled the companies listed on the stock exchange.

After taking Postum public in 1922, the company leaders started on a buying spree, purchasing Jell-O, Baker's Chocolate, and Maxwell House during the 1920s. Orchestrated in 1929 by Mrs. Hutton, the $20 million acquisition of Clarence Birdseye's frozen-food company cemented Postum's future. After that, it became General Foods, joining the ranks of General Motors and Sears, Roebuck and Company on the Dow Jones Industrial Average.

In a show of exuberance during that summer of 1929, the Huttons hired golf course architect Donald Ross to usher in Palm Beach's first private links. Fresh from the fairways of St. Andrews, the Scot designed nine holes on the lake side of Mar-a-Lago.

From his desk at E. F. Hutton & Company, the self-made investment advisor saw a new zenith in stock trading late that summer. During a four-month window in mid-1929, the Dow gained more than 20 percent. It had multiplied sixfold since the dawn of the 1920s. And with it rose the financial standing of monied families who traded investment tips while walking on the sandy shores of Palm Beach.

As the decade of America's strongest growth margins drew to a close, though, gray clouds loomed. The nation's factories had slowed production and sent workers home. Farmers struggled and debt mounted. Economists voiced concerns that stock prices had far exceeded their value.

Troubled economic forecasts had the potential to undo at least some of the wealth of Manhattan, Palm Beach, and other exclusive locales. Even Florida's economy suffered from not only sharp land devaluation but also from its citrus crop dropping by 60 percent in 1929 with the invasion of Mediterranean fruit flies. Roadblocks and quarantines were put in place to try to contain the destruction.

Backed by a financial empire that seemed solid, the main stakeholders of General Foods had just splurged on a series of corporate acquisitions. Fortunes of all kinds were made and lost on Wall Street every day. The trouble brewing in the financial sector now had the potential to strike a blow against several of the giants along Ocean Boulevard.

As the stock exchange ushered in what would be its most cataclysmic month, E. F. Hutton & Company distanced itself from more bullish investment groups by calling for cooler heads. In newspaper columns published around the country on October 3, 1929, Hutton's brokerage advised: "We do not think the time has come for the average trader to follow rallies." In other words, only wizened investors should risk stock buys. The falling market was no place for amateurs.

A week before the largest crash in the history of the stock exchange, the daily investment roundup in newspaper financial pages projected overall rallies for Monday, October 21.

Hutton's group contrarily took a more conservative position: "The market is still in a critical position."

On that Monday, the market dropped more than 3 percent with phone lines jammed and record trading during the first two hours. What came next would bolster some investors but signal instability to others. On Tuesday, the market shot up almost 2 percent. Then it crashed by more than 6 percent on Wednesday and spiraled further with mass sell-offs during what would become known as Black Thursday, October 24. That's when a pool of investors propped up the market with bulk buys.

A chorus of respected voices sought to tamp down the jitters of sell-off panic. US president Hoover assured his countrymen that America's bedrock of production and distribution was secure. Steel industrialist Charles Schwab told a group that the balance between production and consumption was at equilibrium. The top executive at Sears, Roebuck and Company said he expected the company's biggest month ever.

Some investment advisors told the public that the worst was behind them. The day after Black Thursday, the firm Love, Bryan & Company wrote in its newspaper advisories:

"Our belief is in continued prosperity and that he who has sufficient funds can today find innumerable stocks that can be purchased with sound management and continued prosperity in view."

Hutton's group tempered its enthusiasm. That same Friday, Sidney Loeb of E. F. Hutton & Company wrote:

> Eventually the good stocks should find their way back to more reasonable levels, but middle-grade and second-grade issues that were being so enthusiastically bid up only a short time ago are apt to do nothing or sell lower.

Insiders at E. F. Hutton & Company had extracted themselves from the melee. Founding firm member Gerald M. Loeb, Sydney's older brother, famously predicted the crash, pulling out all his funds and those of his clients. He would go on to write classic investment books and found a namesake program honoring business journalists, but his deft move in advance of the October 29,

1929, crash became the headline on his *New York Times* obituary almost half a century later.

Few, though, had that kind of foresight. Bank closures swept the nation and the financial backbone propping up the Palm Beach area began to fail. As the Roaring Twenties closed, a dozen banks in Palm Beach County failed. Families lost their savings, and unemployment swelled. The grip of the following Depression squeezed almost a hundred thousand families in the Sunshine State. Railway companies that had ushered wealth into Palm Beach suddenly declared bankruptcy.

For Post and others who were central in New York's "cafe society," displays of philanthropy quickly took the place of shows of wealth. Post stowed away her flashy jewels and created namesake food banks in Hell's Kitchen and meals on wheels programs for impoverished, older residents of New York City. She raised more than $50,000 for the Salvation Army and bolstered other charities supporting families stripped of income as unemployment struck a quarter of the working class.

Claudia "Lady Bird" Johnson later recounted hearing Post talk about getting advice to cut off the funds she had been pouring into Mar-a-Lago: "There was still work going on when the crash came . . . and advisors told Mrs. Post that she ought to stop. She said, no indeed, Palm Beach needed it now more than ever, so she went right on, giving employment to many with work on the surrounding grounds and the houses [sic]."

Longtime Mar-a-Lago superintendent James Griffin said the crash ended up shaping the house in a more crafted way:

> What they did do, of all this stuff you see around here, the cypress banisters and the pilasters and all of this stuff. They done that all by hand. Now they could have very easily done it and had a lathe and cut these things all out with machinery and machined it . . . . Now it didn't have to be

done that way. . . . [T]he superintendent brought this up.
And she said, "Listen, I want to give people work. I know. I
was brought up in construction. I want it all done by hand
so people can have a salary."

Even though bankruptcy and closures plagued and killed businesses, General Foods survived better than most. Profits slowed at
the company but it was still making money. Food, it seemed, was
not a discretionary expense.

And so the party in Palm Beach slowed even less than a chauffeur glancing at a roadside crash.

New York Times staffer Tom Buckley later wrote:

For the old established rich of Palm Beach, of course,
recessions and depressions are economic phenomena that
happen to other people. Their fortunes are too large, too
widely diversified and too carefully managed to be seriously
affected by swings in the business cycle. About the worst
that can happen is that for a year or two they may have to
live on the interest rather than the interest of the interest.

For months following the nation's financial collapse, there were
few outward signs of a downturn for Palm Beach's grand dame.
Eva Stotesbury celebrated her husband's birthday with hundreds
of guests. Their El Mirasol estate was more than double the size of
Mar-a-Lago, and it wore the esteemed brand of Addison Mizner,
the architect who helped define South Florida's most notable
residences with his spin on Mediterranean Revival and Spanish
Colonial Revival building styles.

Under sun-dappled palm fronds draped over El Mirasol's
courtyard, hundreds of men dressed in summer suits chatted with
stylish women donned in pearl necklaces and summer cloche hats.
They milled.

They sipped.

They gossiped.

And they congratulated the guest of honor on his birthday. As the dapper eighty-one-year-old financier received the Huttons and other esteemed guests, white-gloved servants wearing tuxedos presented appetizers and glasses of punch. "What Is This Thing Called Love?" played in the background.

During that first season after the crash, dozens of ground-workers pruned, planted, and pampered the prized Stotesbury estate. They relocated rubber trees, trimmed the oleander, and managed almond trees. The men shipped avocados and mangoes to the family's primary estate in Philadelphia. And they cared for more than a dozen monkeys and an aviary with thirty-five bird species, including macaws and cockatoos. Architect Maurice Fatio oversaw renovations there in 1930, designing a grand entrance gate off North County Road. And in the fall of 1931, the workers installed a kitchen garden "in keeping with the general popularity of the thrift movement."

Yes, Palm Beach society gave a nod to the "thrift movement." Clearly, it was not a time to fly the flag of personal riches—at least not in the public eye.

While the renowned cereal princess and Wall Street magnate together won attention for their work establishing soup kitchens in New York and writing checks to otherwise failing charities, more privately, they awaited what was to be the ultimate jewel in their covey of trophy properties.

Ostensibly as a belated wedding gift to his wife, Hutton commissioned a German company to construct one of the largest yachts in the Western Hemisphere. In 1931, the million-dollar *Hussar V* was about to be christened even as hard-faced mobs filled the streets of Manhattan protesting against locked-down banks.

They first saw the yacht in Bermuda the week after Thanksgiving and accepted delivery in New York weeks later.

Just as they began relishing their new prize, the *Palm Beach Post* reported the couple would not be returning to the island town at least until January "in the interests of their work for the unemployed of that city."

What had truly captivated them was a ship like no other. Designed by New York's Gibbs & Cox with the classic lines of an American clipper ship, *Hussar V* was born in excess. It was to be the largest, tallest, safest, and most modern vessel of its kind.

For the first time, shipboard guests could chat on automatic-dial telephone systems. The latest in Hutton's series of Hussars came with its own barbershop and a hospital equipped for surgeries. Jukebox music from thirty-six records could be piped into any cabin or salon. For the adventurous, she came with her own fleet of eight smaller boats, including a motorized whaleboat.

With interiors described in the local press as "opulent," bedrooms featured marble fireplaces, rare antique dressers, swag-topped headboards, and ceilings studded with Louis XV relief work framing glass chandeliers.

As long as a football field and staffed with a crew of more than sixty, the four-masted vessel was a beauty unsurpassed in future generations. Serving up ever-changing views at every shore, the head-turner was the Huttons' ticket out of the spoils of a soured economy.

Starting in 1932, the couple sailed the world, porting in Cuba, Panama, Galapagos, Tahiti, Alaska, and elsewhere. They entertained royalty with the ship's movie theater and bar.

As the yacht sailed, one of the country's most significant residences idled. The darkened mammoth of a house on South Ocean Boulevard cast a shadow on Palm Beach's winter party. A famed *New York Daily News* columnist, who wrote under the name Nancy Randolph, likened Post's absence to a half-cast Shakespearian play. The writer noted the demands of Post's charity work in Manhattan and then compared the Palm Beach scene in 1932 to "a performance of *Hamlet* minus the Prince of Denmark."

"Mrs. Hutton is so much a part of the gay and glittering life of the Southern colony that it is almost impossible to imagine Palm Beach without her," the famed gossip writer mused. "Palm Beach has been dependent upon Mr. and Mrs. Hutton for its biggest and best parties for several seasons past."

Mar-a-Lago wasn't Palm Beach's only darkened ode to better times. Emilie Keyes, a writer for the *Palm Beach Post*, described the empty, haunting manses of those Depression years as "here and there light flooding from windows and maybe next door a gargantuan pile of darkness."

Offshore, meanwhile, the Huttons' ostentatious secret began to get out with the *Hussar*'s international swagger and parade of newsworthy guests. Newspaper items began to mention they were distracted from their fundraising duties, being otherwise occupied.

As the Palm Beach season was ending in 1932, the Huttons returned to New York from a ten-week cruise in the West Indies. Marjorie returned just in time to help oversee a charity carnival at Madison Square Garden the next month.

Heading into the next winter season, the pattern continued. *New York Daily News* society columnist Nancy Randolph reported in December 1932 that the *Hussar V* was being rolled out, and it looked like Mar-a-Lago would once again remain mothballed, hurting the local economy: They did not open this costly home last year and, oh, what a difference that made in both colonists and the tradespeople.

If the Huttons worked to evoke an image of Depression-era good works, Palm Beach worked on an image that the nation's worst financial crash blew right past the winter retreat.

Newspapers around the country published stories about Palm Beach society's apparent ban on the word "depression" in the dead of winter 1933. Beachgoers sported colorful parasols, houses featured riotously striped awnings, and "residents parading about in handsome, gaudy beach costumes." Winter resident Colonel Edward R. Bradley opined in a newspaper column that Palm Beach was largely untouched by the Depression, other than a downturn in hotel guests due to companies cutting their dividends.

"Come to Florida and live twenty years longer," he said.

One family that steadfastly embraced their winter life in the Palm Beach tropics, of course, was Ned and Eva Stotesbury, although the rumors circulated that their children might take over El Mirasol. The Palm Beach stalwarts entertained with luncheons, teas, and parties with Russian royalty.

By that winter of 1933, the Huttons gave passing homage to the Palm Beach winter scene. Hutton spent time at his hunting lodge and later in New York before joining his wife in Palm Beach for a few parties and dinners. That summer, Long Island physician George S. King cruised with Hutton aboard the *Hussar*, cutting into ports in Egypt, Turkey, and Russia.

Depression-era decadence elicited a dim view from the public. The *Minneapolis Tribune* published a piece in August 1933, putting it this way:

> Mar-a-Lago, the $3,000,000 house designed for Mr. and Mrs. Edward F. Hutton by the late Joseph Urban was closed this past Winter, too, while its owners cruised the Pacific in their four-masted schooner, *Hussar*. But the equally pretentious Cielito Lindo, the estate of the Woolworth heiress, Mrs. James P. Donahue, was open again this season.

Simply put, the Huttons had lost interest in the vision they crafted over a period of four years.

In an apparent bid to gauge market interest, aerial photographs of the palatial estate started showing up on society pages. *New*

York Daily News writer Nancy Randolph said the couple wanted out.

"It's no secret that the Huttons would like to get rid of the estate in which they sank some four million dollars," Randolph wrote. "This is the third season the Huttons, potential leaders of the colony a few years ago, have shunned Palm Beach."

One of America's leading residences was shuttered and locked for years, not because its owners could not afford it but because they apparently were bored with it all, the columnist continued.

CHAPTER 6

"AN INSOUCIANT MINX"

Over the decades, they would come and eventually go. The spouses who held court as seeming royalty at Mar-a-Lago all reveled for a time as the master—or mistress—of the house. They commanded that attention for a time, at least until the real head of the house dismissed them. Some reigned over 1100 South Ocean Boulevard for a generation while others lasted there only a handful of years. One was a diplomat, one a former model, and one delivered a baby months before her wedding. Throughout it all, the continual string of breakups, embarrassments, and high-ticket divorces all carved their way into the lore of a place forever baked in social pressures.

The first in that line was a man who stood watching as this place of history was born.

Marjorie Post Hutton had scoured the seashore for the untamed land where she wanted to build her winter estate. She had bankrolled the multimillion-dollar project with her family money. She sat for countless hours with her architect brainstorming its design. Yet Post, one of the wealthiest female entrepreneurs in the world, didn't own her Florida home, at least not in her early years there. For reasons that aren't entirely clear, Mar-a-Lago came into the world under the sole ownership of the man of the house.

"Mar-a-Lago was originally in the name of Edward F. Hutton, alone," according to 1969 correspondence between Circuit Judge James R. Knott and General Foods chief attorney Lester E. Waterbury.

The practice of titling property to husbands wasn't at all uncommon just a half dozen years after American women won the right to vote. Florida, in particular, was one of the holdouts that hung onto unequal property rights for married women. It wasn't until 1943—almost a century after other states began passing the gender-equality legal rights—that Florida followed suit and even then only under pressure from the state's sole female legislator, Mary Lou Baker. In those years before Baker won property-ownership protection rights for female Floridians, Post and her attorneys had to navigate the state's choppy waters for women. They had good reason.

In the winter of 1934, Marjorie Post Hutton headed south to Palm Beach but, rather than going to the trouble of opening Mar-a-Lago, she stayed with Wall Street investor Jay F. Carlisle and his wife at their winter retreat on Golf View Road, not far from where the Huttons had built Hogarcito. Dinner party guests at the Carlisles' that February included Washington attorney Joseph E. Davies, former chairman of the Federal Trade Commission and part of the Franklin Delano Roosevelt inner crowd. He was a man brimming with Democratic ideas that had been dismissed by Post's increasingly conservative husband.

As Mar-a-Lago sat empty for a third winter season, the Huttons traveled to Phoenix for a retreat at the Arizona Biltmore Hotel, which was just a few years old at the time. The desert city was becoming the new playground for sportsmen and tony members of the New York stock exchange. Unlike his wife, Hutton was staunchly opposed to Roosevelt's New Deal package of economic reform efforts, writing for newspapers that a 25 percent tax cut on businesses could be passed down to help workers earn greater wages. He joined the American Liberty League, which championed individual liberties and private-property rights.

Whether politics contributed to an unsurpassable divide or their interests had simply drifted, the union of Marjorie and Edward Hutton eroded. Their renowned retreats, trips, cruises, and parties were coming to an end. A celebrated marriage that bore a beautiful daughter and untold riches now teetered. In the newspapers, blame fell on the dallying husband, but both spouses appeared to have had other interests.

Just three months after their respite in Phoenix, one of the nation's highest-profile couples announced their separation. Rumors circulated about the extramarital affairs of the dashing chairman of General Foods. The split left them apart but not distant. Marjorie and the couple's only child, eleven-year-old Nedenia, stayed in Rosyln, Long Island, with Hutton living nearby. He still oversaw General Foods.

For an American public devastated by the Great Depression, news of such marital affairs and undoings became a delicious distraction. In an era predating television, the breakfast cereal heiress and General Foods tycoon served as the soap opera stars of the day. Realizing the appetite, newspaper editors fed their stories to the masses.

New York Daily News columnist Jack Alexander reported the culprit for the split was "the tapping of a pair of pert, French heels belonging to an insouciant minx of 19 or 20." Hutton was fifty-eight years old.

When the divorce was finalized in September 1935—two months after Marjorie and Edward's fifteenth wedding anniversary—courts sealed the divorce papers. The cause was cited as adultery and the spoils went to Marjorie. The grand dame took full ownership of the Hillwood estate in Long Island, the Manhattan penthouse, the sprawling estate in upstate New York, and the *Hussar V*. She also claimed Mar-a-Lago.

A campaign quickly ensued to put a good face on the dissolution. Newspapers ran photos of a beaming fifty-eight-year-old Hutton, decked in a double-breasted suit and two-tone shoes and with his arm around his preteen daughter. The chin-up image may have been an attempt to shore up respect for the New York financial magnate. In reality, Hutton's visitation with his only child became limited to alternating Christmas and spring breaks, as well as one summer month each year.

Neither party wasted time committing to new partners. The same month the divorce was finalized, news circulated that Marjorie Post Close Hutton soon would add yet another last name to the list. She was to wed the man she had met barely half a year earlier at a Palm Beach party—Joe Davies.

In a swirl of related newspaper reports running throughout the country during the fall of 1935, Americans followed news of the highbrow divorces and marriages almost as Brits track the royal family.

Marjorie's new beau had divorced his wife just weeks after the Huttons' divorce. He and E. F. Hutton were similar in age but Davies was recognized as a pivotal player in national political circles, serving earlier as an economic advisor to President Woodrow Wilson and soon to represent the United States in Soviet Union diplomatic circles. The press described him as charming and opulent.

In October, one month after the dissolution of the Huttons' marriage, another divorce would free Edward Hutton's love interest—Dorothy Metzger. She had met Edward Hutton a year earlier when she and her then-husband were guests of one of Marjorie's daughters at Hillwood. The woman who would become Hutton's twenty-eight-year-old fiancée filed for divorce on the grounds of cruelty from her husband, former Brown University football player Homer Metzger. Coincidentally leading up to the divorce, the former collegiate athlete had just landed a job at the New York–based medical company Zonite Products Corporation. Hutton was Zonite's chairman of the board.

Two months after the divorce of Marjorie and Ned, Hutton bungled his chairmanship of General Foods. In an opinion piece for a public utility industry publication, he called for businesses to "gang up" against Roosevelt's New Deal politics. It was, in short, a grand miscalculation. Just when Hutton's anti-Roosevelt sentiment reached new public heights, his ex-wife and reigning shareholder of General Foods was about to marry a high-level Roosevelt appointee.

General Foods quickly went into damage control mode. Company president Colby M. Chester wrote to Commerce Secretary Daniel Roper that Hutton did not speak for General Foods and that the company preferred to stay out of politics. Hutton publicly apologized, saying he wrote the piece months earlier and things had changed with the Roosevelt administration since then. He said that he had been ill just before publication or he would have pulled it:

> All the statements I have made in recent months have been issued by me as an individual citizen and are not to be taken in any way as the views of the General Foods Corp., of whose board I happen to be chairman.

By then, though, it was too late.

Hutton remained on the board but no longer as chairman of the corporation he had helped grow from a cereal company into a diverse, global food conglomerate. Under his direction, the company had acquired the Jell-O Company and companies producing

Minute Tapioca, Baker's Chocolate, Log Cabin Syrup, Maxwell House Coffee, and Calumet Baking Powder. He had helped cement the company's financial success at a time when many businesses were forced to close during the Depression's stranglehold on commerce. Marjorie had long been an important part of the decisions that helped form and grow General Foods, particularly with the purchase of the Birdseye company. Women at the time, though, were educated to become wives. They weren't welcomed into the world of corporate-speak and were typically sidelined by boards of directors. But the divorce and Edward Hutton's political gaffe gave her the opportunity to publicly lead a company in which she had the greatest stake. So, in 1936, she became one of the first women to serve as a director of a major corporation.

While Post gained stature, Hutton lost both status and prized possessions. Heading into the holidays in 1935, he went to the yacht slips in Georgetown, where his beloved *Hussar* sat docked. It had been his grandest in a line of yachts but, on this day, he came to collect his belongings from it. Marjorie was prepping it for an extended honeymoon cruise with her new husband.

At the age of forty-eight, the moneyed matron's third wedding was a relatively intimate affair in her penthouse. Someone was charged with calling down to the legion of reporters that gathered outside on the drizzling day. In play-by-play fashion, he called to them: "Now they're walking down the aisle . . . now they're getting married . . . it's all over, he kissed her twice, once on each cheek." After the wedding, Marjorie's finger-waved trusses and manicured brows framed an elegant smile as Davies sat next to her and beamed to the squadron of reporters and photographers on the sidewalk.

Even Marjorie's new stepdaughters seemed open-minded about their father's new spouse. Eleanor Ditzen, the oldest of the three, told the *Washington Post* in a 1978 interview that she could not blame her father:

"It was sad," recalled Eleanor Ditzen, eldest of Davies's three daughters and eldest surviving family member, "I did not go to the wedding. I stayed with my mother and took care of her. My mother was an angel. . . . My father and mother were absolutely devoted and it was a terrific shock but he fell madly in love with (Marjorie) and I don't blame him—she was a terrific gal.

In January, Marjorie and her new husband inhaled international coastal breezes aboard the newly renamed *Sea Cloud*. That same month, Hutton married Dorothy Metzger. The pair honeymooned in Palm Beach—not in the palatial Mar-a-Lago but instead at the "little house," Hogarcito.

For Mar-a-Lago, the guard changed from the bon vivant who was pivotal in the mansion's creation to a political operative more at home in Washington, DC.

News reports and society columnists long referred to it as E. F. Hutton's Mar-a-Lago, even though it had been built with his wife's wealth. In the aftermath of the divorce, no one mistook it for E. F. Hutton's house. From its gold-leafed living-room ceiling to the Post ancestry coat of arms in bas relief above the fireplace, the residence was the product of Marjorie Merriweather Post's travels, tastes, and sensibilities. She had secured twenty thousand roof tiles and the twenty-two hundred black-and-white marble floor blocks that originated in a Cuban castle. She had conceived the idea of melding together Spanish, Venetian, and Portuguese styles. Future generations might forever link the four-masted *Sea Cloud* yacht with Hutton, but Mar-a-Lago was Post's own unique combination of stately pearls and dazzling diamonds. For her, it seemed a kind of gift for the people of Palm Beach, and she tended it with due respect.

Like husbands, houses would come and go throughout her life. This residential creation, though, was about to embark on a new future that no one could have foretold. For Mar-a-Lago, the Hutton divorce wedged open the manse's round-arched main entrance to a long parade of unlikely individuals and high-profile battles that would eventually come to define its very character.

• • •

In Palm Beach, about a half-mile of waterway separates mansions from mainland, but the distance must have seemed much farther in those early days of the 1930s. While families scrounged for food in West Palm Beach, the darkened mansion with fifty-eight bedrooms across Lake Worth on the island sat unused. As hard-scrabble itinerants walked dusty South Florida roads seeking work picking crops, a skeleton crew of caretakers tended Mar-a-Lago and pruned Mrs. Davies's prized cutting garden. Trying to keep the worlds of poverty and privilege from colliding, Florida State Police patrolled state border crossings and turned away families with no resources or place to stay.

In what must have seemed an alternative universe from the realities of the Depression, the faint sounds of big bands wafted across Lake Worth in Palm Beach. By night, swing music enlivened the dance floor of the Everglades Club. By day, the sound of rub-ber tennis balls still thudded on the courts at the Bath & Tennis Club. The Breakers brimmed with winter vacationers. Rolls-Royce Phantoms and Mercedes-Benz Roadsters sometimes hummed along Ocean Boulevard. The only apparent struggle was between the old and new guards clashing at the polo fields, golf tourneys, and the Palm Beach Yacht Club regatta.

The wealthy still played at their winter playground, but the frivolity differed from the high-riding party days of Flo Ziegfeld's Midnight Frolic and the costumed Washington Birthday Ball at The Breakers. A patina began to coat the hamlet of seventeen hun-dred residents. Or could it have been a fine film of dust? During those days in the early 1930s, Palm Beach's evening coastline became eerily dotted with an occasional light emanating from one of the residences along Ocean Boulevard while black hulking mansions claimed the nighttime coast. The great winter homes that were the calling card of Palm Beach just a decade earlier had morphed into a collection of oversized relics.

For some of those massive mansions, the Depression was the beginning of the end. "With the Great Depression," wrote Bethany Lyttle of the *New York Times,* "the cost of keeping and maintaining these homes became untenable for most residents. Many of the homes were broken up and sold as separate residences. And many, if they were unaffordable and lacked landmark status, were knocked down."

By the mid-1930s, though, some signs of life resurfaced on Ocean Boulevard. The sound of hammers and saws came from workers making repairs at Cielito Lindo. Workmen prepped for the return of Mrs. James P. Donahue. Like Mar-a-Lago, the Donahues' winter home had been designed by Marion Sims Wyeth. The two houses, both topped with towers, were built at a similar time. Most important, each stretched from the Atlantic to the Intracoastal Waterway on limited-edition land. The house had gone dark as the heiress to the Woolworth fortune came to prefer her yacht to the luxury manse.

Addison Mizner's masterpiece Playa Riente, also built more than a decade earlier, shined with new furnishings in 1936 when it opened for the first time in years. During that previous shuttered period, few footsteps echoed in an entry hall that spanned sixty feet with thirty-foot ceilings in homage to the stock exchange building in Valencia, Spain.

Even as expectations rose for Palm Beach's most notable addresses, the decade-old mansion at 1100 South Ocean Boulevard sat shuttered. In fact, Mar-a-Lago's newly remarried owner stayed elsewhere in Palm Beach. Mr. and Mrs. Joseph

Davies were guests of Eva and Ned Stotesbury at their winter address—El Mirasol. For weeks, the newlyweds were feted and honored by friends and foreign dignitaries. They were guests of honor at a dinner in the Bath & Tennis Club and then embraced at an honorary luncheon in Malmaison restaurant. They reigned at the season's largest private event, a reception for them at El Mirasol.

In comparison, Palm Beach's greeting was cooler for Marjorie's ex-husband and his new bride. Hutton and Dorothy Metzger Hutton had ample time for togetherness during their Palm Beach honeymoon.

"The Hutton name has not been particularly conspicuous on the guest lists which it once ornamented," wrote *New York Daily News* society columnist Nancy Randolph.

The writer went on to predict a fallout for anyone hoping to entertain both Hutton and his ex-wife: "Whether it wishes to or not, the colony will have to divide and take sides, for no friendship survived the Hutton divorce."

The former chairman of General Foods still called the tropical island his winter home. In 1937, he built a house less than a mile from the landmark he and Marjorie had built a decade earlier. The rambling, white structure hinted of Greek classical style. It centered on a courtyard that terraced two hundred feet down to the lake. Twenty-inch cypress boards framed part of the off-white house. Guests strode up a marble entry stairway and walked through marble-paved corridors. Even with the elegant touches, the one-story winter residence was a mere shadow of Mar-a-Lago. The new, wood-frame structure cost a fraction of the Palm Beach home he lost in the divorce.

For years, Marjorie and "Ned" Hutton had been the darlings of Palm Beach. They invigorated the tony settlement with society sizzle, costume balls, and orchestral galas. More than the parties, dinners, benefits, and dances, they had validated the island by building a multimillion-dollar vacation home at a time when Florida's land values had soured. They bestowed one of the last monuments to the country's pre-Depression era of elegance and opulence.

When Joseph Davies entered Palm Beach society with Marjorie on his arm that winter season, he saw a different world than the one that had enchanted his new wife decades earlier. The Stotesburys had long reigned as the center of celestial Palm Beach but Ned Stotesbury was now approaching ninety and a new hierarchy was forming with Consuelo Vanderbilt at the helm.

The new denizens of the order saw little value in building cavernous houses that sat empty most of the year. Those days were officially over. In the depths of the Depression, Vanderbilt staked her claim to South Florida by hiring architect Maurice Fatio to create Casa Alva in honor of her mother. While true to the Moorish Mediterranean architecture of the day, the winter retreat was about a third the size of Mar-a-Lago and ten miles south of Palm Beach on an island in the tiny village of Manalapan.

Then, white-haired Palm Beach society suffered a blow in 1938 with the death of its reigning patriarch, Ned Stotesbury.

Buying a waterfront footprint of forty acres (more than double the size of the Mar-a-Lago property) and hiring architect Addison Mizner to design the house may have been the genesis of the "Spanish palaces" that came to define the island. Tourists drove to Palm Beach just to marvel at the conifer-lined drive leading to El Mirasol. Postcards of hand-painted photographs showed off its tropical setting. The 1920 manse had long riveted the colony's attention as home to the pinnacle event of the season— Stotesbury's birthday party.

"Everyone from the haughtiest visiting titles to the local grocer has been invited to the mammoth birthday party," wrote *New York Daily News* writer Nancy Randolph in February 1939.

After his death, the fate of Stotesbury's El Mirasol took a turn. The economic crash cut deeply into family fortunes, which shrank from an estimated $100 million before the Depression to just $4 million less than a decade later. The dismantling of the prized estate would begin within two years of Stotesbury's death when a member of the Pulitzer family purchased two hundred feet of choice oceanfront property for a residence. Rather than hiring the legacy architect Addison Mizner, the new owners contracted architect John L. Volk. For the first—and most consequential—of the estates that made Palm Beach famous, the sale marked the initial blow in what would be a long, slow death of iconic homes along Florida's Gold Coast.

Two months later, the grande dame of the Stotesbury family dynasty sold more than half of El Mirasol's forty-two acres to a developer for $170,000. Grounds so recently revered by the colony were quickly carved into fifty-five homesites called Stotesbury Park.

Privileged children who once called those quixotic estates of old Palm Beach "home" rarely thought enough of their childhood haunts to want to preserve them. So, then the mansions, unwanted by heirs, faced the open real estate market. The rare, qualified buyer who could afford them preferred to build his own residential legacy rather than live with the vision and tastes of others. The prized land they wanted to build on had been snatched long ago by the first wave of elite Palm Beach pioneers. While the aged mansions defining the island became stodgier with every passing year, the land beneath them only became more seductive.

Just as the ex-wives who later ruled Mar-a-Lago would eventually return there for family celebrations, E. F. Hutton came back in the spring of 1939 to throw a lavish dinner in honor of his niece, who had married into the title of Countess Barbara Hutton Haugwitz-Reventlow. Why might the Woolworth heiress, one of America's wealthiest citizens, visit the epic house her uncle helped build?

"The Gold Coast, particularly those who attended the dinner, decided that the only possible reason for opening the villa was that Barbara was planning on buying a house in Palm Beach," wrote Nancy Randolph in May 1939.

If Mar-a-Lago was to find a champion, it would not be Post's third husband, Joe Davies. The South Florida playground where industrialists, heirs, and investors spent their winter leisure time sport fishing and sailing may have been a little foreign to the Roosevelt appointee, who was firmly entrenched in Washington and its Democratic presidency. Wintering with the "colony" may have seemed provincial for the new ambassador to the Soviet Union. With World War II mounting, Europe and Washington beckoned him more than did an island off the coast of Florida.

One thing was for certain: The darkened hulk of Mar-a-Lago didn't violate the shoreline blackout restrictions that had been prescribed to avoid German U-boat attacks.

When the Davieses finally visited Mar-a-Lago in early January 1940, the couple arrived in Palm Beach wearing winter dress hats, dark overcoats, and heavy jackets that looked more appropriate for the formality of Washington than for the flowering seaside island. For the first time in almost five years of marriage, they opened their winter home. The ambience of sportsmanship and frivolity that once emanated through the halls was replaced by a more political bent. Within days of their arrival, they threw a dinner party and then immediately returned to the nation's capital. The power couple returned only periodically to host an Animal Rescue League benefit or address the Everglades Club on war matters.

The new man of the house at Mar-a-Lago was otherwise occupied by the FDR administration. The president entrusted his longtime friend to oversee the third-term inauguration ceremony. In addition to serving as Soviet ambassador, Davies served as ambassador to Belgium and Luxembourg. As World War II loomed, he helped oversee war policy and issues for the State Department.

In Washington, the Davieses settled on a rolling, twenty-acre estate with a red-brick, Georgian-style house and named it Tregaron in honor of Davies's ancestral home in Wales. Just three miles northwest of the White House, the home put Davies near the center of US discussions on the war. They installed a nine-hole golf course and fountains, painting the bottom of a lily pond turquoise. Over the ensuing years, they entertained three US presidents and a host of international power brokers there.

By the winter of 1940, with temperatures in Palm Beach climbing up into the eighties, Davies was ready for a change of scenery and headed south.

"I'm down for a rest I feel I much needed after three and a half years in Europe," he told the *Palm Beach Post*. "Coming home is like going to heaven from an inferno. No one can realize the horror and devastation and hopelessness of the people in Europe today."

Sitting in his wood-paneled library, Davies espoused the virtues of American liberties and European views on America. He told the reporter that he and Marjorie considered Palm Beach the "most beautiful spot in the world" and hoped to spend "more and more time here, taking a real part in the community life. Only the pressure of official duty could drag me away."

Yet Mar-a-Lago held his attention for only a week or two of a ninety-day leave of absence from his federal post. Soon, he would chair the president's committee on war relief.

For Davies, his wife's palatial Palm Beach estate served a purpose. During their rare visits, the couple invited the usual cast of winter characters for dinners and parties. In addition to the regulars, though, new names appeared on the guest list. Democratic senator Millard E. Tydings and Democratic Senate Majority Leader Alben W. Barkley were among houseguests. Former ambassador Joseph P. Kennedy, the patriarch of what would become one of the nation's leading Democratic families, attended parties. Those years etched Mar-a-Lago's entry into a new era, setting the stage for formative political talks shaping national and international affairs.

Fireside chats at the one-ton dining room table undoubtedly centered on US involvement in the war that escalated after the December 7, 1941, bombing of Pearl Harbor.

Throughout the United States, war ration books soon dictated supplies of sugar, coffee, and canned goods for all families. People had to declare if they possessed more than the monthly allotment of a pound of coffee or five cans of food per person. Women worked in factory jobs vacated by men who were serving overseas.

If monied families steered away from flaunting their excesses during the Depression, they honed an image of self-sacrifice during the war.

Mrs. Davies waved farewell to her New York City penthouse atop what had been the old Burden Mansion. For years, she had rented it for $75,000 annually, but her attention now turned to renovating her Tregaron estate in Washington, DC.

In Palm Beach, Eva Stotesbury opened El Mirasol's pool during select summer days for military officers and their families.

The Davieses offered up Mar-a-Lago as a ticket to help raise much-needed war funds. In late February 1941, the manse was displayed for the paying public as part of a five-home tour benefiting a mobile canteen operation for Great Britain. They donated their yacht, the *Sea Cloud*, to the Coast Guard for war-related efforts and would soon offer up their grand Palm Beach residence yet again as a patriotic gesture.

In Palm Beach during 1942, the owners of The Breakers leased it to the federal government. It became Ream General Hospital, providing treatment for war casualties. The owners tucked away valuable art, carpets, chandeliers, draperies, and other trappings. For two years, nurses, physicians, and surgeons treated 750 injured service members in oceanside quarters once reserved for the privileged class. Palm Beach matrons volunteered. First Lady

Eleanor Roosevelt and Senator Harry S. Truman, a Missouri Democrat, graced the seaside military hospital.

Even as casualties mounted, the $250,000-plus annual lease was set to expire in June 1944. The War Department and hotel owners hit a stalemate during lease negotiations, setting the stage for unflattering images of wounded soldiers being evicted from the elite hotel. A Senate committee, headed by Truman, questioned what seemed a heartless move.

In keeping with other part-time islanders, the Davieses offered up the grounds of Mar-a-Lago. The offer made no mention of soldiers recouping among the mansion's fifty-eight bedrooms. The evicted members of the military were at least invited, though, to use sea-stretching acreage and bathing facilities.

For decades to come, wars would touch this place in indirect ways, from events honoring war veterans to a dinner for the leader of a country the United States had once battled. Even Mar-a-Lago's partnership with its supposed savior—the Department of the Interior—occurred under the shadow of the Vietnam War. And the giant house itself would lose favor as its owner amassed Revolutionary War artifacts from the other side of the world.

CHAPTER 7

MONUMENTAL ALBATROSSES

Gusting May winds brushed against El Mirasol's ocean-view bedroom windows in late spring 1945. A shadow cast over the winter home that once stood at the center of Palm Beach society and inspired Marjorie Merriweather Post's vision for her own winter estate. Inside, Eva Stotesbury languished from pneumonia. Usually, by late spring, she would have migrated back to her main home—the three-hundred-acre estate of Whitemarsh Hall in Philadelphia. This year, the octogenarian could not make the move.

Outside her sickroom, the whipping winds carried more than midges and maypop pollen. From the shores of the island to the mainland and throughout the country, the May breezes of 1945 wafted with the sounds of horns honking, children squealing, and marching bands blaring. World War II had ended for Europe. Lying in her bed and struggling to breathe, Eva Stotesbury may not have contemplated the full breadth of the moment—or what it would hold for her own world. But even in her compromised state, she was well aware that this wind held change for her longtime claim to island life.

A month after the war ended, an "invasion attempt" occurred on the very spot where Mrs. Stotesbury convalesced. A St. Petersburg group known as the Hayes Foundation planned to purchase the grand estate on the condition that the Town Council support plans to transform it into a sanatorium. Neighbors, including newspaper magnate Herbert Pulitzer, protested the rezoning. The very town officials weighing the request lived nearby the proposed sanatorium. Mayor James M. Owens Jr. and Town Manager L. Trevette Lockwood had purchased homesites at Stotesbury Park. Certainly, the regal old homes that branded Palm Beach may have lost some of their charm, but could it actually become a hospital ward? Mrs. Stotesbury later denounced the proposal, saying she had no knowledge of the zoning request. Plans died in June when the Palm Beach Town Council responded that it considered rezonings only December through May.

The mansion would not become a hospital. Instead, another fate awaited. The eighty-one-year-old owner's health failed. She stayed in the home she and her husband had built between the ocean and the waters of the Intracoastal Waterway a quarter-century earlier. In mid-May, she suffered a heart attack and died a week later. Newspapers in a dozen states published stories noting her death. Across the continent, a piece in the Spokane, Washington, newspaper memorialized her as the end of an era: "Mrs. Stotesbury was the last of the great dowagers who for years ruled Philadelphia Society with an iron hand and a velvet glove, and long had been a figure in the social life of Palm Beach."

Listed for sale at a half-million dollars, the estate could be had for just $350,000 without the furnishings. Despite its regal setting and waterfront views, it sat for months with no respectable offers.

Then the auction came.

Billboard signs advertising the sale of its furnishings loomed next to the driveway. The heart of the estate—the trove of legacy furniture originating from Italy, Spain, France, and Germany—went to the highest bidder. Rugs dating back to the sixteenth century could be had. Paintings from the French, Dutch, and Italian schools awaited new owners. The eye-popping stash of valuables became its own tourist attraction. Even with a two-dollar admission fee, more than four thousand people came. Owning a piece of El Mirasol drove prices sky-high; a rug appraised at $500 sold for $3,700, and a $750 oil painting went for four times that much. The trove generated $156,000, which was equivalent to millions of dollars in 2023.

The carefully selected pieces that gave the house its identity were now gone from the echoing halls. Under the headline "Half-Empty El Mirasol Stands as a Monument to Era of Luxury Living," the *Palm Beach Post* published a residential obituary to the house following the auction.

"Stark and half-empty, El Mirasol, once the setting for some of Palm Beach's most elaborate social gatherings, stood last night, a shell of its former self, with all its paraphernalia for luxurious living passed into alien hands," wrote the *Post* on March 4, 1947.

Famed American portrait painter and intellectual Frances Cranmer Greenman wrote a piece about the auction for the *Minneapolis Star Tribune*:

Remember that shiver of sadness which strikes your heart when in a forest you hear the cry of "TIMBER" and a pine tree which for years has been a landmark comes crashing down, breathing its last prone upon the ground, taken from its temple of blue and the wind and the stars.

When the auctioneers' cry of "Sold" rang out over and over again, selling the furnishings of "El Mirasol," that's the way I felt.

The house and property were, of course, next. They fetched a few hundred thousand dollars to be divvied among fourteen divisive heirs. One syndicated newspaper columnist wrote that the fate of El Mirasol had been assured by a trio of fun-loving children "with their lackadaisical nonchalance at seeing the family home left to dust and disrepair."

The bottom line told the story. While the furnishings sold at auction for 70 percent more than appraised value, the house and 370 feet of its oceanfront property sold for just 15 percent above appraisal. An affiliate of Pittsburgh investor Michael Phipps bought the house and land. Rather than claiming the aging Stotesbury mansion, he would build his own place on the property on the southern end— with the rest carved up for other houses. Among the homesite buyers were Palm Beach Mayor Owens and Town Manager Lockwood.

The spectacle cast a long shadow over Mar-a-Lago and the other remaining grand residences built decades earlier. The sheer lack of interest in saving such a residence was disconcerting. Elsewhere in the country, groups of residents, architects, and historians had started banding together to prevent destruction of historic buildings. Charleston, South Carolina, and the French Quarter in New Orleans had led preservation efforts. Even in Florida, the state had granted protections for buildings in St. Augustine, where tourism stoked the local economy. But local and state officials were slow to protect aging mansions that sat atop commercially viable oceanfront property.

Chicago Tribune writer Helen Van Hoy Smith wrote of the emerging battle between the old and the new. She lamented that the residential giants of Palm Beach sat empty while a settlement of small pastel homes clustered in the northern end of Palm Beach "like bon-bons in a box."

New York Daily News columnist Nancy Randolph asked the obvious question: "Will this 24-carat whistle-stop, which used to draw two-thirds of the country's wealth, ever be the place it was? What happens to vacated estates is anyone's guess."

El Mirasol wasn't alone. Like century-old live oak trees rooted in the corridor of a planned highway, the estates Playa Riente, Casa Bendita, The Towers, Casa Florencia, Casa Joseto, and La Fontana all faced bleak futures. Sometimes called the white elephants of Palm Beach, they aged atop waterfront property coveted by ambitious developers. Within a few years, the properties would all be destroyed or dismantled to make way for housing developments and high-rise condominiums.

Many owners saw these vestiges of the Gilded Age as anachronisms—too large to air-condition, too expensive to maintain, and too hard to staff.

• • •

In certain pockets of the country, preservationists made ground in saving a few unique estates. In Palm Beach, the attitude was different. Townspeople considered it a victory to preserve parts of Mrs. James P. Donahue's Cielito Lindo by carving the residence into five separate houses.

The Woolworth heiress's winter home emptied out after a three-day sale of her belongings. Demolition seemed obvious, making room for about twenty lots with a road running through the middle of the property, where the mansion stood. But architect Byron F. Simonson suggested dividing the home and its buildings into five dwellings.

"Dining halls became living rooms in the partitioning, servants' quarters were converted to bedrooms, and even an incinerator flue became a fireplace large enough to burn twelve-foot logs," read a January 1949 article in *Palm Beach Life* magazine. "Bedrooms were fashioned from loggias and entire kitchens from the laundry of the large house. In every instance something old becoming something new in the skillful partition of a mansion."

In monied enclaves throughout the country, a shadow loomed over architectural gems like Cielito Lindo and El Mirasol. And as the grand estates along South Florida's coastline and elsewhere met their fate, Marjorie Post Davies would quickly learn the toll that preservation can take.

Seemingly on the other side of the universe from Mar-a-Lago, midway in the summer of 1947, a din of voices began to echo off auditorium walls. The chairman of the Oyster Bay Zoning Board repeatedly threatened to shut down the meeting if the cacophony continued.

Anxieties had been so high during that heated showdown that officials had moved the meeting to Oyster Bay High School. Cars overflowed the parking lot as about a thousand residents came to oppose Long Island University's plans to purchase and repurpose the Davieses' 120-acre Davies Hillwood estate into a campus. It was the retreat Marjorie had bought and rebuilt with her ex-husband Edward Hutton after he lost what was then his only child during an equestrian accident at his Long Island retreat.

Now, for the first time, Marjorie Post Davies faced a mob that was angered by her plans to sell one of her estates to a buyer with other plans for the 120 acres.

This was not your typical neighborhood protest.

Post's country getaway was nestled in the so-called Gold Coast, where the Vanderbilts, Astors, Whitneys, Woolworths, J. P. Morgan, and hundreds of other wealthy families had built hillside mansions overlooking famed beaches of sculpted boulders threaded with sandy pockets of shore. By some counts, five hundred mansions stood upon seventy square miles. Investment banker Otto Kahn's castle far exceeded anything Palm Beach had seen and was possibly second only to the Biltmore for its girth and grandeur. Theodore Roosevelt built what would be called his

Summer White House there—Sagamore Hill, with its clapboard siding and shingles signaling Yankee craftsmanship. The rolling seaside hills cast the legendary setting for F. Scott Fitzgerald's novel *The Great Gatsby*: "The parties were bigger. The pace was faster, the shows were broader, the buildings were higher, the morals were looser, the liquor was cheaper."

Hillwood was a sort of stepsister to Mar-a-Lago, both crafted for Marjorie and Edward Hutton as places to escape the city and entertain. Unlike the grand estate in Florida, Hillwood centered on a Tudor house surrounded by cedars and holly trees. They planted fruit trees and vegetable gardens. Hillwood's own dairy farm also helped sustain the estate.

Now, the Davieses had other interests.

At home in the nation's capital, they were entrenched in the political and power circles of Washington. They hosted all levels of politicians who were in town for presidential inaugurations. Socialites vied for invitations to Marjorie's garden parties.

"The key reason why Marjorie decided to sell was very simple," said Kenneth Mensing, former historian for Post's Long Island University. "Her interests had moved to Washington, DC, and she was just not using the estate any longer. She felt that it was a waste to have the house mothballed."

Back in Long Island, the staff at Hillwood must have known it was over in 1941 when Marjorie shipped her bedroom furniture from there to her home in Washington. She tried to sell her old North Shore country estate, but buyers were more scarce than eligible bachelors during the war. Sentimental strings may have tugged too. Her teenage daughter, Nedenia Hutton, dreamed of marrying and hosting her wedding reception at her childhood summer home. In 1946, E. F. Hutton walked "Dina" down the matrimonial aisle and celebrated with busloads of guests at the Gold Coast haven. The old manse, it seemed, had finally served its purpose.

Now, all that remained for Post's Long Island home was its disposal.

Long Island's old-money ranks must have watched in awe as one of the island's giants fell leading up to Hillwood's rezoning fight. In the spring of 1947, wreckers began the six-week job of demolishing Harbor Hill, one of the largest homes ever built in America. It once hosted the Prince of Wales and celebrated Charles Lindbergh's transcontinental flight. After owner Clarence Mackay died, his son leased part of the six-hundred-plus acres to the military for an Air Force station in 1940. Vandalism and neglect claimed the grand halls that had been erected at the turn of the century. The wooded haven would become a housing development.

"Another fabulous old mansion, which housed a multimillionaire in the gaudy era when the servants numbered 100 and the party guests reached 1,000, is on the way down the dusty trail to the special junkyards reserved for the colossal 'white elephants' that dot Nassau's North Shore," *Newsday* writer Helen Dudar wrote in April 1947.

Yesterday's magnificent wonder. Today's laboring white elephant.

Two months after Harbor Hill's demise, Long Island University offered to buy Marjorie's summer estate for the full asking price of about $200,000. Officials planned to keep buildings intact for a campus. Hillwood, it seemed, could get a second life as a place of education and enlightenment for future generations.

If the Davieses celebrated Hillwood's pending sale by uncorking champagne, they likely needed only a few glasses. The privileged elite and local residents feared they would face a parade of delivery trucks, collegiate revelers, and the littered residue of campus life. They mounted a campaign against Hillwood's next life.

Tempers flared among the throngs of angry Long Islanders at the Hillwood rezoning meeting. For six hours, residents pleaded that the college campus would add traffic, noise, and bars to the stately North Shore. Trustees of nearby villages testified against it. An attorney mounting the charge against the new campus said the plans would drastically alter the very character of Oyster Bay and its villages.

University president Tristram Walker Metcalfe responded by saying he didn't want to go where he was unwelcome. He also reminded the crowd that the North Shore already had higher education institutions. Construction would be minimal because Hillwood was in such good condition that classes could open in just a few months. The main manor house would transform with twenty-eight dorm rooms and additional dormitories in Hillwood's farm buildings. Education groups and the American Legion rallied for the new campus, which was to serve 600 local students and 125 veterans home from the War.

The Davieses let the university president do the talking. It would be four years of navigating challenges, protests, and litigation before the deal closed.

The fight would have left anyone scarred and exhausted, particularly when one might have to go through the whole ordeal several times again with Topridge (previously named Hutridge) and Mar-a-Lago. Even if she could find suitable buyers for those two storied residences, could Post really endure more battles like the last one? At the age of sixty, she could see the challenges ahead. Her three daughters showed no interest in preserving their mother's regal vacation quarters of bygone eras. If the properties were left to them, they'd be sold and bulldozed to make way for clusters of quaint little mansionettes.

The world would always know Marjorie Merriweather Post as the heiress who reinvented her father's company and one of the first women to command a global corporation. The famed jewels and Russian artifacts she collected would forever be admired in museums, exhibitions, and collections. But the houses she created as her ultimate stamp of success had increasingly few chances of surviving.

More was at stake than losing a foothold for family memories. The homes of the General Foods empress helped brand entire communities—just as the Vanderbilts' Biltmore estate shaped Asheville, North Carolina, and Hearst Castle came to define San Simeon, California. Those increasingly rare properties helped benefit local economies with visitors anxious to see the last vestiges of the era of America's industrial wealth.

Gone were the days of feather boas glancing off Mar-a-Lago's sweeping staircase railings. Where big band brass once serenaded guests against a backdrop of February sunsets, only seagulls squawked on the southern banks of Lake Worth. The mansion that had so successfully funneled money into local and international charities remained shuttered as its owners entertained elsewhere.

The protracted sale of Hillwood cast a harsh light into the dark recesses of Mar-a-Lago, which had barely opened during the last decade. Was the Palm Beach manse really worth the time, trouble, and expense to keep? Would anyone want to take it on? Was there any hope to preserve one of the country's most impressive examples of Gilded Age glory?

At the time, Post's youngest daughter, budding actress Dina Merrill, had married the heir to the Colgate-Palmolive fortune. Her older sisters, Adelaide Brevoort Close and Eleanor Post Close, also had their own lives and succession of husbands to attend.

Merrill would later say that it just didn't make sense to her, or to any of her sisters, to take it on:

Life being what it is, one goes on to the next stage. Life is not stationary. That was a wonderful part of my life, and memories that I will always treasure. Before Mother died, she gave all of us a choice of having the house left to us, with all its responsibility and costs, or not. That house supports a lifestyle that certainly I'm not interested in. That's part of the past. And it's wonderful to have been part of that past, but it's not my life or my lifestyle—never was since I was a child. I started as a working actress at a very young age and continued with that. My sisters are the same. One raises horses and dogs in Maryland; the other lives in France and has no intention of coming back to the States. It just wasn't right for us.

Mother recognized that, and that's why she figured something else to do with it.

Years later, the subsequent owner of Mar-a-Lago accused Merrill of turning her back on the opportunity to honor her renowned mother. Said Donald Trump in November 1997: "She should have been the one to save Mar-a-Lago. Mommy had given her money and it would have been an easy and popular thing to have done."

To many, answers to the pressing questions about Mar-a-Lago seem obvious. It may have been almost expected when, in November 1951, news broke of its pending demise. After surviving hurricanes, Florida's real estate bust, the Great Depression, divorce, and disinterested heirs, it appeared that developers would finally get their hands on Marjorie's pride and joy.

Just three months after the battle ended over Long Island University's purchase and rezoning of Post's old Hillwood country estate, newspapers from Miami to Montana reported that the Davieses would level their seldom-used winter home and make way for a subdivision.

"The plan is to raze the mansion," the *Miami News* reported, "but if the cost is too great they will try to get a zoning permit to divide both the villa and the gardens into a subdivision." The house that had captivated a generation of America's wealthiest denizens was set to be carved up, just as developers had divided Mrs. James P. Donahue's Cielito Lindo house in Palm Beach.

A New York syndicated columnist wrote: "The Davies have issued orders to raze their fabulous Palm Beach oceanfront villa." The column went on to note the owners could tear down the entire place rather than see it quartered up so that some retired "bookmaker could boast that he bought the Davies place."

The story faded, and along with it, a marriage that put Marjorie near the center of US political circles but paired her with a husband she would find too controlling to bear. Within a year of the initial reports, news circulated that she would divorce Davies.

She later told a reporter for the *Pittsburgh Press* that her children didn't want Mar-a-Lago and she "couldn't bear the thought of it being torn down."

Watching El Mirasol's demise and Hillwood's troubled sale didn't deter Marjorie Merriweather Post from investing in homes that would eventually become hard to unload.

Perhaps the darkest day for Mar-a-Lago, and its ultimate fate, was January 31, 1955. There was no Category 5 hurricane on the horizon, no hair-slicked developer in the anteroom, and no contentious ex-husband at the attorneys' offices. There was, though, a new addition to the Post portfolio of properties.

Extracting herself from her two-decade-long marriage to Davies had come at a price. As part of their 1955 split, she got Mar-a-Lago and Camp Topridge while he got their twenty-acre spread in Washington, DC. For an heiress to a food fortune, the DC property was easily replaced with another home that would keep her near the country's center of political power. Even before an Idaho judge granted her the divorce, on the grounds of mental cruelty and incompatibility, Post found another Washington estate to suit her needs. For $650,000, she arranged for the purchase of the old Arbremont estate and its twenty-four gently rolling acres overlooking Rock Creek Park in northwestern Washington, DC.

She anointed it Hillwood, in honor of her onetime estate on Long Island.

Unlike its predecessor, this Hillwood would become the darling—serving as more than Post's home for springs and autumns.

For more than two years, she renovated and crafted extensive gardens with views of the Washington Memorial. The thirty-six-room home transformed into a venue for parties, teas, and fundraisers. She opened Hillwood's doors to student groups and art historians. Her gardeners cultivated rare greenhouse orchids, using them in floral displays throughout the house.

Most important, it showcased the priceless imperial Russian and Orthodox artifacts the venerable collector garnered during—and beyond—her years with Davies. He had served as Soviet ambassador in the late 1930s during the Stalin regime, known for its violent Great Purge. At the time, the dictatorship had limited cash but ample access to valuables from the days of Imperial Russia and treasures of the Romanovs.

Among Hillwood's ninety Fabergé pieces are two imperial Easter eggs that Post purchased while Davies was in Moscow. Above a table in the breakfast room hangs a green and crystal chandelier from Empress Catherine's palace.

Post described her breakfast room in her booklet *Notes on Hillwood*: "In this charming little room I would like to draw your attention to the glass and ormolu chandelier, a Russian one from the palace of Pavlovsk near St. Petersburg."

While the priceless collection long helped Hillwood visitors better understand the riches and lifestyles of a renowned historic era, it has had its controversies. Hillwood curators have carefully documented provenances of the pieces. The issue, according to some scholars, is that the grand hostess and philanthropist turned a blind eye to the atrocities committed under Stalin in order to build her collection.

"Post essentially ignored the destructive Soviet policies that made these artifacts available for purchase," wrote University of Maryland scholar Lindsay T. Inge in 2016. "Post chose to purchase cultural objects that she knew had been seized from the Orthodox Church and private Russian citizens."

Harvard University's Dumbarton Oaks research library put it more gently: "This art was available due to the Soviet Union's official policy of financing its industrialization plans by selling off paintings and objects that had been confiscated from the imperial family, the aristocracy, churches, and some museums."

Even with some raised brows over its collections, Hillwood quickly upstaged Mar-a-Lago. With its red brick elevation and white-columned entry, the neo-Georgian style lacked the imagination, heft, and significance of its older sister in Florida. But it had what Mar-a-Lago could never attain with any amount of money—location. It was plugged into the nation's power elite with a diverse and seemingly endless supply of provocative guests and, later, monied benefactors. A constant menu of symphonies, ballets, and concerts lay at its doorstep. While West Palm Beach had its Norton Museum of Art, designed by Mar-a-Lago architect Marion Sims Wyeth, Hillwood had proximity to the National Mall studded with Smithsonian museums, gardens, and presidential monuments.

Mar-a-Lago commanded views of one of the world's largest bodies of water. It backed to a waterway navigable up the entire Eastern Seaboard. It offered a haven from the perennial ice storms, blizzards, and winter malaise of the North. Aesthetically, few examples of American architecture could compare with Mar-a-Lago's design delicacies or its authentic mix of Dorian stone, centuries-old Moorish tiles, and hand-crafted relief. Yet it was still a one-season wonder. Its main strength could be its main weakness—island exclusivity far removed from the engines that pushed the country forward.

But why was there a sibling rivalry at all between Hillwood and Mar-a-Lago? Certainly, a woman who would be a billionaire by twenty-first-century standards could afford any number of residences. And certainly, it seemed that Post could manage multiple estates. At least that was the case while she was alive.

CHAPTER 8

"LUSTER'S LAST STAND"

With the exception of one "attractive blonde," the Florida Council of 100—an elite group of power brokers—was composed of all white males appointed by then-segregationist governor C. Farris Bryant.

The membership roster was studded with names like CBS news anchor Walter Cronkite, radio and television celebrity Arthur Godfrey, the president of ABC News, and the heads of dozens of the biggest corporate engines in the state. State Comptroller Fred Dickinson chaired the group and called it "the most influential group of industrial and business leaders ever assembled in the history of Florida."

Their job generally was to find that sweet spot of private enterprise and government partnership. Boosting tourism and profits generally drove the agenda.

Missing from this esteemed table, though, was a most notable Floridian who had helped build one of the largest conglomerates in the world and likely had more wealth than anyone on the select council, possibly even all of them combined. That would be the person credited with founding General Foods—Marjorie Merriweather Post.

She ushered in the 1960s with a new love—her fourth husband, Westinghouse Airbrake executive Herb May. While he sat on the prestigious Florida Council of 100, his far more successful wife was relegated on the council's membership address list to the column titled "Residences" and simply noted there as "Wife, Marjorie."

During that time, car radios began blaring Bob Dylan singing, "The answer, my friend, is blowin' in the wind." Birmingham police enlisted fire hoses and dogs to control protesters, including children. NASA bid adieu to its Mercury space program. Amidst this budding undercurrent of change in spring 1963, a mail stream carrying hundreds of invitations landed at the homes of the most powerful men in Florida, entreating members of the Florida Council of 100 to bring their wives to a luncheon at Mar-a-Lago on April 5.

It was no secret that the owner of 1100 South Ocean Boulevard in Palm Beach had been trying for years to save her South Florida casa.

The home's silk needlework panels, Bristol chandeliers, antique Spanish rug, and other furnishings had been prepped for auction in 1958 when a Florida restaurateur planned to buy the property. Those plans were thwarted by Palm Beach's iron fist on the property, dictating zoning restrictions. Syracuse University had been interested in it a few years earlier.

Syndicated columnist Charles Ventura wrote in his *Manhattan Memo* in January 1958: "Gold Coast die-hards may feel that it is luster's last stand when they learn here that Mrs. Marjorie Merriweather Post has agreed to surrender Mar-a-Lago, the old guard's sole remaining ocean-to-lake stronghold in Palm Beach, to the new guard."

The storied little town buzzed that Middle Eastern royalty would soon be sharing their beach. A Saudi king, perhaps Saud bin Abdulaziz Al Saud, first tried to rent the sprawling spread and then wanted to purchase it. Nancy Randolph, gossip-queen columnist for the *New York Daily News*, put it this way: "Resorters are predicting that when King Saud sees the 128-room Mar-a-Lago, it 'will be a case of the right man meeting the right mansion.' And that he'll want to buy it for his future American resort home."

The "resorters" were wrong.

"On the Saudi king, there was an inquiry," Marjorie Post recounted years later. "They wanted to rent it. But we were coming down. Well, they offered almost anything and they finally ended up wanting to buy it. I wasn't interested."

The king rented elsewhere, she added, bringing with him thirty-nine wives.

"Charming," commented the governess of social decorum in a tone dripping with disdain.

A few years earlier, the *New York Daily News* reported that Post "has let it be known that the place can be bought for $3 million. She has put $10 million into it. But Mrs. May will not sell Mar-a-Lago except to someone who will maintain her own standard of living. Otherwise she will give it to her church (Christian Science)."

By any measure, Mar-a-Lago was "in play." It is interesting that so was its amply appointed younger sister in DC.

As the Florida Council of 100's April 5 date with Marjorie loomed, the tables at Mar-a-Lago were set with an underlying truth: Post planned to leave her Hillwood residence in DC, along with its museum-quality collections, to the Smithsonian. In May 1961, she entertained the Smithsonian Board of Regents with a dinner so they could see the house, grounds, and artifacts she intended to bequeath to the museum. She had long fostered a relationship with the institution and knew Smithsonian Secretary

Leonard Carmichael from their time together on the Mount Vernon Seminary and College Board of Trustees.

Far from leaving the Smithsonian with a costly albatross, Post committed millions and millions of dollars to care for it. She promised income from a $10 million trust fund. If that ran out, there was a multimillion-dollar backup fund. Hillwood had a chance at survival.

Now, with the power elite prepping to sit at her Florida table, it was Mar-a-Lago's turn for salvation.

As one hundred suited-up Council of 100 members and seventy-five well-dressed wives entered the estate grounds on the morning of April 5, 1963, blue skies framed its signature rooftop tower. A sprinkling of spring showers cast a glistening finish on the grounds and loggia. The sea breeze had cooled the temperature, which was stretching into the eighties. Past the massive iron-grille front doors, they entered a front hall lit by hanging Spanish lanterns and reflecting light off walls and historic Moorish tiles.

"Everywhere there are flowers, which with family photographs and ingenious furniture arrangements, lend the room an air of intimacy and charm despite its large size," one frequent guest later described.

With her silver tresses coiffed and her neck bejeweled in a multitiered necklace of gems, Post looked exquisite as she welcomed her guests.

Small talk likely touched on the Soviets' chances for a moon landing with *Luna 4* or teenage daughters' bedroom posters of The Beach Boys. "You know, Marjorie banned the Twist from her dance floor last year," they may have whispered.

"Well, she offers women covers for their stiletto heels so they don't damage the dance floor. Can you imagine?"

Maybe guests raised eyebrows at the mention of the $115,000 donation their hostess had just made to the organization that would spawn the John F. Kennedy Center for the Performing Arts.

Chitchat was the side dressing. What would be remembered about that day was an announcement from Council Chairman Fred O. Dickinson, a rising star in state politics. What the West Palm Beach native had to say would make headlines in newspapers across Florida and as far away as Pennsylvania, Ohio, Texas, and Michigan. The news was both decided and celebratory. Led by this august body of council members, the path had opened for Floridians to protect Mar-a-Lago. Post had willed this gift, valued at $10 million, to the state upon her death. Headlines included:

PALATIAL PALM BEACH HOME DEEDED
TO FLORIDA BY THE MAYS

—*Fort Lauderdale News*, April 5, 1963

LAVISH MAY ESTATE DEEDED TO FLORIDA

—*Pittsburgh Press*, April 6, 1963

MAR-A-LAGO PRESENTED TO STATE BY HERBERT MAYS

—*Palm Beach Post*, April 6, 1963

STATE TO RECEIVE PALATIAL ESTATE

—*St. Petersburg Times*, April 6, 1963

STATE GETS MAGNIFICENT ESTATE

—*Tampa Tribune*, April 7, 1963

News articles gushed about the massive piece of real estate and the state's good fortune to receive such a gift.

"The Mediterranean architecture includes reproductions of some of the most famous buildings and palaces in Italy and Spain," reported the *St. Petersburg Times*. "The property also has a pavilion auditorium seating 200, staff buildings, a short nine-hole golf course and a 35,000-gallon swimming pool. The estate has its own water supply, from two 8,000-gallon tanks."

But whatever would be the role and purpose of this massive souvenir of the 1920s? How to best put this domestic castle to use in a way that would benefit the state? Holding educational seminars, entertaining visiting kings and dignitaries, hosting the Southern Governors' Conference, and opening a museum were among initial ideas. Even crafting a botanical garden for the public was in the mix.

The governor appointed a committee, led by none other than the incoming president of the council, to recommend a new role for the stately, old residence. Recommendations were due by June. But even by November, only the bare buds of a concept started to emerge from the leadership group. They proposed transforming Mar-a-Lago into a center for high-level diplomatic meetings and educational seminars. It would be part of the new Florida Atlantic University in Boca Raton, which had been dedicated by President Johnson just a few years earlier. The concept of an academic powerhouse blossomed into plans for a research center where scholars could avail themselves of Florida universities and the entire region.

The governor's staff produced a twenty-four-page booklet titled *The Mar-a-Lago Center for Advanced Scholars*. This would be Florida's chance to compete with some of the Ivy League schools to attract top intellectual talent. Select scholars could delve into the sciences and humanities while enjoying unparalleled quarters sitting between the lake and the sea. Across the United States, only the Princeton Center for Advanced Studies and the Institute for Behavioral Science in Palo Alto, California, offered such an intellectual platform, backers said.

"Under this program," the governor outlined, "the Center could literally be a great nerve center of excellence for the South, feeding out to institutions really seeking excellence in their graduate programs."

Beyond minted scholars, the doors of the Mar-a-Lago center would also welcome "gifted adults" who could add to this learning arena. This could be Florida's opportunity to distinguish itself in the field of thoughtful pursuits and polish a reputation beyond bikinis and gators. Southern businessmen could stay for a week or so and glean new insights about their fields. Plans called for seminars and conferences aimed at tackling economic and societal ills, including traffic, water supply, sewage disposal, decay of city centers, and spreading slums.

In short, this rebirth of Mar-a-Lago would be a boon to the culture of not just Florida but all America. Post heartily approved of this scholarly pursuit. Mar-a-Lago would become a house of serious learning.

University of Florida history professor Rembert W. Patrick put it this way: The expense would be worth the opportunity for Florida to attract scientists, literati, artists, professors, doctors, and lawyers.

Little could they know that their inaction would open the doors of Mar-a-Lago not to the great scholars of the time but instead to ideologues interested in bleach injections to ward off the COVID-19 pandemic or forecasts of the ocean rising a mere eighth of an inch during the next few hundred years.

At the time, these political appointees charged ahead with a plan: The governor won cabinet support to create a $5 million fundraising drive that would finance the estate's upkeep and operations. A team including a state Supreme Court justice and the president emeritus of Florida State University would help steer this slow-moving, bureaucratic ship.

"This resort town's most magnificent estate moved a bit nearer Friday to its renaissance as a scholarly retreat for Florida's men of letters and sciences," reported Jerry Parker of the *Miami Herald*. "But for Mar-a-Lago, the old palace cereal heiress Mrs. Marjorie Merriweather Post May wishes to give to the state, the transition will be a slow one."

Managed by Florida Atlantic University, the Mar-a-Lago Institute would be overseen by a board including the director of Florida's State Board of Parks, the Palm Beach mayor, a Palm Beach County legislator, a Post family representative, and leadership from the Historical Society of Palm Beach County.

State officials cast the institute as "a center for continuing cultural pursuits and educational programs for the entitlement and enjoyment of mankind."

Dealmakers called for about a thousand visitors to tour the estate over a period of three days each month, grossing an estimated $25,000 annually in fees. In addition, nonprofits including the American National Theatre and Academy and Florida Atlantic University would lease space there. They planned more revenues, with $5,000–$10,000 monthly registrations for seminars at the university's Institute of Arts and Letters.

The process itself, though, could have been a scientific study in Newton's third law of motion—put simply, for every action, there is an equal and opposite reaction. Just as excitement mounted for the new scholarly center, concerns about it rose too. First, the old-money resort town of Palm Beach complained about losing $35,000 in annual tax revenues. No one countered those concerns with an economic impact study—the mathematical multiplier-effect studies that would later become a staple to justify every big-ticket proposal considered by government.

Despite later claims that reopening Mar-a-Lago would be too pricey, advocates laid out a solid proposal fat with multitiered revenue. The university's music guild would contribute $5,000 from concert and musical theater ticket sales. Additional seminars for the university's Advanced Studies Center would bring in another $15,000. Even the state would contribute, serving up $75,000 annually based on an endowment from Post.

Contentious zoning battles can tie up projects for years, but Mar-a-Lago sidled up next to a longtime commercial enterprise known as the Bath & Tennis Club. Rezoning to allow a learning institute next to an athletic club seemed only logical. Overall, local issues seemed manageable when compared to the ultimate benefits that awaited Florida and the nation.

There was, though, a nimbus cloud forming quietly over Post's winter home. It had little to do with zoning or taxes. The shadow cast on the Mar-a-Lago Center for Advanced Scholars focused on the resort's highly guarded veil of exclusivity and the importance of protecting Palm Beach for the select few who could afford to winter there.

In the two years that passed since the Florida Council of 100's gala luncheon at Mar-a-Lago, the old guard of Palm Beach seized upon a poison pill that could kill the deal: The estate could cost about $260,000 a year to operate and maintain. Costs included:

- Employing a staff of up to eighty and providing more than twenty-six bedrooms for them—a six-figure venture
- Repairs and maintenance—$61,000
- Keeping the gardens and greenhouses in shape—$18,000
- Window cleaning during the season—$1,000
- And the utility bill—more than $11,000

The state edged forward with plans to raise millions of dollars to run the place. In addition, costs could be trimmed. Say, for instance, guests wouldn't each require a maid and butler. Even so, the costs smelled of excess and possibly government waste. Florida's legal counsel advised that the state couldn't pay the tab, and suggested a group like the Ford Foundation might help. But for the matriarch of General Foods to seek operational funds from the Ford group seemed a little, well, disingenuous.

Despite Mar-a-Lago's emerging reputation as a bottomless pit of need, Post's estate actually had the money to float its operations. The only problem was that the funds were earmarked to care for another of Post's residences—Hillwood:

> Mrs. May told Gov. Bryant all she can do is "give the property." She explained she endowed her Washington, DC, home, Hillwood, when she turned it over to the Smithsonian Institution a few years ago. She says her estate is "not large enough" for another endowment.
>
> —*Palm Beach Post*, October 4, 1964

Hillwood, with its view of the Washington Monument, had decisively upstaged Mar-a-Lago by garnering funds that otherwise could have gone toward a Mar-a-Lago Center for Advanced Scholars.

One solution would be to open Palm Beach's premier work of architecture to the masses for an entrance fee. But as Palm Beachers might say, "Absolutely appalling."

As the *Palm Beach Post* noted, "When word leaked out some months ago that Mar-a-Lago might be turned into a museum, which the owner suggested 'might be opened to the public (to) produce quite a good income . . .' well the idea went over with permanent residents of Palm Beach like a lead balloon."

Post's efforts to save her prized Florida home only baited the same kind of protesters who fought the rezoning of her original

Hillwood in Long Island a dozen years earlier. Handing over that estate to Long Island University took years. For Post, the clock ticked loudly. The seventy-seven-year-old had surpassed the average life expectancy for women at the time. Who knew how much longer she had?

Even that uncertainty clouded plans: She might die tomorrow or decades later, leaving the state at a loss as to how to plan for the scholarly center they would only get when she died.

The tide had shifted and even the *Palm Beach Post* called out the pretensions of its audience: "This public expression of sentiment to keep Palm Beach exclusive and generally uncluttered by tourists" sparked another idea. One of the members of the state's Mar-a-Lago committee suggested selling the estate's beachside property to help pay for upkeep of the house and grounds.

In New York, *Newsday* reported that Post's Mar-a-Lago neighbors had been "stunned, horrified and finally articulately hostile about the whole thing." As nationally syndicated columnist Lynn Sands wrote, "They rose en masse to protest her action on the grounds they did not want the public cluttering up the beach; they didn't want the estate taken off the tax rolls and they did not feel the gift was given in the proper spirit."

Further worsening her chances, two of her biggest allies were gone. About the same time Mar-a-Lago's upkeep costs became known in the early summer of 1964, her marriage to Herb May ended. She divorced him following six years of matrimony and lost any goodwill he might have built with the all-important Florida Council of 100.

Months later, Miami financier Stanton D. Sanson died aboard the *Queen Elizabeth* at the end of a ten-day cruise with his wife. The sixty-four-year-old had been a key member of the team pushing for the Advanced Scholar Center. The president of Florida Atlantic University put it this way in a 1962 letter to Sanson: "Surely you have done more than any other person to stimulate

interest and activity in higher education on the part of the out-
standing business and industrial leaders of Florida."

Angry islanders, zoning battles, lost allies, and Hillwood's
maintenance tab—the combination proved too toxic even for a
woman who had commanded an international corporation. On
January 14, 1965, Post surrendered her Mar-a-Lago quest with
the state.

"Many Palm Beachers—including the town officials—had
made it clear they resist putting the property to any other use than
a private residence," wrote *Miami Herald* staffer Jerry Parker in
bolded typeface.

Lynn Sands called Florida's $10 million blunder "a real gaffe"
and laid blame squarely on Post's neighbors who didn't want the
wrong element in their midst.

Other monied buyers eyed the residential jewel. Palm Beach
real estate agent Gwen Fearing heard from Rollins College president Hugh McKean about acquiring it. Together with his wife,
Jeannette Morse, the couple sought "to have the estate for their
own for the future." A board member of Palm Beach's new
Kennedy hospital (now known as the HCA Florida JFK North
Hospital) inquired about Post donating it for eventual use as a
museum. The Bath & Tennis Club president re-avowed interest
in buying the place. Even the Palm Beach Town Council tried to
snag it: "We feel that there is a possibility that something can be
worked out between the owner and the Town whereby the property can be given to the Town of Palm Beach to be maintained as
a Park."

The string of would-be owners came and then disappeared like
sand crabs down a hole, either swatted away by Post's contingent
or dissuaded by the enormity of the deal.

Publicly, the state patted Post on the head by making her an
honorary Florida citizen just a year after they spurned her offer.
She had long ago renounced her longtime Florida residency when

the state created a new wealth tax. On the day of her citizenry ceremony at the state capitol, some suggested resurrecting plans for Mar-a-Lago.

Privately, talks with the state continued for years. Even three years after Florida rejected Mar-a-Lago, the Florida State University Foundation joined forces with the state and its Board of Parks and Historical Memorials to accept the estate. The deal had been recommended by a committee laden with prestigious Floridians, including Florida State University President Emeritus Doak S. Campbell.

Two months later, those plans were scrapped. Judge Knott wrote that Florida governor Claude R. Kirk would gladly "accept" the gift of Mar-a-Lago if not for the "tremendous blast of publicity" that would follow.

CHAPTER 9

LADY BIRD LANDS

Everyone got a small gift to start out the trip. Well, to be fair, the present for Lady Bird Johnson wasn't so small. It was a three-foot-tall Easter bunny for her grandson, Patrick. In addition to the presents, also there for the flight from Washington, DC, to Palm Beach was Johnson's press secretary, Liz Carpenter. She had joined the First Lady as they walked up the dozen steps leading from the tarmac to the door of a turbojet aircraft. With each step, they could better see, next to the door, the flag emblems of about twenty countries where Post's Vickers Viscount airliner had landed.

George and Helen Hartzog had already boarded.

Former ambassador and White House Protocol Chief Angier "Angie" Biddle Duke would soon join them. His wife, Robin, was there already. The White House billed the trip as a break for Mrs. Johnson before she embarked on a five-day Texas trip. Also inside the plane were Post's attorney, Henry Dudley, and his wife, Lavinia. They must have felt particularly at home in the spacious aircraft, which was appointed with lush carpet, upholstered chairs, and lounges, along with flowers and food from Hillwood.

With everyone secured in their plush seats, the First Lady could hear the hum of its Rolls-Royce engines, which "set the tone," as she would later say.

The hum of the *Merriweather*'s engines had long ago changed the way Post used her constellation of high-end escapes. For more than a decade, the million-dollar jet ferried her family, old friends, guests, and even flowers from one estate to the other.

The *Merriweather* was more than transportation. It opened up startling views—aerial panoramas not just of Mar-a-Lago sunning itself next to the Atlantic but sharp visuals of the butchered island of Palm Beach, which she had cherished even as a young woman. The Stotesburys' El Mirasol and other grand estates that once claimed much of the barrier island, stretching from their Atlantic beachfronts all the way westward to their riverbanks, had disappeared among a sea of lesser rooftops conjured up over the decades by profiteering real estate developers.

Mar-a-Lago still unfolded amidst its expansive, rolling lawns, almost defiantly claiming the space as Palm Beach's last remaining symbol of what American ingenuity once bore. The fortress built to defy hurricanes once again welcomed politicians and businessmen just as it opened generously to charities and nonprofits that would decades later pay as much as a quarter of a million dollars to throw a bash there.

From cloud level, the house below stood not just as a display of wealth and inheritance but as a product shaped by the many influences in Post's life. Without her parents' efforts to educate her through world travels, the vision for the house might have been more parochial. Without the legal insights of her first husband, Edward Close, she might have lost a large chunk of her father's assets to her stepmother. Without E. F. Hutton's appetite for power and influence, Mar-a-Lago might have been just a far-fetched idea. And without Marjorie's own strategic willingness to grow the General Foods empire—including the purchase of Clarence Birdseye's company, which had pioneered the process of quick-freezing food products—the money to sustain the mansion over the decades might have disappeared. Even the sudden deaths of Hutton's first wife and son, coupled with the terrorist explosions on Wall Street, underscored life's fleeting nature and likely shaped the decision to build one of the grandest residential statements the country has ever seen.

Whenever the *Merriweather* descended into Palm Beach International Airport, she could see another important mansion on the shores of Lake Worth. Over the years, Henry Flagler's old Whitehall mansion had become a mangled atrocity that seemed to mock the long-dead railroad developer who opened up South Florida to the world. About a dozen years after he built the house as a tribute to his second wife, he died after falling down a flight of stairs at the mansion. His widow remarried within a few years but then died, leaving the seventy-five-room mansion to a niece. In a move that some family members would regret, she sold it to hoteliers. They obliterated key parts of the home and built a ten-story, three-hundred-room hotel on the site. They churned room nights with an eye for profits and disregard for Flagler's sanctums.

The reinvented Flagler estate, though, had something Post's lacked—a champion. As dim prospects loomed on the railroad tycoon's Palm Beach mansion in 1959, his granddaughter stepped up with a plan. Jean Flagler Matthews formed the nonprofit Henry M. Flagler Museum and organized a plan to save this piece of Florida history.

Marjorie Post had often stayed at the Whitehall Hotel, as it was called. Flying into Palm Beach in the early 1960s, Post could see evidence that Flagler family members, preservationists, and locals had stepped in to restore the grand old house. Hundreds attended the Restoration Ball for the museum, including National

Trust for Historic Preservation president Richard H. Howland and Florida governor Leroy Collins and his wife. On Post's flights in and out of Palm Beach, she could only ponder how the Flagler family had succeeded at something that seemed so elusive for Mar-a-Lago.

But here lay another chance. On this second day of April 1968, the queen of society in both the nation's capital and Palm Beach banked on her long-fostered relations with the power elite of Washington, DC. Those ties could now open a path for the preservation of Mar-a-Lago. As the afterglow of the sunset hung in the sky, the *Merriweather* touched down with its White House entourage at Palm Beach International Airport. Her guests' short, chauffeured ride from the airport across the Intracoastal Waterway ended at Mar-a-Lago with an abrupt honk, which signaled America's version of royalty to step outside to greet them.

"There was indirect lighting," Lady Bird Johnson recalled, "and I could see the palms soaring skyward and there was Mrs. Post at the door, calm and regal, the last of the queens in a setting that probably will not continue or be duplicated in this country in the lifetime of my children."

The two women knew each other from the parties and galas of Washington. Later in her life, Johnson told an interviewer that "one of the most glittering" parts of her life had been attending Post's annual garden parties.

Post escorted her guest to the estate's most storied chambers—Deenie's room which was named in honor of Post's youngest daughter, Nedenia. Painted in delicate pinks and blues with sprays of flowers, perhaps Dogwood, etched in bas relief across the wall, the room centered on a bed canopied in blue taffeta rising to a crown at the center.

"When I stood at the door, I thought, I am once more in the bower of a fairy princess, but this is a very young princess," Johnson said.

With the help of a personal attendant, which was a requisite for Mar-a-Lago guests, Johnson donned her flowered Adele Simpson gown and headed to the dining room punctually at 8:30 p.m. for dinner. Post's majordomo, Frank Moffat, announced guests in a pronounced way so even the hearing-challenged hostess could understand. There was fellow Texan and ardent LBJ supporter Fred Korth, former secretary of the Navy and dear friend to Post. Johnson's escort was Circuit Judge James R. Knott, a preservationist who had voiced support for Florida's thwarted plans to preserve Mar-a-Lago as a place of scholarly learning.

Appetizers floated past guests on trays offered by servers. Then, upon walking into the fresco-walled dining room, footmen flanked both sides of a massive dining table laden with caviar blinis paired with Russian vodka. The aroma of mushrooms and beef filet emanated from the room. Cherry-glazed carrots and asparagus in hollandaise glistened on plates. Wineglasses were filled with 1961 Château Haut-Brion and 1965 Puligny-Montrachet. Dom Perignon and Grand Marnier complemented the dessert soufflé as an accordionist and violinists played Calypso numbers. The party retired to a drawing room for after-dinner cordials, brandy, and coffee.

The flight in the private jet, tour of the house, time with Post, and elegant meal all made an impression. The next morning, with the sunlight framing their coiffed hair, Post guided the First Lady down the semicircular staircase from the loggia to see the grounds. The tour, dinner, and crafted suite all worked their magic on the First Lady, who quickly set into motion to protect Mar-a-Lago from the same fate that had demolished so many other estates. A week later, newspapers around the country reported a deal in the making.

MULTIMILLION DOLLAR ESTATE MAY BE SOLD
TO THE FEDERAL GOVERNMENT

—*Post Crescent*, Appleton,
Wisconsin, April 12, 1968

CASTLE MAY BE GIFTED TO THE U.S.
—Charlotte Observer, April 14, 1968

HEIRESS OFFERS RETREAT TO LBJ
—Lancing State Journal, April 14, 1968

GIFT OF PALACE IS PONDERED
—Spokane Review, April 15, 1968

Unlike the failed Florida plan to use Mar-a-Lago as a center of scholarly learning, this concept envisioned a more luxurious version of the Camp David presidential retreat for high-level officials and visiting world leaders, who often want to extend their US stay after departing Washington and the Blair House. *Washington Post* writer Maxine Chester went so far as to describe Mar-a-Lago as the better option than the "white-washed Georgian structure at 1600 Pennsylvania Ave."

Far from the reaction of Florida's leaders when they considered the manse, federal officials were initially guarded about prospects. A spokesperson for the First Lady, presumably Liz Carpenter, said: "Anything written about it will risk losing a potential gift. It is a dream ten years away."

"Quite true the preservation of historic homes and sites is becoming an increasingly important part of our national life and culture and therefore something to be fostered and worked at by the First Lady," she said at the time. "But for this particular First Lady, it's no duty—it's a pleasure."

Johnson started pushing both Stu Udall and her fellow guest at Mar-a-Lago, National Park Service Director George Hartzog, for Post's Palm Beach property to become part of the National Park Service.

A month after the beef-filet dinner in the company of Marjorie Merriweather Post and Lady Bird Johnson, Hartzog once again heard the hum of the *Merriweather*'s Rolls-Royce engines as it taxied down the runway in DC. This time, it headed south to Palm Beach on the business of expanding the Park Service.

Post knew this play of hers would likely be the last best hope for a showcase she had orchestrated when she was just half the age she was now. The matter now rested in the hands of a presidential administration mired in distractions as the nation prepped for its replacement.

In the last week of the Johnson administration, Udall had within his reach not just the preservation of a thirty-year-old winter vacation home in Florida but, more important, a separate deal that could be the pinnacle of his entire career.

It was Alaska—just a decade as a star on the US flag, it covered more land than Texas, California, and Montana combined. Udall was close on a deal protecting six million acres of federal lands there and another million in his home state of Arizona. He was all but assured of getting President Johnson's signature on the order naming the lands as national monuments. The move would keep some of the country's most pristine frontiers safe from commercial logging, mining, oil exploration, and other uses often allowed on federal lands. Coming to this moment, Udall had worked with key Democrats and Republicans to gain support for the initiative. With just weeks left in his administration, LBJ told Americans that more land would be set aside "before this administration ends." The clock was ticking.

Designating Mar-a-Lago, so admired by the First Lady ever since her visit the previous year, as a National Historic Site could only help get President Johnson on board with Udall's eleventh-hour national monument effort.

Udall likely knew that even the Kennedy clan had eyed Mar-a-Lago. Joseph P. Kennedy reportedly made a lowball offer of $1 million about a year after his son was elected president. The Massachusetts family had outgrown the fourteen-room Palm Beach compound that served as their winter retreat for decades. The president's mother started visiting the resort town even before there was a Mar-a-Lago. His tanned father famously worked deals and connections from the palm-draped patio, nicknamed the "bullpen." It was where JFK healed from back surgery and wrote much of his Pulitzer Prize–winning book, *Profiles in Courage*. Even though he lost the state of Florida and its ten electoral votes, Kennedy immediately celebrated his presidential victory by retreating to his Florida home after defeating Richard Nixon in November 1960.

Not even a month after Kennedy's inauguration, rumors persisted that his family would buy Mar-a-Lago for a Winter White House.

Even Palm Beach officials lobbied Post to deed it over for use by the Kennedys and subsequent presidents.

Even though Mar-a-Lago could grant the entire Kennedy crew ample space and a regal feel, its period architecture and pretensions somehow seemed off cue for a young First Family intent on updating the aging White House in Washington. And then there were the perennial upkeep costs and din of jets flying overhead to think about.

The idea of presidential retreats was gaining acceptance among Americans. While George Washington, John Adams, and James Monroe often stayed close to home, air travel and phone service soon loosened the presidential leash that tethered leaders to DC. Theodore Roosevelt and his family had retreated to their rambling Sagamore Hill estate in Long Island's Oyster Bay community, just a few miles from the original Hillwood estate that Post sold to Long Island University. Dwight Eisenhower stayed at the Augusta National Golf Club in Georgia, and Harry Truman revived in the warmth of his quarters in Key West, Florida. For Kennedy, his Winter White House was more the overall playground of Palm Beach aboard his yacht, *Honey Fitz.*

During Palm Beach's debut as a presidential vacation spot, the "colony" endured traffic, protests, and the media spotlight. When Kennedy's plane first landed at Palm Beach International Airport just four days after his election, thousands of people descended on the aviation port to greet him. Cuban exiles held signs, "Down with Castro."

Thousands more would come.

Not even a year into Kennedy's presidency, the *Palm Beach Post* reported that fifty thousand tourists—about eight visitors for every resident—had descended on the island resort, peering at the high garden walls and weather-beaten driveway leading to the winter residence for the Kennedy clan.

They drove their progenies in Comets and Plymouth Valiants along palm-lined Ocean Boulevard for a peek at the island's most famous part-time resident. Throngs jammed the streets when he arrived. Kodak Instamatics flashed in restaurants and bars. The colony's cherished privacy was lost at that time.

Overall, Florida had pretty much shed its "land bust" reputation from the 1920s. American astronaut Alan Shepard had been launched into space from Cape Canaveral Space Center. Now the nation's tenth largest state, Florida's population had more than quadrupled to five million from the post-bust crash in 1928. Its tourism industry burgeoned with Busch Gardens opening in Tampa. Universities were launching in Orlando, Boca Raton, and Pensacola. Despite its failed attempt to revive Mar-a-Lago for scholars, the state was gaining a certain cache.

Members of the Joint Chiefs of Staff lunched at Mar-a-Lago after budgetary meetings down the boulevard at the president's retreat. All levels of government officials, curiosity seekers, and journalists invaded the sidewalks of Worth Avenue.

Of course, along with the spotlight comes dark shadows. Navy Seabees constructed a presidential bomb shelter at nearby Peanut Island. Barely a month after the election, Palm Beach police apprehended and arrested a retired postal worker with plans to blow up the president-elect at the Kennedy compound. In addition to his confession, seventy-two-year-old Richard Pavlick carried seven sticks of dynamite, detonators, blasting caps, and four large cans of gasoline in his old Buick. Deemed mentally ill by the courts, Pavlick served six years in a psychiatric hospital.

Kennedy's last visit there was just four days before he met his fate in Dallas. And while Palm Beach basked in the light of international exposure, it had also seen a mentally ill man bent on dynamiting the presidential motorcade. For a hamlet honed long before fashionable gated developments blocked outsiders, those memories would not fade anytime soon.

Sitting at his desk years later, Udall could appreciate the intertwined threads of Jack Kennedy, Palm Beach, and Mar-a-Lago. Leading up to the 1960 election, the popular congressman from Arizona helped deliver enough electoral votes from that state to get the young Democratic candidate into the White House. Kennedy quickly rewarded Udall with the Interior post.

This was also Udall's chance to give a nod to the bereaved Kennedys and his now-deceased friend Bobby. Using his position, Udall orchestrated a name change for the stadium that was home to the Washington Redskins and Senators. It would henceforth be the Robert F. Kennedy Memorial Stadium. Word of the new stadium name spread quickly.

"A few hours later, LBJ telephoned Udall and angrily informed him that he would not after all sign the [Alaska wilderness] order. Udall offered his resignation on the spot," wrote reporters Frank Mankiewicz and Tom Braden in a story published on January 26, 1969, in California's *Sacramento Bee* newspaper.

Trying to please the Johnsons with protection status for Mar-a-Lago may have just been a stepping stone to Udall's now-quashed plans for greater wilderness protections. Whatever the political pressures that made it happen, Mar-a-Lago joined the ranks of National Historic Sites in January 1969—less than a year after Lady Bird Johnson's visit. In creating the Mar-a-Lago National Historic Site, Udall's Department of the Interior cited the nation's policy to preserve historic sites "for public use." And yet for this newest addition to the nation's collection of historic sites, the idea of preservation for public use would forever ring hollow.

Even though the Alaskan frontier plans died, Mar-a-Lago now bore the brand of a National Historic Site. It deserved protections. The nation's designated historic sites usually fall under the watchful eyes of the National Park Service—usually. The details of how Mar-a-Lago would become part of the nation's parks would be slow to emerge. Questions lingered of an endowment, regarding operations, and even surrounding Post's own use of the property, because she planned to use it throughout the rest of her life.

For the octogenarian Marjorie Merriweather Post on this occasion, there was much to celebrate. Immediately after securing the historic designation for Mar-a-Lago from the Johnson administration, the eighty-two-year-old belle celebrated Richard Nixon's presidency at an inaugural ball. Her box, by the way, was next to Richard and Pat's. Earlier in the month, she further celebrated in Palm Beach, treating ten houseguests to a cocktail gala for the new Findlay Gallery, headed by Wally Findlay, the third generation to lead the business that bore one of the oldest names in the American art scene.

"Still beautiful in her 80s, Mrs. Post has never lost her touch," one newspaper columnist wrote about her outing.

Continuing her tradition of hosting charity events at Mar-a-Lago, she prepped for a February fundraiser for the Animal Rescue

League of the Palm Beaches. She also oversaw the Palm Beach Red Cross international gala.

After shedding four husbands, the serial divorcée and matriarch of General Foods now devoted herself largely to philanthropy and trying to save her three remaining homes from destruction.

Finally on her own again, she reopened Mar-a-Lago with a bang, adding a bomb shelter that could protect Post, loyal staff, and select valuables. It could even serve as a hiding place for any important documents that might ever need to be stashed. Also new was a $250,000 pavilion to keep guests dry during her famed square dances. A staff of forty served three dinners and two dances a week.

When she welcomed the public to her grounds years earlier as part of a five-home tour sponsored by the Garden Club of Palm Beach, club leaders touted: "It is the last of the great estates of Palm Beach that is still occupied by its original owner." Mrs. Marion Sims Wyeth, wife of the architect who designed the house, led the Mar-a-Lago portion of the tour.

Through those years, Post entertained the Duke and Duchess of Windsor with a dinner for thirty guests. Designer shoes grazed a dance floor installed atop the patio; tube roses scented the air and lush palms edged the scene. Alcohol and cigarettes seldom passed her lips, yet she indulged guests with their requested hors d'oeuvres, cocktails, desserts, and favorite songs. When Princess Astrid of Norway visited, Post even invited Edward Hutton and his wife for an evening of revelry. The beat was back, echoing off the stone walls of the last of the Palm Beach great ones.

There was one seeming casualty among her collection of residences. With energies thrown into her new DC address and two revived vacation retreats, it was time to unload the storied old yacht *Sea Cloud*. One of the largest ships of its kind in the world, it had once attracted potential buyers, including Greek shipping magnate Aristotle Onassis, Cuban dictator Fulgencio Batista, the crown prince of Saudi Arabia, and the governments of Iran, Portugal, and Argentina, according to reports of tax deductions filed by Post. Six months after divorcing Davies, she sold it to Jacksonville shipyard owner George Gibbs for a half-million dollars. He then profited from selling it to Dominican Republic military strongman Rafael Trujillo, who became legendary for one of the bloodiest dictatorships on record.

Among other things, it served as a reminder that the prized possessions she had protected for so long could land in the hands of just about anyone.

CHAPTER 10

THE PRESIDENT
AND BEBE

The thunderous sounds of two helicopters overhead grew louder as they neared the nine-hole putting course at a long-closed mansion on South Ocean Boulevard. They came up the Intracoastal Waterway from the south, violating local rules. The downwash from the rotors whipped at the fronds of palm trees and drowned out even the noise from planes ascending into the flight path of nearby Palm Beach International Airport.

President Richard Nixon and his entourage—most notably including his old friend Charles Gregory Rebozo, perhaps better known as "Bebe"—looked out as the landing skids touched down in a backyard that had once enthralled everyone from locals to royals.

For the thirty-seventh president of the United States, this excursion was a much-needed break from the increasing pressures of Washington, DC. Ever since he had refused to turn over tapes of recorded meetings a year earlier, his presidency had spiraled. Impeachment hearings had started two months before, and now it looked like the whole matter could end up in the Supreme Court.

His antidote? South Florida with its ruddy tans, salty waters, and general disregard for convention. Just a few days was all he could manage, staying at his bayside Key Biscayne compound, popping into the Jamaica Inn for lunch, and boating with Bebe on the Cuban's houseboat, the *Cocolobo III*.

It wouldn't hurt to take a quick trip up to see the Palm Beach estate that he had brought into the National Park Service. The sixty-mile flight from his island retreat off the coast of Miami edging north up the coast would just take a half hour. Bebe might not be schooled in architecture, design, and diplomacy, but he knew real estate and might see a way to enliven the place.

Nixon's diary for that day—July 7, 1974—summed up the visit: "The President, accompanied by C.G. Rebozo, looked over the property to determine its potential for possible use by US Presidents for visiting foreign dignitaries."

The presidential helicopters clearly intruded on the resort's studied morning quiet. People fishing nearby said they mistook it for the Army and commented on the "men in suits" at Mar-a-Lago. Secret Service agents, Bebe, an assistant, and Nixon's personal physician all peered down as their aircraft slowed over the Intracoastal Waterway as the downwash stirred small wakes on the water's surface. Yes, it was a bit of a public show, but there was no need to make the press aware of the day trip, really.

They had tried to keep Clem Conger's trip to Mar-a-Lago quiet back in 1970. Nixon knew he could trust the White House curator to gauge the mansion and its furnishings without making his visit there fodder for the media. Even so, on the first day of Conger's long weekend visit there, the *Washington Post* had tracked him down almost immediately.

"I suppose every time I show up in some great house that needs saving, everyone is going to shout: 'Whoopee! The day is saved,'" he had quipped to the reporter.

Whoopee, indeed.

Clem and his boss had seemingly saved the day for the last "great house" on the winter island of millionaires. Congress had managed what the state of Florida botched—protection for this place of import. Congressman Wayne Aspinall of Colorado, together with US representatives Paul Rogers of Palm Beach and Roy Taylor of North Carolina, won passage of the Mar-a-Lago National Historic Site bill. Finally, the property eyed by many a developer was now safely in the hands of the National Park Service. As chairman of the House Interior Committee, Aspinall conveyed to Congress on October 10, 1972, the critical need to make the estate a national treasure: "Mr. Speaker, I have visited Mar-a-Lago and can tell my colleagues that it is a national treasure. No other place in the country equals it and it is unlikely that any comparable place will ever be built in the future. Here . . . we have an opportunity to protect a property before it slips into disrepair or before it is altered in some way as to render it less valuable to the American people. It is a great opportunity and a minimum risk. I heartily endorse the project and urge its adoption by the members of the House."

During those early years of the Nixon administration, when Post gave Mar-a-Lago to the Interior Department, the deed from December 1972 called it "a gift to the people of the United States." Unlike any other such gift to the National Park Service, this one even came with a trust fund for operations. By all accounts, it was in impeccable condition. Now the sprawling winter home of General Foods cofounder Marjorie Merriweather Post could serve generations as an example of how America's wealthiest society lived.

But with Nixon and his old friend looking upon it now, just two years later, this gift to the public had clearly languished under Florida's searing summer rays. Years after it joined the Park Service, Mar-a-Lago remained closed to all. As Nixon and Rebozo stood there staring at this abandoned estate, the waste must have seemed like a glaring example of government ineptitude. Or was it just a prize slow in the making? Two years earlier, when Nixon had signed the measure making this tower-topped icon part of the Park Service, officials had painted verbal pictures of it being used for seminars and diplomatic meetings. It was supposed to be a place where foreign dignitaries, heads of state, and high-level federal officials could stay. Now only a few groundskeepers and household staffers puttered about. Resident caretaker James Griffin, who inherited the job from his father in the 1950s, came out to greet the president and his companions that morning in early July 1974.

"He was very pleasant and thought the place was marvelous but didn't indicate one way or another whether he'd want to use it," Griffin later said.

Nixon's last-minute trip to Palm Beach didn't endear him to the local officials, who complained about the lack of notice. It was little wonder they were thrown off, considering the town's efforts to keep Mar-a-Lago off-limits. Even before the legislation came to the Oval Office for Nixon's signature, its cosponsor—Paul Rogers of Palm Beach—offered to take his name off the bill in hopes of appeasing angry islanders. Without the hometown boy's support, the bill would likely die.

But instead of pulling his support for the Mar-a-Lago park site, Rogers simply watered down the measure. Wording changed from: The federal government "shall develop and administer" the estate.

To this: The government "may accept and maintain" the site.

Word shifts that seemed so small were indeed deadly to preservation efforts.

If any regular member of the public tried to use the public property, they would need permission from the Interior secretary, who would need to check with a special commission appointed to oversee the historic site. Looking now at the mothballed estate, it was clear the commission hadn't been very busy.

Maybe the continued closure was just the product of a slow-moving bureaucracy. Perhaps the Park Service made an unwise choice to wait for Post's death before devising a plan to open Mar-a-Lago.

The inevitable had occurred soon enough. On September 12, 1973—ten months before Nixon visited the nation's closed-off treasure—Post had died at the age of eighty-six in her Washington, DC, home of Hillwood. Nixon had known the celebrated philanthropist through various DC social circles and worked to get her prized winter home preserved for the public to admire. Perhaps he even admired her wisdom for delaying her gift of Mar-a-Lago to the country until after her death. Then she couldn't see it sitting abandoned. In the time before her death, Post may have taken pride in accomplishing one of her life's missions—to save her three homes in perpetuity for the greater good of society. Hillwood and its rare treasures were safely in the hands of the Smithsonian Institution. And, at the time of her death, the state of New York was about to acquire her fabulous Camp Topridge.

What would she have thought now, with Mar-a-Lago's doors locked instead of welcoming esteemed guests as she intended? Of course, she had been keenly aware of her Palm Beach neighbors' efforts to block her plans. But the swift opposition to Mar-a-Lago's federal use had differed from the battle she had endured in Long Island, where her neighbors fought against plans to transform her weekend estate into a university campus.

No, the Palm Beach dissension differed from typical not-in-my-backyard discord. It started near the top with ringleader Robert Grace, Palm Beach Town Council member.

"Where are the casinos and night spots? The place is dead. That's the way we want it," Grace said.

The town wanted control of Mar-a-Lago, and Grace suggested the manse of international acclaim be used for town meetings and offices for the mayor. These weren't just any townsfolk throwing their weight around. Earl Edward Tailer Smith was likely America's only small-town mayor who had served as ambassador to Cuba, graduated from an Ivy League school, and lunched with the likes of Lilly Pulitzer.

A troika of town officials, including a Town Council member who had been ambassador to Pakistan, flew to Washington, DC, to fight plans for regular Americans to visit a National Historic Site on their island.

In response, Marjorie Merriweather Post's longtime lawyer flew to Palm Beach to defend the plans. Hunched, balding, and gray, the bespectacled Henry Dudley told the Town Council that they had hurt the late heiress "by the misunderstanding of facts so rampant in the town she loves.

"I just cannot understand the onslaught on the character of a lady like Mrs. Post," Dudley admonished.

Dudley was not alone in criticizing town leaders bent on excluding the public. Local and national media pilloried town officials and said the men were out of line. The lead editorial in the *Palm Beach Post* on December 29, 1969, advocated opening the mansion.

"There is no reason why the grandeur of Mar-a-Lago can't be shared by people not fortunate enough to be presidential guests," the piece read. "Taxpayers deserve as much accessibility to Mar-a-Lago as possible—and certainly more than envisioned by Palm Beach officials."

New York Daily News columnist Aileen Mehle put it this way in the "Suzy Says" column: "What really worries dwellers in the little Florida oasis is that hordes of peasants (disguised as tourists of course) will descend, and destroy the quiet elegance and status quo upon which that nest place of the rich prides itself. . . . Their blood freezes, even in that climate, when they consider that the house and its 17 acres of prime property may be open to the public."

Clearly, on this seventh day of July 1974, standing in the back-yard of Mar-a-Lago, Richard Millhouse Nixon had more on his mind than some resort town trying to thwart the public's access to a National Historic Site. Tomorrow at this time he would meet with the vice president and then the media. They were relentless in hounding him. A decision on articles of impeachment haunted him. If anything, this shuttered mansion hulking before him may have seemed just a metaphor for the direction of his own presidency.

Post's youngest daughter, Dina Merrill, later said Mar-a-Lago was a victim of poor presidential timing: "My sadness was that Watergate happened when it did, because President Nixon had come to visit, and thought this was far nicer than Key Biscayne and was prepared to move in. And then Watergate happened. And then we got President Ford. Then we got President Carter. As a result, before the election of President Reagan, who would have adored it, Congress passed a bill giving it back to the family. We were notified by mail that it was being returned to us. And we were horrified."

The helicopters' rotary blades started whirring. Heading back now, Nixon might have time to join Bebe for a cruise on the *Cocolobo* before heading back to DC in the evening. Thirty-one minutes after their helicopter landed at Mar-a-Lago, the president and his group boarded again for their trip back to Key Biscayne.

A month after his trip to Mar-a-Lago, the president who had welcomed it into the National Park Service and watched the first manned moon landing would resign from office under a cloud of scandal.

"I'm sure President Nixon will never use the estate," Post's attorney told a *Palm Beach Post* reporter following the president's visit.

He didn't.

After Nixon and his entourage helicoptered away from Mar-a-Lago on that searing summer day in 1974, no one might have imagined that he would play a role in what would become perhaps the blackest day for the house on South Beach Boulevard.

When Richard Nixon left Washington, DC, to return to his "La Casa Pacifica" home in San Clemente, California, he left behind the unfinished business of Mar-a-Lago. And, like other presidents, he took with him records and recordings of his years in the White House. Recognizing the importance of the material, Congress quickly passed a law prohibiting Nixon from taking the materials. It went on to pass the larger Presidential Records Act of 1978, ensuring that future presidents would transfer to the National Archives all official materials—particularly top secret documents—when they leave office.

In that way, Nixon's footsteps would echo in the halls of Mar-a-Lago long after his visit there on that searing day in early July 1974.

CHAPTER 11

SMITHSONIAN SWAY

Ling-Ling, the female, was a little more exuberant than her intended mate, Hsing-Hsing, according to zookeepers. Together the juvenile giant pandas stole the hearts of millions of guests at the Smithsonian Institution's National Zoo. Visitors came in droves, at a rate of twelve hundred people per hour. The pair of ebony-and-ivory creatures gifted by China drew twenty-four-thousand fans on their debut weekend in mid-April 1972.

At the time, the Equal Rights Amendment started making its way through the states; Americans stood in line at the cinema to see *The Godfather*; and NASA revved up its space shuttle program. The cultural heartbeat of Washington, DC, the Smithsonian, redefined itself too. It had just opened a Marine Station off Florida's southeastern coast, about an hour north of Palm Beach. The Hirshhorn Museum and Sculpture Garden in Washington would soon open with its tableau of modern and contemporary works. Perhaps most impressive, the National Air and Space Museum was underway with an architectural and design scheme that had much more than history in mind.

Nestled in the subdued hills of northwestern Washington, Post's Hillwood estate—and its cache of royal Russian treasures—didn't really epitomize America's revolutionary "Me Generation," as author Tom Wolfe called it. But the stately manse was now distantly related to the celebrated Ling-Ling and Hsing-Hsing as members of the Smithsonian family.

In January 1969—the same month US Interior Secretary Stewart Udall accepted Mar-a-Lago—US Supreme Court Justice Earl Warren accepted the deed to Hillwood in his position as chancellor of the Smithsonian. By all appearances, Post's famed residences would at last be protected and studied for generations to come.

Entering the 1970s with new approaches to offering museum experiences, the seasoned hands at the Smithsonian tightened Hillwood security, weighed admission rates, and debated how to best showcase Post's jewels that told historic stories of riches both lost and found. On the Smithsonian's 125th anniversary in 1971, Hillwood was featured as one of the Institution's new ventures.

In 1974, when the grand dame of business, culture, and philanthropy died at the age of eighty-six, newspapers in every corner of the country hailed her and noted the new owners of Mar-a-Lago and Hillwood. Expectations for a Hillwood opening mounted now that it was no longer Post's residence.

"While Smithsonian directors declined last week to say when the public would be able to view the collection called the finest outside of the Soviet Union's own Hermitage Museum, sources close to the project predicted Hillwood would be open in about six months," reported *Washington Post* writer Nancy L. Ross days after Post's death.

Little now stood in the way of visitors who might, for once in their lives, see the nuptial crown worn by generations of Russian royalty or orthodox chalices dating as far back as 1666. Post said it took some work to even begin to understand the value of the trove.

"When I first saw some of these chalices in a shop in Moscow they looked as though they were made of pewter because they were so heavily tarnished and covered with dirt," reads Post's *Notes on Hillwood* booklet published in 1979.

She got permission to take them to the US embassy and "we put it in a bath to remove the tarnish and found it was made of silver gilt decorated with miniatures and Ural Mountain stones," she wrote. The chalices had been heavily scratched when they were tested to see if they were made of gold. Being instead made of silver, they were not melted down to get bullion for the Five-Year Plan to fuel the new communist economy.

Just as Mar-a-Lago's future seemed in limbo, the same held for Hillwood. Six months turned into a year, with no Hillwood opening set. Still, Smithsonian executives trumpeted their work on the project.

"We have stepped up the security a great deal since the time of her death," said renowned curator Richard Howland. "We have so many guards and devices, it's unbelievable." Most of her jewels that were on loan to other Smithsonian museums would be returned to Hillwood, he added.

Museum experts buzzed about the jewels Post donated— the diamond necklace Napoleon gave Marie Louise and Marie Antoinette's tear-shaped diamond earrings of thirty-six carats, an Indian necklace of diamonds and fat, multifaceted emeralds. Where should they go? How best to protect them?

Yet as Smithsonian experts debated jewel displays, America's interests were shifting from opulence to activism. On the heels of the revolutionary 1960s, women were more likely to go braless than adorn themselves in diamond necklaces. Watergate had forced out a president. A new generation had crushes on panda bears from China. More important, though, families struggled amidst the worst recession since 1937. Rising gas prices made travel difficult. Inflation shot up more than 10 percent in one year and the Dow collapsed.

The working class wasn't the only group affected. In what would become a disastrous collision, Hillwood's annual operating costs climbed from $450,000 to $750,000 at the same time the foundation established by Post to cover the management of Hillwood watched as its stock portfolio revenues fell. Plans for the grand museum on the fringe of Rock Creek Park stalled like traffic entering a Washington, DC, roundabout.

Months ticked by, with Post's longtime attorney, Dudley, failed to create the trust that the Smithsonian needed to run Hillwood. Smithsonian historian Pamela Henson later described it as a "long, long period of delay in setting up the trust, in actually putting the money in the trust."

Smithsonian's point person on the deal, James C. Bradley, said Dudley and his staff had problems with the liquidity of stocks and bonds, the worth of the estate, and the grind of necessary legal steps. Oh, and then there were eroding pressures of inflation and stock market turmoil.

"We began early to have uneasy feelings about the validity of the $10 million bequest because of this," Bradley recounted in 1977.

Popular belief would hold that Hillwood cost too much due to Post's standards for daily fresh flowers and seasonal garden-plot changes. The irony is, though, that the Smithsonian's standards were likely costlier. While Post hired her security guards from the old soldiers home in Washington, the Smithsonian invested in skilled professionals and proven technologies to protect valuables.

The money was, in fact, there to run Hillwood. If Post's $10 million endowment wasn't enough, she gave the Smithsonian "first call" on proceeds from a much larger trust. But for every dollar of Post's money that went into Hillwood, the Smithsonian spent another dollar. It was supposed to be up to the Smithsonian to proactively work with the trust, flagging any deficit.

"When the Smithsonian did so, the foundation refused," wrote scholars in a 2020 paper authored by Smithsonian Assistant General Counsel Laura Damerville and two others.

Any other organization might have pushed the matter, but the Smithsonian had long been beholden to the Posts. If you were in the fundraising business, it wasn't a family you wanted to lose.

Since no one wanted to ask Congress for more money to keep Hillwood going, the two sides hit an impasse. In what can only be considered an extremely rare move, the Institution in July 1976 gave back a fully appointed estate that had been a museum in the making for years.

Hillwood's fate stood as a failure for both the Smithsonian and the Marjorie Merriweather Post Foundation. Not only had the Post heirs failed to execute the wishes of their benefactress, but the Smithsonian didn't want to send out the message that donors might waste time and money pursuing an ill-fated arrangement with the Institution. Considering what was at stake, the news garnered relatively little attention. The *New York Times* reported: "The Smithsonian Institution, having looked a gift horse in the mouth, has reluctantly decided that inflation has transformed it into a white elephant."

Costs became the scapegoat, but something larger was at play than a few hundred thousand dollars on the tab of an organization with the world's largest collection of museums and research centers. Hillwood's prized collection of Russian trophies had become out of step with a growing celebration of American art, scientific breakthroughs, and entire classes of people overcoming challenges.

When Post first started talking with Smithsonian Secretary Leonard Carmichael about Hillwood back in the early 1960s, she did what seemed natural—she entertained. She invited the Smithsonian regents to her celebrated home for a luncheon and tour. The reviews, however, were mixed.

"There were some who thought that this almost priceless real estate and collection of art and furnishings would be prized by the American people as a jewel in the crown of the Smithsonian's offerings of exhibitions," wrote former Smithsonian Under Secretary James C. Bradley. "Quite to the contrary, there were other regents who felt that the Smithsonian would be stepping out of character to become the sponsor and administrator of so opulent an estate."

The scales of changing priorities tipped further when S. Dillon Ripley took over the Smithsonian in 1964.

"The Smithsonian was no longer interested in maintaining a 'precious' memorial to a millionaire on the outskirts of DC that had essentially no research value and little public appeal," according to the 2020 piece cowritten by the Smithsonian's legal counsel.

Instead of fulfilling Post's dream for Hillwood to become a beloved part of the Smithsonian family, it became known instead as a "problematic donation" and held up publicly by the Smithsonian as a "shrine." This came at a time when the Institution began to see a new vision for its mission. Reflecting the social change of the 1970s, Ripley preferred dedicating Smithsonian resources on programs like the Folklife Festival. He would rather embrace a museum highlighting the struggles and accomplishments of Washington, DC's working-class Anacostia community than highlight "a shrine to a single wealthy American collector," reads a 2013 Smithsonian article titled, "Don't Look a Gift Horse in the Mouth."

For Mar-a-Lago, the prospect loomed that Hillwood would suddenly require more resources to care for it. It could now need more attention to reshape as a museum on its own—without the support of the Smithsonian. Pressures mounted on Post's trust even at a time when Mar-a-Lago languished in the hands of federal officials who complained about upkeep funds. If the group entrusted with honoring Post was forced to choose between caring for Hillwood or funneling additional funds into Mar-a-Lago, which would it be?

John Goldsmith Phillips, longtime departmental chair for New York's Metropolitan Museum of Art, resided in Palm Beach and wrote to the foundation about the "depressing" prospects for Mar-a-Lago.

"We in this town—as does the Nation—have few enough architectural monuments," Phillips wrote to the foundation in February 1978. "Many of us continue to feel that Mar-a-Lago has given a certain distinction to Palm Beach."

After conferring with National Trust for Historic Preservation president James Biddle and Norton Museum of Art director Richard Madigan, Phillips suggested selling Hillwood and transferring its "stunning" collections of Fabergé jewels and "superb" Russian porcelains to the historically acclaimed showcase of Mar-a-Lago. With financial help from the Hillwood sale, the seaside manse in Palm Beach could open as a museum serving just a hundred paid visitors daily.

The intoxicating combination of Post's treasured Russian collections, "remarkable" house, and "incomparable" setting would position the Marjorie Merriweather Post Museum at Mar-a-Lago as a "very special institution" for present and future generations, wrote the man who helped shape the Met over four decades.

Yet the words of one of the top art minds in the country echoed into nothingness. Getting dumped by the Smithsonian didn't mean that Hillwood and its rare collection would be sold, donated, or sidelined from public view. It meant that the Post Foundation was suddenly in the museum business. And it needed cash quickly.

Even as a young woman, Marjorie Post embraced style during a time when women quickly evolved from the Victorian Era. UNIVERSITY OF MICHIGAN LIBRARY DIGITAL COLLECTIONS.

(BELOW) *Before the millionaires of the 1920s began constructing massive winter homes on the shores of Palm Beach, the barrier island stood largely undeveloped as a sliver off the mainland, whereas West Palm Beach began to emerge with grid streets and the seeds of a tourist economy.* PLEUTHNER, W. K. LIBRARY OF CONGRESS, GEOGRAPHY AND MAP DIVISION.

(ABOVE) *Early "colonists," including Marjorie Post, hired men to cart them through what was known as Palm Beach's Jungle Trail in the days before mass development.* DETROIT PUBLISHING COMPANY COLLECTION. LIBRARY OF CONGRESS, PRINTS & PHOTOGRAPHS DIVISION.

(RIGHT) *In the years before they even conceived of undertaking a project as massive as Mar-a-Lago, Marjorie and Edward Hutton set out in style on the sands of Palm Beach.* UNIVERSITY OF MICHIGAN LIBRARY DIGITAL COLLECTIONS.

Mar-a-Lago set the stage for costume parties dating back to its earliest days—a tradition that would live on. Festooned in finery, the display stands as a rare look at the revelry enjoyed by some of America's wealthiest families as the Roaring Twenties drew to a close. HISTORICAL SOCIETY OF PALM BEACH COUNTY.

Marjorie Post's 1935 wedding to her second husband, Washington, DC, diplomat Joseph E. Davies, took the couple to Moscow but seldom to her winter home in Palm Beach. EVERETT COLLECTION HISTORICAL / ALAMY.

One of the most prestigious addresses in America—in the heart of tony Palm Beach—regularly transformed into a venue for square dancing at the hands of Marjorie Merriweather Post, an Illinois native with a penchant for recreation. HISTORICAL SOCIETY OF PALM BEACH COUNTY.

Lady Bird Johnson on the Mar-a-Lago patio with Marjorie Merriweather Post. Lady Bird's April 1968 visit marked the beginning of a commitment by her husband's administration to bring Mar-a-Lago into the National Park Service. HISTORICAL SOCIETY OF PALM BEACH COUNTY.

*Marjorie Post at one of the fundraisers she long held at Mar-a-Lago for the
American Red Cross. She is escorted by her fourth (and final) husband, Herb May.*
HISTORICAL SOCIETY OF PALM BEACH COUNTY.

Within months of the Trumps' 1986 purchase of Mar-a-Lago, Ivana Trump posed for a Town & Country *magazine spread declaring her the new mistress of the manse, which had belonged to the American public a half-dozen years earlier.* NORMAN PARKINSON, ICONIC LICENSING.

(ABOVE) *Mar-a-Lago became the unofficial Winter White House during the presidency of Donald Trump, who regularly conducted official state business there. Pictured here, he shakes hands with Chinese president Xi Jinping at an April 6, 2017, dinner at the President's Club in Palm Beach, Florida.* ALAMY.

(BELOW) *First Lady Melania Trump stands at the columned, arched porte-cochere of Mar-a-Lago between the US and Venezuelan flags. She bids farewell to Fabiana Rosales de Guaidó, the first lady of the Bolivarian Republic of Venezuela after a visit in March 2019.* ALAMY.

Teleprompters, set lighting, video cameras, and television screens contrast the gilded and hand-carved architectural details of an estate reinvented as a stage for a president. Pictured here, President Trump speaks with the military during a videoconference on Christmas in 2020. ALAMY.

During the Trump presidency, protesters regularly took over streets, sidewalks, and even waterways of a town that worked to get Mar-a-Lago delisted from the National Park Service. Town leaders worried that even limited park-visitor access might hurt property values. This photo shows protesters overtaking Ocean Boulevard in Palm Beach during January 2018. ALAMY.

Within hours of his April 4, 2023 arrest in New York City, Donald Trump held court at Mar-a-Lago with hundreds of guests celebrating him as he made his way to the ballroom stage. The audience chanted "U-S-A! U-S-A!" as he took the podium and denounced charges related to business fraud. He proclaimed his innocence and political persecution on those thirty-four counts, as well as investigations into his role in the January 6, 2021, Capitol riots and the illegal storage of top-secret documents at Mar-a-Lago. AP IMAGES.

CHAPTER 12

MAR-A-LAGO NATIONAL PARK

FULL-LENGTH TOUR OF MAR-A-LAGO*—$9.50
ABBREVIATED TOUR*—$4.25
* RESERVATIONS REQUIRED

Only two hundred visitors could enter daily, getting shuttled from West Palm Beach, past the Bath & Tennis Club and into the estate. Ten people would be allowed at a time via shuttle vans that collected passengers on the mainland, according to a preliminary options study from the National Park Service. Better reserve early because it would be closed four months a year.

Judging by the prices, a trip to Mar-a-Lago seemed similar to visiting the Hearst Castle in San Simeon, California, the Biltmore Estate in North Carolina, or Vizcaya in Miami. With minimal impact on the enclave of Palm Beach, everyone from schoolchildren to scholars to collectors could see for themselves what life looked like for America's wealthiest society during those decadent days leading up to the Great Depression.

National Park Service officials from southeast regional offices in Atlanta saw public ticket sales as a way to make Mar-a-Lago financially viable. Of course, they knew the Palm Beach Town Council had trouble pronouncing the word "public."

The *Miami Herald* in March 1975 parodied the Palm Beach council and civic association by writing that they united in "unanimous horror" at the prospects of seventy thousand tourists "storming the island" to see Mar-a-Lago National Park.

"The fine print of the Park Service report revealed that the agency had exerted only the minimal effort required in order to deflect any criticism that it was squandering a national treasure. Instead of overseeing admissions, the service would delegate that cumbersome task to the volunteers at the Historical Society of Palm Beach County. Such an arrangement was basically unheard of in the management of federal parks."

Long gone were the days of Stewart Udall building up the Department of the Interior, and the legendary Geroge Hartzog guiding the Park Service. A succession of political appointees rotated through the big corner offices. Some insiders commented that Marjorie Merriweather Post wore down Udall and Hartzog by flying them several times from DC to Mar-a-Lago in her private jet. One Park Service official wrote in a memo, six months before Post died, that Mar-a-Lago failed to meet the mark of national significance and should have never been brought into the fold. Regardless of departmental scuttle, the Park Service is charged with carrying out laws enacted by Congress rather than undercutting the legislative body's decisions.

"For a new site to be on a senior Park Service official's hit list at all is bad news," said longtime public servant and former National Park Service administrator Dwight F. Rettie, who studied the Mar-a-Lago debacle for his 1995 book on the national park system.

A Park Service renowned for delivering experiences with precious lands held disdain for an opulent example of enormous wealth and conspicuous consumption, according to Rettie. The park system's apathy became apparent to all. By the end of 1974, the *Palm Beach Post* published a piece stating: "Although Mar-a-Lago was designated a national historic site by Congress, Park Service officials say its main value serves as a curiosity or an example of a defunct lifestyle."

Those same values—exemplifying bygone lifestyles—might also be ascribed to Versailles or Catherine the Great's palace near St. Petersburg, Russia.

Had Mar-a-Lago been billed as the estate of E. F. Hutton—the veritable voice of American investment—would the male-dominated upper ranks of the Park Service have viewed it differently? History will never know, but too rare was the example of a woman's accomplishments among the Park Service's portfolio.

Charged with managing Palm Beach's "palace," the Park Service largely ignored its task to create a master operating plan, which would have addressed public concerns. The service never managed financial problems. Estimates for annual upkeep ranged like the daily tidal charts, rising from $98,350 to $170,000 within two years.

The upkeep astonished the director of the Flagler Museum, which had once been the home of railroad tycoon Henry Flagler. "I've wanted to know for a long time why it costs the government so much just to keep Mar-a-Lago in mothballs," said Charles Simmons, who ran the museum.

As Mar-a-Lago evolved from a family-style operation to a government one, costs went up, said longtime supervisor James Griffin.

Unlike the Smithsonian petitioning the Post Foundation when operating funds for Hillwood fell short, it appears no one from the Park Service asked the foundation for more financial help with Mar-a-Lago.

"In any case, Congress should never authorize a park system unit without retaining oversight of its care and financing," Rettie wrote.

Mar-a-Lago's new overlord did not bother to erect a National Park Service sign on the premises. A 1972 National Parks Guidebook, published by Chatham Press, listed Mar-a-Lago's location as Tallahassee, which was hundreds and hundreds of miles away from Palm Beach. It was perhaps the only national park property where the handful of employees working there did not even wear the uniform of their employer.

Instead of fulfilling its basic mission to preserve the estate as it had been charged, the Park Service failed to preserve Mar-a-Lago's beachside swimming pool.

Another thud was the Mar-a-Lago National Historic Site Advisory Commission, which could have been prodded into action by the Park Service. With appointees by federal, state, and local leaders, the group was sanctioned by Congress. Such groups can wield powers of persuasion, build public awareness, and navigate controversial issues, according to Rettie.

Perhaps not surprisingly, the Mar-a-Lago Commission never even met, leaving its namesake without a needed voice. The commission's resistance to move forward left the great estate to languish.

Cresting westward, the full moon still illuminated the inlaid black stones so carefully installed on Mar-a-Lago's riverside courtyard at the height of the Roaring Twenties. Throughout five decades, this homage to elegance had hosted socialite parties, political luncheons, charity teas, formal dinners, and orchestral dances. Romances had kindled in its sunset views and marriages had crumbled under its towering weight. This product of architects Marion Sims Wyeth and Joseph Urban welcomed royalty and plebeians alike. Unlike its sister seaside estates of the same era, Mar-a-Lago had survived smashing hurricanes and the appetites of salivating developers.

Now, as the nation neared its bicentennial, the public owned a prized property but could not enter. Not even elite diplomatic corps could convene there.

Palm Beach Post columnist Steve Mitchell drove his beat-up Ford Pinto sedan up the driveway in the early summer of 1975. Under the headline "Mar-a-Lago: I Own It but I Can't Visit It," he wrote: "It presently is owned by the federal government, but the Americans whose tax dollars help maintain it can't get a look inside to see what they're paying for. This is a source of some embarrassment to the National Park Service."

A caretaker told him it wasn't open to the public "and probably won't ever be opened to the public."

If Mar-a-Lago had too few friends in the National Park Service, it lost a key supporter in Congress. Inside the ranks of the service, managers sometimes joked about congressmen trading votes in order to create a national park in their district. They called it getting on "the NPS teat." By snagging a national park status back home, the politicians could take credit for boosting tourism and the local economy. But on an island where leaders once considered charging tolls to nonresidents, no one was really looking to get on the government "teat" if it meant bringing outsiders into their world.

The hometown congressman for Palm Beach, Paul Rogers, tipped his hat to the jewel on South Ocean Boulevard when he cosponsored the legislation making it part of the National Park Service in 1972. At the time, he said: "In every respect, this property is a national treasure worthy of preservation and recognition. While it is not associated with the early history of the nation, it is representative of an era of more modern times which will continue to grow in value in the generations to come."

Two years later, he backflipped and pushed a bill to delist his "national treasure" from the Park Service—a rare humiliation doled out only for a handful of properties deemed substandard or simply not worth the trouble.

Why surrender a storied mansion commanding some of the most stunning views on the Eastern Seaboard, particularly when bulldozers readied nearby to replace it with a subdivision of residential insignificance?

Town Council members had complained to Rogers that having a national park, albeit one next to the Bath & Tennis Club, could mean declining property values for the millionaires' milieu. Palm Beach leadership also bemoaned losing tax dollars because governments don't pay property taxes. Somehow that didn't seem to be a problem for the mayor's request that Palm Beach take over the manse. The Vanderbilt Mansion in New York, Vizcaya in Miami, the Biltmore in North Carolina all generated millions of dollars annually for their local economies. And while Mar-a-Lago opponents cited a lack of security on the grounds, the Secret Service insisted it never came to that conclusion.

Town Council members also objected to Mar-a-Lago's federal upkeep costs. But why? Those costs would not increase Palm Beach tax bills. They would be borne largely by the Post Foundation unless officials made the case for more government support. The Post mansion was hardly alone in its local tax exemption. Every church, government, nonprofit organization, and school got the same tax break—even the prized Palm Beach Atlantic University that the town had courted.

At one time, Palm Beach had been the answer to the Riviera, wrote Norton Museum of Art director Christina Orr-Cahall for the publication *Historic Preservation Washington*.

"It is a spa in the European tradition with a distinctly American tone and it is unparalleled in the United States," she continued. But with controls left up to developers who are intent on demolition, the "architectural identity of Palm Beach is being destroyed."

And with the federal government unwilling to keep Mar-a-Lago, the fate of this "principal landmark on the island of Palm Beach" rests with a town that wants the estate back in private hands rather than risk the island's "cherished" privacy.

"Certainly the American public has the right to retain and see this important residence, which indeed it has owned for the past five years," the museum executive said as the island's emblem floundered in federal hands.

Dissension swelled not just within the Park Service and town but also among the Post contingent. While the Post Foundation wanted Mar-a-Lago back (in order to sell it), the executors of the estate wanted the winter home protected by the government, a Park Service spokesperson told the *Washington Post*.

Henry Dudley, Post's loyal attorney who had long battled to help her save her homes, insisted that Post's Mar-a-Lago trust included plenty of money for upkeep.

"We've got sufficient money to maintain the place, and we are maintaining it, at no cost to the taxpayers," he told the *Palm Beach Post* in December 1974, adding that about twenty groundskeepers, painters, and handymen kept it up. "Unless they can show that we're reneging on our part of the agreement, the Park Service can't do anything."

Post's intention, he said, was always to maintain Mar-a-Lago at her own expense for future generations.

Yet months after Dudley avowed Post's commitment to Mar-a-Lago, Post Foundation director David Close said the grand mansion would have to be sold because the Interior Department complained about a lack of funds. At the time, the Washington-based Post Foundation had bigger worries than a high-maintenance winter home languishing hundreds of miles away in Florida. First and foremost, it needed to save Hillwood, which stood in the center of the power circles. It looked as though the Smithsonian might return Hillwood, and they could use the money from a Mar-a-Lago sale to help float Hillwood.

Ah, Mar-a-Lago, forsaken by its benefactors, owners, and neighbors. James "Jimmy" Griffin spent his entire life at Mar-a-Lago. He followed his father's footsteps to become the superintendent caring for it. He could recite the location of every air filter and electrical panel. In the years after his boss died, he worked to keep it in the kind of condition Post would appreciate. A reporter for the *Palm Beach Post* surmised in September 1977 that the place looked pretty much as it did in its heyday.

"Mar-a-Lago is just as it was four years ago this week when Marjorie Merriweather Post died—manicured, immaculate and livable," wrote Tim O'Melia of the *Post*. "James Griffin and Frank Moffat, the superintendent and the steward for Mrs. Post's 17-acre estate for more than 30 years each, keep it that way because it is their home."

Griffin blamed Mar-a-Lago's bleak future on intervention from Washington officials, who had been lobbied by Palm Beachers. And one of the few people who had the perspective of not just federal lawmakers but also Palm Beach was the congressman who first championed the Mar-a-Lago National Historic Site.

Wearing signature glasses that framed his soft features, Paul Rogers was winding down from a political career that started when he replaced his late father as congressman for the area. That had been decades earlier. The middle-aged attorney from West Palm Beach said it was his job in Congress to reflect the views of the people of the town. His loyalties rested squarely with locals who were proud to have an icon like Mar-a-Lago in their midst— they just didn't want to share it with anyone else. Rogers seemed less interested in representing his constituents who supported Mar-a-Lago's new national honor. They included former circuit judge James R. Knott, who had escorted Lady Bird Johnson to her Mar-a-Lago dinner and presided over the local historic society. Barbara D. Hoffstot, a trustee of the National Trust for Historic Preservation and author of a popular book on Palm Beach architecture, also favored the long game for Mar-a-Lago.

The handful of supporters was no match for disengaged owners, isolationist neighbors, and bored family members. At the

White House, President Gerald Ford sent a missive to his chief of staff, Don Rumsfeld, following December 1974 press reports that the federal government would return Mar-a-Lago to the Post Foundation.

"What's [the] story," wrote Ford, who had expressed no interest in retreating to Mar-a-Lago for respites. He was being lobbied by, among others, the mayor of Palm Beach. And Palm Beach resident Laurent Varnum wrote his White House friend, Phil Buchen, suggesting uses for Mar-a-Lago and sending well-wishes to Buchen's wife, "Bunny."

Aide Dick Cheney sent directives down the line of the executive branch, seeking intel on the prized estate that no one seemed to prize. Bureaucrats laid out four options, but added that three of them were too costly.

The fourth, and seemingly only viable, option was to return Mar-a-Lago's keys to the family foundation intent on selling something their matriarch had fought decades to save.

CHAPTER 13

PARK BARREL POLITICS

Bombastic and crude—those were some of the nicer ways people described the man who stood as, perhaps, Mar-a-Lago's last remaining champion.

Phil Burton liked his vodka straight up, in a tall glass. A chain smoker, the congressional power broker collected enemies like he did friends. Deference, decorum, and diplomacy were not his brands, according to biographer John Jacobs.

American political history scholar Norman E. Tutorow captured him this way: "Undoubtedly the most abrasive, tempestuous, uncouth, vulgar, dictatorial, obnoxious, boorish and ill-mannered politician who ever appeared on the American political scene."

A congressman from California, Burton once told Wilderness Society director Bill Turnage that he revered only Cesar Chavez and Ansel Adams and tried to emulate their dedication to helping humankind. "But they did it without being mean, nasty sons of bitches like me."

This imposing political figure stood for years as Mar-a-Lago's last hope for survival. As chairman of the House subcommittee on national parks, Burton had long flicked away Palm Beach's attempts to heave the estate away from the public. But first, Congressman Paul Rogers repeatedly did his best to protect Palm Beach from the prospect of public access to Mar-a-Lago. Better to give it to the Post Foundation, even though it would likely sell it to developers.

Congressman Rogers engineered cuts to federal funds that would have helped keep up Mar-a-Lago. By May 1975, he cosponsored legislation to return it to the Marjorie Merriweather Post Foundation because of upkeep costs, even though the costs to the public by that point had only been the salary of one National Park Service employee.

Burton fought back, saying, "You don't solve a budget problem by giving away valuable assets of the US government." His office raised the question, reported by the *Palm Beach Post*: If the country surrendered Mar-a-Lago "because of local political pressure," the United States could one day lose the Lincoln home, Hyde Park, and other treasures.

Then, nearing the end of his twelfth term, the hometown congressman who was intent on rooting Mar-a-Lago out of the Park Service decided not to run for reelection. The news shook the Palm Beach Town Council, which had relied on him to protect their island. But the fight over the manse was far from over. It was only getting started. Rogers's understudy, his former chief of staff Dan Mica, won his boss's old seat and took over where Rogers had left off. Mica said he made his position on Mar-a-Lago clear during the campaign.

"I had announced in the campaign that I would do everything I could to get it back on the tax rolls," Mica said years later. More flamboyant than his old boss, the thirty-four-year-old freshman congressman once said his personal style combined "the incendiary tactics of extremists with a moderate political philosophy.

"I'm a mainstream Floridian," Mica later described himself to the *Orlando Sentinel*. "But I can also set a three-alarm blaze."

Within a few days of his election, Mica got a call from none other than his nemesis on the Mar-a-Lago issue—the hard-charging chairman of the national parks subcommittee, Phil Burton. The congressman from California said he had been following the Mar-a-Lago issue and intimated that he was amenable to working on getting the mansion back on the tax rolls. At least that's what Mica heard. According to Mica, there was even talk about Mica's office putting out a press release suggesting the stalemate could be over.

"We were elated," Mica recounted later. "We announced it to the press. The town was elated."

Then, Mica added, things began to get questionable. Burton suggested Mica assign one of his staffers to chauffeur Burton around during a visit to Palm Beach and Mar-a-Lago. There was a request for a hotel that served breakfast and even a special pillow to ease the pain of hemorrhoids.

"Well, whatever the chairman wants, I'll deliver," Mica said.

A few weeks before the trip, Burton requested a reception for himself and his wife at the Everglades Club, which did not serve Jews. Burton was Jewish. What to do? Mica conferred with his old boss and also with the town manager but, alas, a reception was unlikely.

Still, Mica was optimistic. He reintroduced the old bill divesting Mar-a-Lago from the Park Service and Mica's spokesman said Burton seemed ready to act on it.

As the ground in the District of Columbia petrified in a deep freeze during the dead of winter in early 1979, South Florida was just hitting its prime time. On February 18, Burton left behind temperatures hovering at zero and arrived in the tropics where the air felt like room temperature and sea breezes wafted palm fronds.

After disembarking from his plane on the mainland, Burton soon arrived in the town where mansions hide behind towering, impenetrable rows of coiffed hedges. Shining black Cadillac Eldorados with gleaming chrome grilles chauffeured old money down South Ocean Boulevard and polished-red Corvettes drew the eyes of police patrol cars.

Joining Burton on this Mar-a-Lago exploratory trip was another member of the parks subcommittee, Congressman Austin Murphy of Pennsylvania. Their wives and an entourage of more than a dozen people joined them.

"We get it all set up and the town fathers are elated," Mica said. "We got golf carts to drive through the estate that George Frost, the city manager at the time, had arranged."

As Mica relayed, Burton didn't seem too anxious to turn the keys of Mar-a-Lago over to anyone outside the Park Service: "He comes in with a Columbo-style raincoat and was like a bull in a china shop, to be gracious. . . . I introduced him and he said, 'Can I talk to you for a minute?' There was a bar to the side with swinging doors. 'What is this shit that you are telling people that I'm going to work with you to give this back. I will never work with you on that but I'm coming down every winter to inspect it.'"

Any of Burton's inspections would have revealed the winter estate that Marjorie and Edward Hutton built at the south end of Palm Beach a half-century ago had seen better days. There were now bare spots where dead shrubbery had been pulled. One of the four greenhouses was beyond repair. Few remnants remained of the nine-hole, par-three golf course.

"We're just maintaining Mar-a-Lago in mothball condition," Superintendent James Griffin later commented. "There's no question it's slowly deteriorating, but the building itself is in relatively excellent condition. The biggest deterioration is in the grounds."

Post's signature fresh-cut flowers were missing. There were no servers circulating trays of refreshments for guests or string quartets serenading audiences. Perhaps, though, a glimmer of greatness still emanated.

White cloth coverings protected furnishings, such as Dresden urns and a dining room table of note. But there was no hiding such sights as the living room's gold-leaf Thousand-Wing Ceiling; thousands of black-and-white marble floor tiles that came from a Cuban castle; or cantilevered balconies lifted on shaped brackets and embraced with both round wooden columns and guardrails of turned balusters. Back when the house had been alive for an evening of entertainment, Post would sometimes peer down from there to watch the reaction of first-timers taking in the cavernous room of unparalleled, crafted detail.

Congressman Murphy said it begged to be opened as a museum so that visitors could immerse themselves in a way of life that would never exist again.

"How many of us will ever get a chance to see such splendor in our lifetimes?" he said. "I don't think we want to spend tax dollars on upkeep of this place for the exclusive use of a select few. If anything, it should be for the people."

Mica had countered that a museum was out of the question since the enabling language precluded it. But National Park Service Legislation Office Chief Richard Curry had earlier said the idea of locking the mansion's doors to the public was "poppycock." The Mar-a-Lago advisory commission could have determined ways to accommodate the public without disrupting Palm Beach. Curry cited language that allowed ticket sale proceeds to benefit the property.

After the Burton entourage's two-hour tour of the house and grounds, Burton told reporters that he was undecided about Mar-a-Lago's future. He said he was sure of only one thing—he didn't want to participate in anything that would lead to its destruction.

He had been taken by it.

"You should spend two hours in just one room to do it justice," the rising congressional star from California told the *Miami Herald*. "It's like racing through a Rembrandt."

Within forty-eight hours of the visit, Post ally James R. Knott seized on this fresh, new turn by writing Burton and seeking salvation for Mar-a-Lago. Knott was on hand at Mar-a-Lago when the firebrand from California toured the estate and now implored the congressman: Put restrictions on it so the house and grounds can never be sliced up. Dismantling it in any way would destroy its essence.

"It just wouldn't be the same," Knott wrote. Let some shuttles from the mainland drive limited guests there for just a yearlong trial, he further compelled Burton.

Mica's office, meanwhile, was stung by Burton's tactics.

Mica's chief of staff, Richard McBride, later said the trip to Palm Beach seemed like a "big 'in your face'" from Burton, who championed farmworkers and unions. "I think it had more to do with a class thing," he added.

The idea of Burton wanting to upstage a town of elitists was certainly plausible. Burton's drinking buddy, Maryland congressman Bob Bauman, explained his friend this way: "Phil was for the little guy and talked in terms that were mildly Marxist."

By any measure, the trip had backfired on Mica, who had done everything except fluff Burton's hemorrhoid pillow for him. Instead of Mar-a-Lago falling into the hands of the Post Foundation, the trip had sparked hopes that the grand old residence might still be of some benefit to greater society.

The *Miami Herald* editorial board questioned whether Mica had buckled under pressure of the Town Council. Perhaps he had failed to explore other options. Writers noted that the touring congressmen had marveled at Mar-a-Lago's "palatial beauty" and recognized what was at stake. This National Park Service rarity could be used in other ways, as deemed by the advisory council.

The *Miami Herald* put it this way in February 1979: "Mar-a-Lago is too great a treasure to return to private hands without first exploring other options."

During that spring of 1979, the Space Shuttle *Columbia* prepped for its first launch, television audiences watched John Wayne's final public appearance during the Academy Awards, and a nuclear plant partially melted down at Pennsylvania's Three Mile Island. In the news, there was no mention of President Jimmy Carter from Plains, Georgia, planning a winter break in Palm Beach amongst Marjorie Merriweather Post's carved corbels and bas relief.

The congressional "bull in the china shop," as Mica called Burton, was busy fine-tuning what some called "the national parks and recreation bill of the century." A pure example of "park barrel" politics, it was loaded with dozens and dozens of national parks projects poised to make half of Congress look good with their constituents back home. The bullying that was needed to get the parks shopping list passed was vintage Burton. When Louisiana senator Bob Livingston started to object to Burton's "magnum opus" parks bill, "Burton ran full throttle across the House chamber screaming, 'There will never be another fucking nickel for sugar. I'll get you,'" according to Jacobs's *Rage for Justice* biography of Burton. Senator Harry Byrd called Burton's engineering on the bill reprehensible, but others considered him the consummate strategist. Wisconsin senator Gaylord Nelson would later say Burton was "the one absolute political genius" he had met during more than three decades of elected office.

By all accounts, the man was a temper tantrum just waiting to erupt, and he still refused to budge on Mar-a-Lago, saying he would not partake in the "irreversible act of disposing of it." And he couldn't conceive of the government failing to find a solution.

Even worse for Mica, money actually started shifting toward Mar-a-Lago. Illinois congressman Sidney Yates, who had visited there several times, called for $100,000 to care for the locked-up Park Service property.

The idea of such federal support for Mar-a-Lago appalled Post's elder daughter, who said such spending for her mother's estate would be "taxpayer money down the drain." As president of the tax-exempt foundation that had been bankrolled by her deceased mother, Adelaide Riggs stood ready to undercut her mother's intentions by selling the estate—if only the foundation could tackle Burton and get it back from the federal government.

Why, for heavens to Betsy's sake, as the matrons of Palm Beach might say, was this Mar-a-Lago thing still a problem? The foundation had the Palm Beach Town Council on its side and, also, key members of the National Park Service. It had congressmen on its side. The only thing that seemed to stand in its way was a vile California congressman who loathed the upper class and wielded power like a lumberjack with a chainsaw.

By the late 1970s, the Mar-a-Lago story line had become so tired that newspapers no longer trumpeted updates on the front page, as they had in the past. Even Adelaide Riggs seemed rather disinterested.

"The tidiest thing to do would be to return [Mar-A-Lago] to the foundation," she told a *Miami Herald* reporter. "We've heard optimistic reports over the years [about the expected government action] but nothing's ever come of it. I just don't think about it anymore."

With no support from the family and political opposition in Palm Beach, the end for Mar-a-Lago National Park would be as unceremonious as the day Stewart Udall signed its protections.

Early in December 1980, near the end of the congressional session, a staffer ran up to Phil Burton as the bombastic congressman from California was regaling, on the House floor, about the passage of the bill that would bring further protections for the famed Lake Tahoe area in his home state. At the time, members were anxious to get business behind them so they could head home for the holidays.

On the floor, the staff member approached and whispered something into Burton's ear. It seemed urgent. Whatever it was, it delivered a blow to the temperamental power broker. His eyes widened, face reddened, and veins bulged, according to one witness.

On the advice of Arkansas senator Dale Bumpers, Palm Beach congressman Dan Mica had taken a prime seat to watch whatever was unfolding.

"I wasn't even aware what I was waiting for," Mica recounted years later. Mica had earlier told Bumpers the story about Burton's seemingly disingenuous visit to Palm Beach. Bumpers responded by saying not to worry and that he would "fix it," as Mica later recounted.

The Arkansas senator then slipped into Burton's prized Lake Tahoe preservation bill a provision that would divest Mar-a-Lago from the National Park Service. Killing the Mar-a-Lago amendment could undo Burton's most precious of bills. Trying to remove it would most assuredly destroy an overall measure that was key to Burton. No one had earlier mentioned anything to Burton about the little surprise tucked into the legislation, at least not until the clerk whispered the news into Burton's ear.

Toying with Burton wasn't for the faint of heart. He had just months earlier threatened the career of California congressman John Rousselot for trying to unseat Burton's brother, Congressman John Burton. Phil Burton was quoted as saying: "You tried to beat my brother. Now you'll pay the price. . . . Nobody pisses in my family's sandbox."

Now Burton turned his ire toward Mica.

"I'm sitting there and I can't believe this. He sees me sitting there and walks over and stands in front of me," Mica said. "He starts growling and grabs me by the lapels and picks me up and says, 'I will get you, Mica. I will get you.'"

Mica's "coup," as it was roundly called in Palm Beach, incensed more than Burton. Kansas congressman Keith Sebelius, a leading member of the national parks subcommittee, said he had long fought for Mar-a-Lago to remain in the park system and "deplored" what had just taken place.

"The best interests of the citizens of the United States, and of future generations of Americans yet to come, will suffer a needless and shameful loss as a result of this provision. I am very sorry about it," the Midwest Republican said.

Mar-a-Lago fell from grace as a National Historic Site to become a mere inconsequential National Historic Landmark. Once President Carter signed the act into law on December 23, 1980, the Palm Beach home erected at the hands of six hundred workers over the course of four years lost its federal parent. In about four months, it would be officially delisted from the National Park Service.

Mar-a-Lago would join a humiliating list of about twenty properties that had been unceremoniously dumped from the NPS. Spread across the United States and stretching to the Virgin Islands, the cast-offs of the parks system all bore the same black mark.

Scholar Alan K. Hogenauer would later bemoan the fate of Mar-a-Lago and other gems delisted from the National Park Service.

"All they seem to have in common is their status as relative rarities—natural and historic features whose days of actual or potential glory have ended, forgotten by all who pass by," Hogenauer wrote for the George Wright Forum in 1991. "Considering how laborious a process it is to establish a National

Park Service area, it seems incredible that this many could have subsequently disappeared."

Even though pruning inferior park properties can better prioritize limited resources, was this unparalleled residence really inferior? As the flip-flopping Paul Rogers said when he helped introduce the bill first embracing Mar-a-Lago, it is a "national treasure worthy of preservation and recognition" and one that "will continue to grow in value in the generations to come."

The problem, of course, was the cost of upkeep. And while it would have been costly to keep, it was hardly the costliest of the national park properties, as reported by author Dwight Rettie. The public-lands expert cautioned against making comparisons but still pointed out that the Gates of the Arctic National Park and Preserve in Alaska and the Frederick Law Olmsted National Historic Site in Massachusetts cost hundreds of dollars, per visitor, to maintain. Both of those, by the way, joined the Park Service roster about the same time Mar-a-Lago was expunged.

With the exception of Mar-a-Lago, the fallen stars of the Park Service all moved to a new government home. Many were shuffled among federal agencies, and some were picked up by states or even a city, according to a 1995 study by former National Park Service historian Barry Mackintosh. Most of the transfers shifted the once-prized sites to an arm of government less specialized in managing parks. In contrast, Mar-a-Lago fell back to a foundation that was simply looking for dollars. Other than Mar-a-Lago, the list of dropped park properties compiled by Mackintosh is actually a study of government offices working together. The list includes:

- **Papago Saguaro National Monument**, Arizona—Established by presidential proclamation in 1914 and transferred to the state of Arizona in 1930.

- **Sullys Hill National Park,** North Dakota—Established by Congress in 1904 and transferred to the US Department of Agriculture in 1931.
- **Lewis and Clark Cavern National Monument,** Montana—Established by presidential proclamation in 1908 and transferred to the state of Montana in 1937.
- **Chattanooga National Cemetery,** Tennessee—Established under the War Department by Army general order in 1863 and returned to the War Department in 1944.
- **Shasta Lake Recreation Area,** California—A 1945 federal agreement through the Park Service led to the 1945 transfer to the National Forest Service three years later.
- **Lake Texoma Recreation Area,** Texas/Oklahoma—A 1946 agreement through the Park Service led to a transfer to the Corps of Engineers in 1949.
- **Father Millet Cross National Monument,** New York—Established under the War Department by presidential proclamation in 1925 before the Park Service took over in 1933 and then transferred it to the state of New York in 1949.
- **Wheeler National Monument,** Colorado—Established under the National Forest Service by presidential proclamation in 1908 before the Park Service took it in 1933 and then transferred it back to the Forest Service in 1950.
- **Holy Cross National Monument,** Colorado—Established under the National Forest Service by presidential proclamation in 1929, and then the Park Service took it in 1933 before it was returned to the Forest Service in 1950.
- **New Echota Marker,** Georgia—Authorized under the War Department by Congress in 1930 before the Park Service took it in 1933 and then it transferred to the state of Georgia in 1950.

- **Atlanta Campaign National Historic Site**, Georgia— Established by the Secretary of the Interior's order in 1944 and transferred to the state of Georgia in 1950.
- **Shoshone Cavern National Monument**, Wyoming— Established by presidential proclamation in 1909 and transferred to Cody, Wyoming, in 1954.
- **Old Kasaan National Monument**, Alaska—Established by presidential proclamation in 1916 and transferred to the National Forest Service in 1955.
- **Castle Pinckney National Monument**, South Carolina— Established under the War Department by presidential proclamation in 1924 before falling under the Park Service starting in 1933 and then transferring to the state of South Carolina in 1956.
- **Fossil Cycad National Monument**, South Dakota— Established by presidential proclamation in 1922 before coming under the Bureau of Land Management in 1956.
- **Millerton Lake Recreation Area**, California—A federal agreement through the Park Service in 1945 and then transferred to the state of California in 1957.
- **Flaming Gorge Recreation Area**, Utah-Wyoming—A federal agreement through the Park Service in 1963 and then transferred to the National Forest Service in 1968.
- **St. Thomas National Historic Site**, Virgin Islands— Established by the Secretary of the Interior's order in 1960 and transferred to the Virgin Islands government in 1975.
- **Shadow Mountain Recreation Area**, Colorado—A federal agreement through the Park Service in 1952 and then transferred to the National Forest Service in 1979.
- **Mar-a-Lago National Historic Site**, Florida—Designated by the Secretary of the Interior's order in 1969 and authorized by Congress to the Park Service in 1972. Then returned to the Marjorie Merriweather Post Foundation in 1980.

It's unlikely that Americans truly realized they had just lost ownership of one of the country's rare residential wonders, though stories ran in newspapers in New York, Detroit, Austin, Indianapolis, Fort Worth, Cincinnati, Tucson, Philadelphia, and Baltimore.

The press was skeptical of Mica's reassurances that the architectural trophy could still be purchased by someone who would keep the entire seventeen-acre estate intact. As *New York Daily News* columnist Liz Smith wrote: "But what do you want to bet that holds? Only an Arab potentate could afford such a colossal and beautiful white elephant."

The *Miami Herald* went so far as to editorialize that Mica had made a mistake:

> Rep. Dan Mica, who engineered its return to the private Post Foundation, counts this as a resounding legislative coup, though history, and much of the public, will not judge it that way. No doubt Mica has made a small faction of Palm Beach residents deliriously happy. Any chance that Mar-a-Lago will serve a public use has been all but eradicated. Forget about a grand museum, or performing arts center. The public, once again, has been staved off, no matter that the price, ultimately, may be the grand estate's destruction.

As Palm Beachers nursed hangovers from toasting their good fortune during dinner parties at the Everglades Club, their hometown paper hit with a thud on the driveways of Ocean Boulevard. Their local newspaper relayed the story of a "jubilant" Mica with the headline:

STALEMATE BROKEN, MAR-A-LAGO 'BACK HOME'

—*Palm Beach Post*, December 6, 1980

Back home indeed. Now for the first time in its half-century existence, Mar-a-Lago's fate was completely uncertain. Post Foundation President Adelaide Riggs suffered little sentimentality about the winter home that her mother and stepfather completed just at a time when Adelaide neared adulthood. The foundation hoped to find a buyer who would use it as a private home, but, as Riggs said: "I haven't a clue who would be interested, if anybody."

As the colonists sipped their mimosas and nibbled their eggs Benedict and asparagus tips, they may have turned a few more pages in their local paper to read the editorial board's take on Mar-a-Lago's "return." Rather than applauding or denouncing Mica, *Palm Beach Post* editors simply looked ahead and warned of the estate's precarious new toehold on survival. Unlike the era of the Park Service, they cautioned, the next owners will challenge Palm Beach's attempt to control zoning, traffic, and preservation: "One suspects the real 'battle for Mar-a-Lago' has just begun."

CHAPTER 14

THE SINKING OF THE OUTRAGEOUS

C hatter about two South Florida buyers contracting to purchase Mar-a-Lago in 1984 made the rounds of the dive bars faster than a jukebox could replay Hank Williams Jr.'s "All My Rowdy Friends Are Coming Over Tonight." The backslapping chatter undoubtedly celebrated a pair of guys who were about to make a big statement in Palm Beach society. The bar-talk might have celebrated these new buyers getting their shot at the great ol' place on South Ocean Boulevard:

William Frederick was a beefy slab of a man who I'm sure knew his way around the sauce bar at Sonny's BBQ. He and his partner, Thomas Moye, built a shopping center in Greenacres City, and they named it Trafalgar Square—just like the one in London, you know. It had a Winn-Dixie grocery and an Eckerd Pharmacy. At the grand opening, country music sweetheart Tammy Wynette flew in on a jet helicopter. Her hair was all puffed up on top and looked amazing. Bill and Tom, that's what she called them, looked the part with their beards and cowboy hats. They got to have their picture taken with her. She was kind of looking more at Tom in the photo, but that's OK.

And now, here they are, the new owners of Mar-a-Lago. Is that how you say it? Well, the sale wasn't final yet but the headlines all called them the buyers. The newspaper also called them big-spending, high-living developers and instant celebrities. Just imagine that. It even said the price would be a record—like in the whole country. It was up there with what Kenny Rogers paid for his place. He knows how to hold 'em, doesn't he? One of those New York papers had a headline that said it sold for "A Whole Lotta Box Tops." That's pretty funny. This house is one big deal, for sure. But with a 137-foot yacht, named The Outrageous *(of course), anything that is big kind of works for these guys. They incorporated under the name Mar-a-Lago Estates. It might be a little long but kind of has a ring to it, doesn't it? They should be able to get at least eight new houses next to the big one, maybe one or two on the golf course and there was room for at least a couple more in the orange groves.*

This place was just made for one of their bashes. Sometimes they get 700 people at their parties. Now that's some kind of good time. Think that many cars could fit on the lawn over there? Most of the time, they throw three good ones a year and sometimes they get their friend Tammy or Burt Reynolds to come. Once, Dom Deluise showed up. He cracks me up. The old lady that used to have the place, something or other Post, they say she used to like to square dance here. She'd be real proud of having somebody like Tammy sing at the place.

When they asked the real estate agent to show them a big place near the water, well, they had no idea. William checked it out back in December and bet you anything he went back twenty times. They say closing could be in a month. Those sellers told reporters they accepted the offer so it's pretty official. Of course, there's always the move. What a pain. William lives in a pretty fancy house in Boca now. It's got Whirlpool baths, steam rooms, saunas, and a dock out back that's bigger than most houses. And get this—the wall outside is Florida-style with shells mixed in the concrete. It's six-foot high and painted mauve. Pretty sharp. . . .

The reaction among Palm Beach residents who fought to get Mar-a-Lago back into private hands might have been a little less enthusiastic.

Ah, luvvie, dear, did you see who is buying Marjorie's old place? Say, could you pour me a tipple of Glenlivet— three fingers? No, make it four. Yes, on the rocks, please.

Almost predictably, the town that had snubbed Florida's proposed Mar-a-Lago Center for Advanced Scholars and lobbied Congress to keep the riffraff away from the trophy house on South Ocean Boulevard was about to get new neighbors.

Boca Raton attorney Robert I. MacLaren II described his former clients as "bombastic and unconventional" but added that they were art lovers and not necessarily what you thought when you first met them.

"Bill was very beguiling," said MacLaren, who had worked with the duo arranging to purchase 1100 South Ocean Boulevard. "He was probably one of the first gaslighters I ever met."

The Boca buyers' 1983 contract was the best prospect that the Post Foundation encountered during its early years peddling the country's highest-priced residential property.

Only shoppers presenting an income statement and letter from their personal banker could enter. That winnows things down, for sure. But with a commission as high as $1 million, agents worked hard to find buyers. The Marriott Corporation eyed it for conversion to a resort. Churches considered it as a retreat venue. And a few oilmen "kicked the tires." There were no takers.

With more bedrooms than most homes have flatware, the tower-topped, crescent-shaped dwelling lacked a homey feel. The mishmash of architectural styles lacked a universal appeal. And the seemingly constant stream of jet noise from the airport's flight path didn't help.

As one real estate agent said, "Frankly, it would be difficult to make a home out of someone else's monument."

The Town Council didn't necessarily want the seventeen acres carved up with rows of "McMansions," but it might be persuaded to acquiesce. Courts often sided with property owners for the "highest and best use" of their land. Shopping center developers William Frederick and Thomas Moye would definitely need to subdivide the long-prized estate in order to make the deal work.

"How are we going to pay for it? Well, we are going to pay for it, well, with a loan, the American way," said the attorney who represented the pair of buyers at the time. "That large grassy area leading down to the lake . . . the lots would be sold off for a lot of money and that was going to provide the means to repay the loan."

On the other side of the deal, the attorney representing the Post Foundation was none other than Doyle Rogers—brother of flip-flopping congressman Paul Rogers, who used his position to get Mar-a-Lago out of public hands. The congressman's role in upending Mar-a-Lago was but a brief chapter in a career otherwise known for health-care policy. In 1978, President Jimmy Carter enacted a bill naming the federal courthouse in West Palm Beach for him. Years later, the Paul G. Rogers Federal Building would factor in Mar-a-Lago's most significant controversy. In the Rogers building in August 2022, US Magistrate Judge Bruce Reinhart signed a warrant that set into motion an unprecedented chain of events. He approved an unannounced FBI search for classified and top-secret documents tucked inside the very mansion that Rogers had worked so hard to wrench out of the public's hands. The Mar-a-Lago raid, as it would be called, sparked an instant backlash across the county. People—some armed and wearing tactical gear—protested at various FBI offices. The term "civil unrest" spiked throughout social media channels. In Palm Beach, thousands of flag-waving interlopers descended on the town and South Ocean Boulevard. And any number marched at the Rogers Federal Building.

Long before anyone might have imagined raids and utter chaos at Mar-a-Lago, Post Foundation attorney Doyle Rogers wanted only to unload it. He was so motivated in 1984 to sell the place that he went to the airport to finalize a second contract as the buyers, their lenders, and their attorney had just landed in their private jet from an Atlanta business trip.

"He was hot to trot to get it signed," MacLaren recalled.

In January, Rogers told reporters it would take two to three months to close the sale. Then four months passed. By May, the Post Foundation opened up Mar-a-Lago again for showings.

Even though Frederick and Moye were favored customers of Sunrise Savings, which had lent them more than $120 million, there was no promise they could get permission to divvy up chunks of Mar-a-Lago and make good on the loan.

Without the blessing of the bank, the deal died. The shopping center developers had, not surprisingly, faced some lawsuits and judgments for not paying subcontractors on past projects, the

Miami Herald reported on May 5, 1984. Within a few years, they would plead guilty to federal charges of fraud, records show. Sunrise Savings and Loan Association folded.

Despair can be like alcohol for those with dwindling options. Bankrupt of choices, people lose their judgment and flirt with recklessness. Things that would have been incomprehensible before suddenly seem logical through the lens of desperation. Shopping center developers, leveraged on the fumes of the savings and loan bubble, suddenly look like a viable option to purchase the priciest estate in the country. And a group that once shunned even discreet public use of Mar-a-Lago now practically held out the estate's keys to the bulldozers. Destruction of all the sprawling residences that once made Palm Beach famous was, well, expected. Wasn't that the American way, or at least the Florida way? Certainly the queen of American riches would have empathized. She would have understood that the people she had entrusted to protect her longtime home—the ones she handed it off to—had no other option than to destroy it. Wouldn't she?

After Tammy Wynette's friends bombed at buying the winter villa on South Ocean Boulevard, the next glimmer of salvation to wash ashore was a developer from the rough and ready Texas town of Houston. At his son's suggestion in 1982, Cerf Stanford Ross visited Palm Beach to vacation at The Breakers. An architect by trade, he was immediately smitten not with Mar-a-Lago but instead with the old, closed-down Paramount Theatre just three miles up the road from the estate. He bought the 1920s venue and set about reclaiming the two-story structure by building interior offices encased in glass. Tenants could look out onto first-floor landscaping and art deco murals with underwater scenes of oversized goldfish.

"It would be like looking out your window at scenery," he told a reporter for the *Palm Beach Post.*

How brilliant—glassed offices in the middle of a theater. Why had no one else ever thought of this?

Soon, though, Ross shifted gears and set about restoring the Paramount to its original use with plans to make it "America's greatest theater showplace." And then, six months after he bought it, he bailed out altogether.

But he wasn't done with Palm Beach, oh, no. In the summer of 1984, he started working with the Post Foundation on his vision for the empty estate. He could build eight more mansions on Mar-a-Lago grounds and then wall off the manse and four remaining acres. Sure, it would block the views and make a mockery of its very name, which means "Sea-to-Lake," but look at the rest of Palm Beach! To the heirs of Marjorie Merriweather Post, perhaps the most attractive thing about Ross's plan was that the foundation would no longer have to sink millions of dollars into it when there were so many other worthwhile ways to invest those funds. "I'm delighted that the Post Foundation had that much faith in my ability to develop the property. Naturally we're all quite elated," Ross said at the time.

Cerf Stanford Ross started selling lots for Vistas del Mar-a-Lago, as he had branded it. On a barrier island now long accustomed to the demolition of grand seaside mansions, Ross got a conditional nod from the town to plow ahead. If he failed, commission members said they had a plan for the property. Standing suntanned with his square-framed glasses and wide-lapel, casual shirt, the svelte Cerf beamed in front of this behemoth of an estate. The city even gave him a monthlong extension to give him the time needed to show his financial progress.

For decades, Marjorie Merriweather Post, congressmen, townspeople, and real estate agents had sought a savior—someone who would appreciate the carefully crafted signature property for the rare jewel it was. This ideal buyer would understand that the Hope Diamond rested in a setting of other diamonds for a reason, and that Mar-a-Lago sat amidst acres and acres of sculptured, gently rolling lawns buffered by both lake and sea. Even the *Mona Lisa* has a frame. Mar-a-Lago's hero would be a buyer of substance and taste, preferably with old-money ways.

The epic search for an ideal buyer certainly started before the Post Foundation got the keys to the kingdom. It predated the Park Service's missed opportunity and started even before Post courted Lady Bird Johnson or entertained the Florida Council of 100. Now, the decades-long quest for someone new to assume the mantle of Mar-a-Lago was nearly over.

CHAPTER 15

TRUMP'S
HOUSE OF CARDS

Estée Lauder's diamond earrings cascaded from the pert blonde's earlobes down to the high-neckline gown she wore for Palm Beach's 1986 Preservation Ball at Mar-a-Lago. Across the way stood Chrysler Motors savior Lee Iacocca and, perhaps more interesting, the former flight attendant/publicist he was dating. They would be married in one month and separated in seven.

White-haired Doyle Rogers beamed as he held the delicate hand of his youthful wife. His brother, Paul Rogers, the former congressman who pulled Mar-a-Lago from the public park roster, had maneuvered it back into private hands. Then Doyle Rogers represented the sellers, the Post Foundation, in a four-year odyssey trying to unload the estate. Wearing his vested formalwear, complete with a double-fold pocket swatch, he appeared ready to toast his own good fortunes on this celebratory night.

In the reception line, Ivana Trump's smile was as big as her cascading blonde bouffant with soft, curled tresses that teased her bare shoulders. A tufted, white designer gown hugged her petite frame. At the age of forty, her real estate developer husband still cut a somewhat athletic figure in his black-tie tux. He owned the New Jersey Generals United States Football League team, you know.

Everyone was there. Well, almost everyone. The Preservation Foundation had to return about $40,000 in ticket sales for its sold-out ball because the new owners of Mar-a-Lago cut off the guest list at 350. For three years, Mar-a-Lago had been the venue for the ball—even as the manse aged on the real estate market like an old maid at a retirement home. The idea behind the ball had originally been to treat guests in the same fashion that Marjorie Post would have entertained them. Rivers of champagne flowed. Couples danced to tempoed orchestral numbers. Precious jewels glinted in the lights of entry hall lanterns. Yet there, on this early March evening in 1986, a film crew for the television series *Lifestyles of the Rich and Famous* snaked its way through the room. Marjorie would never have subjected her invitees to such exposure. And rather than guests milling about admiring Mar-a-Lago's wood-paneled parlors, gold-leafed living room ceiling, and two-ton dining room table, they were instead funneled into a large white tent. For heaven's sake, was this Palm Beach or Miami?

Even though the roped-off, paparazzi treatment might have vexed some of the Palm Beach old guard who doddered about, they could not deny that here stood the man who had saved the historic jewel of their island. Unlike the South Florida cowboys and Houston architect who attempted to buy Mar-a-Lago and build houses on its grounds, this buyer and his dazzling wife were going to keep the estate intact.

New York Daily News columnist William Norwich credited the Trumps with keeping the storied estate whole.

"By taking on the annual maintenance expense of nearly $1 million, the Trumps prevented the mansion from being turned into a tacky subdivision, as had been threatened," he wrote in 1986 as the spring season in Palm Beach was winding down.

It had all happened so suddenly.

Just six months earlier, the Town Council had learned that Cerf Ross had forfeited the quarter-million-dollar deposit he made to buy the property. It seemed his plans to build the subdivision Vistas del Mar-a-Lago were but a house of financially top-heavy cards. The next day, news broke that the "flamboyant" real estate magnate Donald Trump was under contract to buy it.

The town's leaders positively crooned at this turn of events, which would absolve them from any accusations that they had a hand in dismantling Mar-a-Lago's ample spread by navigating it out of public hands.

Indeed, standing next to his debutante-looking fourth wife under tent-ballroom chandeliers, which were draped in flowers, former Palm Beach mayor Earl Edward Tailer Smith looked simply elated. Years earlier when it appeared the Park Service might allow ten-person shuttle vans to bring visitors to Mar-a-Lago, Smith pushed for the town to take over the estate rather than see it become national park property. The town had cleared the path leading Trump to become the only private owner of a fallen national park, according to scholars.

Now, after muscling the federal government to surrender Mar-a-Lago, Palm Beach's elders could hold their balding white heads up high at this coming-out party for the Trumps, whose fingerprints would not be on any bulldozers plowing the landscape down on South Ocean Boulevard. There would be no wrecking balls slamming into the Dorian stone walls or even general admission access to the island's precious gem.

The Town Council of Palm Beach had clearly won.

"That's mind boggling that someone is going to come in and live there," Council president Paul Ilyinsky commented to the

Miami Herald in 1985. "But this is what we wanted. This will solve a lot of problems. I'm looking forward to meeting him."

A Mar-a-Lago neighbor, Ilyinsky said Trump "may find himself a very popular hero." The previous buyer, Cerf Stanford Ross, was "very questionable" and "living a pipe dream," a Council member said.

They all deserved this night, especially when considering how closely the overall estate had teetered on the edge of ruin. The Town Council and Landmarks Commission had all earlier tentatively approved plans for a series of small "villas" to be built on the grounds where gardens, golf-putting greens, and greenhouses now stood. Would the shades of Mar-a-Lago be thus polluted, as Jane Austen's *Pride and Prejudice* character Lady Catherine de Bourgh might have asked. But carving up the island to squeeze in more houses was as predictable as the tides eroding the famous beach.

Underneath the tent's chiffon-draped ceiling, guests dined on poached salmon and veal with strawberry-apricot mousse for dessert. If they weren't feeling special enough by this point, each guest then got a little silver box of chocolates.

"It was a magical night," one guest later said.

Town officials and the Post Foundation's Doyle Rogers seemed to exude a certain air of relief that night. Meanwhile the evening's young center of attention held court atop the tent's white floors. By the next year, this dealmaking New Yorker would have a book out touting just what a good deal he got in picking up Marjorie's old place.

As he would come to tell the story in his bestseller *Art of the Deal*, Mar-a-Lago was a "great deal" as a home, more than an investment. The book's description of the deal, though, was more artful than factual.

- Trump's claims that he purchased it as a residence rather than a moneymaker appear disingenuous considering his first offer

was turned down when he proposed building fourteen houses
on the property.

- Even though his book stated that Post gave it to the federal
government as a presidential retreat, she had, in fact, given
it to Americans expressly as "a temporary residence for visiting foreign dignitaries, heads of states or members of the
Executive Branch." Any other uses could be granted through
a special commission, which never met. The idea that it was
intended as a presidential retreat was a half-truth, at best.

- The book stated the original asking price was $25 million
but, in fact, court records show the price was $20 million.
And while his book cited an initial offer of $15 million, it was
closer to $9 million.

- As he described: "Over the next few years, the foundation
signed contracts with several other buyers at higher prices
than I'd offered, only to have them fall through before closing. Each time that happened, I put in another bid, but always
at a lower sum than before." In reality, as the *Palm Beach
Post* reported, Trump made an offer in October 1983 and
again two years later. During the four times buyers contracted
with the foundation to buy Mar-a-Lago, Trump never made
a counteroffer.

- Trump relayed that he finally succeeded with a cash offer.
Newspaper reports of old court filings, however, show he
got 99.97 percent financing from Chase Manhattan Bank
and used less than $3,000 of his own money. *Palm Beach
Post* reporters later quoted Palm Beach property appraiser
and attorney Gaylord Wood Jr. saying, "You would have to
put out more of your own cash to buy a rabbit-warren condo
in Haverhill."

Perhaps the biggest departure from full disclosure was
Trump's failure to mention the $2 million he spent for 403 feet of

beachfront that was once a part of Mar-a-Lago. After Post died, her foundation had sold it according to her wishes. Next-door neighbor Jack Massey, former owner of the Kentucky Fried Chicken Corporation, bought it from the foundation for $348,321 in 1974. As the parade of Mar-a-Lago's would-be buyers came and went over the years, Massey sat with the ability to build a house blocking Mar-a-Lago's view.

As Doyle Rogers would later say about Massey, "He had . . . an awful lot of leverage on anyone who bought Mar-a-Lago."

In hopes of finally unloading the estate, the Post Foundation bought the land back from Massey for $2 million—more than five times Massey's purchase price just a decade earlier. In addition to paying just $5 million for the Mar-a-Lago estate and $3 million for the furnishings, Trump paid another $2 million for Mar-a-Lago's beach.

No matter how you added it up, though, the self-promoting dealer got a good deal. Trump would ridicule the former US president who gave up Mar-a-Lago because it was too expensive to keep up.

"That was Jimmy Carter's mentality," commented Trump, an ardent critic of government bureaucracy.

Even as former president Carter was nearing the end of his life, a spokesperson for his foundation in 2023 declined to say whether he had ever expressed regret about delisting Mar-a-Lago from the National Park Service.

On this night of revelry at Mar-a-Lago, though, the important thing was that Marjorie's old place had avoided what seemed an inevitable date with obliteration. Fueled by a seemingly unending line of credit from Boston Safe Deposit and Trust Co. and others, the Trumps crafted plans to revive the golf course and install a resort-style pool. Flutes filled with Dom Perignon clinked in toasting the dashing couple. Their host was from Queens, the son of real estate developer Fred Trump. Even though he lacked the pedigree of the Vanderbilts and du Ponts, he was accomplished, with impressive building projects in New York and casinos in Atlantic City bearing his name.

The evening's polite chatter likely touched on tennis phenom Martina Navratilova. Like their hostess for this ball, the queen of grand slams was of Czech descent. And she was now the first tennis player to earn $10 million. Hadn't women come a long way since Billie Jean King's defeat of Bobby Riggs a decade ago?

The politicos and septuagenarians might have raised their brows over a bill floating around the Florida senate. It would require drivers age seventy and up to renew their licenses every two years. Can you imagine? Well, certainly Senate President Harry Johnson, from right across the river in West Palm Beach, would see to it that it wouldn't become reality. Having a driver ferry you around in Manhattan was one thing, but cruising your Benz or Porsche Carrera down Ocean Boulevard was truly one of life's finer experiences.

The chattering crowd included *TV Guide* heiress Janet Annenberg Hooker, who could live large off the interest earnings from interest earnings. No doubt some of these monied guests whispered to one another about falling investment rates and the fast-declining value of the dollar. A few may have even quietly nudged each other about the insolvency of savings and loans. Would today's ripples churn into tomorrow's crashing waves? Were these financial red flags the champagne bubbles that would rise to the surface and pop?

Oh, but why worry about such things on this night as pianist Peter Duchin serenaded the "colony" in a historic nest that was enveloped by evening breezes floating near seventy degrees under the sliver of a crescent moon? Talk of insolvency, after all, was best served with strong coffee and fresh eclairs before noon.

The hangover didn't take long. Just a few years after the locals clinked their champagne flutes with The Donald and his wife over their many successes, a different message wafted across the island.

. . .

For a pledge of just fifty cents, listeners of WJNO radio in West Palm Beach could contribute to the Donald Trump Bail Out Fund and do their part to help save Mar-a-Lago's once-celebrated owner from bankruptcy. The bon vivant, who had been hailed just a few years earlier as the town's hero, now stood billions of dollars in debt with creditors hounding him and banks policing his spending.

Trump's financial benefactors eyed his $2,000 suits and limited him to just $450,000 spending a month, which didn't even include the million-dollar monthly tab for his jetliner and yacht. Mar-a-Lago cost $229,625 a month in interest and expenses, according to his financial firm, Kenneth Leventhal & Company. Lenders got dibs if he rented out the manse or filed an insurance claim—a fire had caused $50,000 in damages less than a year before. And he could not claim it as his personal residence because that would keep it out of the reach of bankers in case he filed for bankruptcy.

"He's waiving every single right in favor of the bank," said Michael Y. Cannon, a Miami real estate analyst. "One wonders if this isn't the beginning of the end."

Hurricanes, the Great Depression, divorces, failed government ownership, scheming buyers, and a foundation with loyalties to Hillwood in Washington, DC—Mar-a-Lago had endured much in its sixty-plus years of existence. But it never before had an owner on the brink of financial ruin.

Certainly, there had been pricier South Florida winter villas he could have purchased. There were larger ones too. But this architect of self-promotion managed to buy the most famous of addresses in one of America's most exclusive enclaves. His own personal brand now incorporated the storied legend of an American icon—Marjorie Post.

No, he wasn't about to lose that cachet.

Trump could still recall first laying eyes on Mar-a-Lago. It had been a rainy day in 1982. Droplets pelted the driveway pavers of The Breakers, where he and Ivana had retreated from New York's bitter cold. The view from their hotel room that day was a monochromatic gray. They hired a limo and the driver toured them around on a Palm Beach parade of oceanfront mansions, stopping at one particular estate on South Ocean Boulevard. "This one's for sale," the driver told them. Quickly proffering financial statements to the listing agent, the couple stepped inside. Unlike some other mansion shoppers, Ivana appreciated the mix of Spanish, Portuguese, Dutch, Norwegian, Italian, English, and even Chinese influences.

Opulent? Yes. Overstated? Yes. Ostentatious? Well, yes. They'll take it. Trump reportedly offered $15 million. At the time, the foundation was plotting Mar-a-Lago's sale to the inventive architect Cerf Stanford Ross from Houston. Two years later, Trump managed to land the grand house that stood as a last emblem of America's industrial-era riches.

Now, almost a decade later, the locals were jokingly pitching in quarters to bail him out and pondering who might buy the old Post place from him.

Even the Preservation Foundation decided to move its signature ball from Mar-a-Lago to the Henry Morrison Flagler Museum, although Trump would later insist he was the one who booted them.

Surely there must be a way he could hang onto this unparalleled piece of American history.

He tried collecting royalties on a new luxury line of furniture called the Mar-a-Lago Collection, with eighteen replicas and adaptations. The carvings were intricate; the fabric was rich, and the splashes of gold hinted at elegance. Now, anyone with a few thousand dollars could have their own replica of a piece of the famed mansion. Even though an armoire cost as much as a half dozen of Trump's suits, a chair could be had for just a few thousand dollars.

The bigger play, of course, was cashing in on the dirt. Everyone who had tried to buy Mar-a-Lago knew that simple math. And, of course, the Town Council had even tentatively approved plans for a previous buyer—Ross—to build nine new houses on the estate.

Development of Mar-a-Lago's grounds had been foreseen more than a decade earlier as the federal government let it slip away. State representative Jim Watt of West Palm Beach had urged Congressman Dan Burton to protect Mar-a-Lago from development pressures. Someone will try to subdivide it and ruin it.

"I seriously doubt this could be done without destroying the essence of Mar-a-Lago," Watt cautioned.

Trump knew that planting a neighborhood on such hallowed ground could, more importantly, damage the Midas-touch image he worked so hard to create. In crafting his reputation, he had even bragged that he bought Mar-a-Lago for enjoyment instead of profit.

"Buying Mar-a-Lago was a great deal even though I bought it to live in, not as a real estate investment," Trump wrote in his book.

Ivana had been even more vocal about keeping their Palm Beach pearl whole.

"No! No! No!" Ivana Trump told a reporter years earlier. "We wouldn't subdivide seventeen acres and build a few houses to sell. When we go into business, we go into big business."

Big business, ah, yes. The Trumps' early talk about keeping the Mar-a-Lago estate intact vanished in the face of creditors calling in the $2 billion they had lent him for various projects. He was no longer even on *Forbes*'s list of the four hundred wealthiest Americans—a steep fall after almost breaking the list's top twenty-five the year before.

Standing there, looking out the Palladian windows of his winter home, he could see acres and acres of property that he owned but that served little purpose other than framing his famed manse. The overall grounds were almost three times the size of the Central Park Zoo. Were the golf course and orange groves really necessary? Leveraging Mar-a-Lago's underutilized land could be his chance to juice up his flagging cash flow and save him from the disgrace of altogether losing this beachfront cradle of lore. He contrived a plan: Appease the locals by keeping the house and satisfy at least some of his creditors by selling off $15 million worth of Mar-a-Lago's grounds as homesites.

If the colony didn't have enough Trump gossip to savor, they soon learned Ivana was now on her way out. Starlet Marla Maples publicly positioned herself to become the next "mistress of Mar-a-Lago," as the tabloids would call her. And as Palm Beach's leisure class buzzed about the Trumps' pending divorce, the town braced for what was about to happen.

As one of about fifteen-hundred structures on the list of National Historic Landmarks, Mar-a-Lago needed local approval for any changes. And so, on February 18, 1991, Trump expressed "love" for Palm Beach as he presented the town with plans to add more than a half dozen homes to the estate that Marjorie Merriweather Post dedicated so much of her life to protect. Not even ten years after the townspeople had toasted him for keeping Mar-a-Lago's footprint intact, they watched as he set about dismantling it.

"Almost from the time I bought Mar-a-Lago, I've tried to think of a way to preserve it, and the subdivision plans are the answer," Trump told the *Palm Beach Daily News*. "Palm Beach deserves to have it preserved forever. When it's all completed in a couple of years, Mar-a-Lago will be as magnificent as it always has been; we're doing this with love."

The sales pitch for the Mansions at Mar-a-Lago, as it was billed, held sweet nectar for a town built on pedigrees—the promise to keep it off limits to the general public.

"What Donald Trump wants to create is one of the most private, secure and exclusive residential enclaves in the world," said his architect Eugene Lawrence, who submitted plans to the town in February 1991.

News of the estate's planned dissection made headlines throughout the country.

DONALD THE SUBDIVIDER

—*Chicago Tribune*, February 21,1991

THE DONALD: 17 LITTLE TRUMPVILLES AT ESTATE

—*Casper Star-Tribune*, February 21, 1991

A CHANCE TO CALL TRUMP A NEIGHBOR

—*New York Times*, February 21, 1991

TRUMP TO SHARE HIS ESTATE

—*Sioux City Journal*, February 21 1991

At first glance, the Mansions at Mar-a-Lago so completely met Palm Beach's requirements that it was a given. Trump's team staked the property to mark the mansion locations. There might be some quibbling over the number of mansions but, to be certain, these "mini-me" houses would soon encroach on the queen mother of Palm Beach residences.

Town officials resigned themselves to the inevitable. After all, Palm Beach had a long history of escorting out the old to make way for the new. They had opened the door for Cerf Stanford Ross to do the same thing that Trump wanted to do. Only Ross couldn't make the deal happen financially.

"Barring any unforeseen occurrences, there will be a subdivision of some sort at Mar-a-Lago. Mr. Trump and his architect have done a wonderful job with their plans for a proposed subdivision of the estate," Palm Beach Planning, Zoning, and Building Director Robert Moore told the *Palm Beach Daily News* in May 1991.

Then, just as the last of the snowbirds retreated north and the crepe myrtles began to show their blooms, something new began to stir in the barrier-island town. In late May 1991, voices of protection and preservation rose anew in a seaside hamlet that had lost much of its character to investors and developers looking to make a buck. Matching the fervor of town leaders who had earlier fought against federal and state control over Mar-a-Lago, a group of preservationists from near and far gathered to mount a campaign against Trump's plans.

"Mr. Trump has a responsibility to preserve for future generations the historical landmark he now owns," Florida Trust for Historic Preservation trustee Frances Bourque advised. "Mr. Trump is the custodian of this great estate, and we would hope he would preserve it."

Vanderbilt University School of Law Dean John J. Costonis, author of two books on the legal aspects of landmark preservation, told officials that Trump had no right to subdivide Mar-a-Lago.

In addition to an array of local and state preservation watchdogs, the National Trust for Historic Preservation opposed Trump's plans.

The American Society of Landscape Architects advised that Trump's looming footprint of development would irreparably damage "this Florida treasure." Even the bureaucracy that had let Mar-a-Lago slip through its hands—the National Park Service—voiced opposition in a letter read to officials during a first public meeting.

"Any subdivision of [Mar-a-Lago] will alter the historic appearance of the Landmark, and large amounts of new construction may cause serious damage to the integrity of Mar-a-Lago despite efforts to be sensitive," wrote Jean Travers from the Preservation Assistance Division of the National Park Service.

The *Miami Herald* would decry Trump's plans to subdivide his oceanic estate as letting "greed win out over good taste" and cramming expensive housing plots without regard to the architecture, horticulture, and history of the National Historic Landmark.

The voices rose together, ascending over the island like a flock of sparrows. This flock, though, had flown into the path of a seasoned hawk. At the time, Trump was facing the pressures of a $64 million debt payment coming due in a month. Talk on Wall Street was that he might have to ask his dad for a bailout. Not only was the hawk accustomed to attacking, but he also had little to lose.

Within days of the opposition advising Trump to back off from development plans, Mar-a-Lago's owner fired off a first salvo, which would leave the islanders quaking in their Louis Vuittons. He claimed their opposition was payback for closing Mar-a-Lago's doors to the Preservation Ball and said he would sue the town.

Then, in a threat more frightening than any lawsuit, he suggested he would sell Mar-a-Lago to the Reverend Sun Myung Moon and his Unification Church of "Moonie" congregants.

"If the town thinks they don't like a subdivision of Mar-a-Lago, what are they going to do when a thousand Moonies descend on Palm Beach every weekend?" a Trump associate asked the *Palm Beach Daily News*.

"Moon wants to make Mar-a-Lago his national retreat."

On a Thursday night in late March 1995, President Bill Clinton greeted donors at Casa Apava on the north end of the island, and Jimmy Buffet entertained them with a special rendition of "Margaritaville."

The Palm Beach crowd could really relate to lyrics about busted flip-flops and guitar strumming on the porch swing, couldn't they? Outside on the patio, as temperatures settled into the low eighties for the evening, perspiration pierced even the most dedicated layers of foundation makeup. Inside, *Miami Vice* television celeb Don Johnson worked the crowd of guests gathered at the estate of Revlon chairman Ronald Perelman.

Down the road at a famous residence on South Ocean Boulevard, conservative columnist George Will bashed Democrats to the delight of almost three hundred members and guests at the Mar-a-Lago Club. Ever since it opened in 1995, the club worked to earn its $50,000–$100,000 membership fees by trotting out big-name entertainment. Singers Tony Bennett and Vic Damone performed there and writer Art Buchwald spoke. Club managers hyped the names of artists "penciled in" for the next season—Luciano Pavarotti, Julio Iglesias, Itzhak Perlman, and Harry Connick Jr.

"It shows the ability I have to get the hottest entertainers. They work for me in Atlantic City and make millions," Trump told a reporter. "And people say, 'Isn't that nice, they come here.' No place in Florida will there be entertainment like this, and it won't be in front of a stadium full of people."

Performers entertained at the front of a white ballroom with walls decorated in glittering gold relief. Out by the pool, a jazz quartet played Irving Berlin and Cole Porter. Guests sipped champagne and sampled a surf-and-turf buffet of jumbo shrimp, lobster tails, stone-crab claws, and beef tenderloins. Over in the drawing room, a string quartet played Mozart and Vivaldi.

In just the last four years, this former national park property had teetered on the edge of becoming a subdivision before actually transforming into a members-only entertainment venue. The journey pitted Mar-a-Lago's owner against the very townspeople who had toasted him not that long ago as it appeared that he purchased the manse as his winter residence. Now, instead of hosting the Palm Beach elitists, he lambasted the town's revered historic society for fighting his plans to subdivide. He bullied anyone who balked at commercialization of the town's treasured, vintage, 1920s, residential star. He sued the town for $50 million. As Trump put it, the preservationists merely sought retribution after he and Ivana suggested they find another place for its Preservation Ball, which had been held at Mar-a-Lago for about a half-dozen years.

"If the Preservation Ball was still being held at Mar-a-Lago, I think the preservationists wouldn't be against me like they are," Trump told the *Palm Beach Daily News*. "But because I own Mar-a-Lago and I wanted the ball moved, they don't want my subdivision," Trump said. "If anyone else owned Mar-a-Lago, you wouldn't see the sort of fight they're putting up."

The grand old place on South Ocean Boulevard no longer belonged to the public, but preservationists still had a say in its future because it was one of fifteen hundred National Historic Landmarks in the country. These officials weren't about to be bullied into submission by a New York personality.

Even the National Trust for Historic Preservation called Trump's plan ill-considered and insensitive, suggesting he sell it to someone who could afford it. As the locals dug in, financial pressures squeezed Mar-a-Lago's owner like two blocks of Dorian stone pressing a dripping layer of mortar. Casino losses and massive real estate debt shadowed him as he fell behind on key loan payments. During that summer of 1990, Boston Safe Deposit and Trust Co. executives famously barged into a Manhattan meeting with dozens of Trump's bankers and lawyers and demanded repayment on borrowed funds for Trump's yacht and Mar-a-Lago debt. Within months of his creditors' door-busting move, Trump waved farewell to his yacht, *The Princess*. He would also lose The Plaza in New York.

Saving himself from the humiliation of losing Mar-a-Lago became paramount.

"Mar-a-Lago is mine," he told the *Miami Herald* in 1991. "It'll always be mine."

Tell that to a town that had undercut the federal government's ownership of Mar-a-Lago. Town power brokers blocked him from cashing out on his estate just at a time when the loan on Mar-a-Lago was coming due and he was behind on the payments, as reported by the New Jersey Division of Gaming Enforcement.

A Palm Beach attorney had been telling Trump that he could save Mar-a-Lago by turning the estate into a club. What—a club? What imbecile would try that? Of course, now that he stared down the barrel of a due date for a $12 million payment, maybe it was worth considering. Meanwhile, he was able to stave off foreclosure in 1992 by paying interest on the Mar-a-Lago note.

And yet, the challenge of paying creditors was nothing compared to the magic it would take to get the Palm Beach Town Council on board with transforming Mar-a-Lago into a club.

The townspeople would undoubtedly fight him. His calling card—seemingly endless access to credit—didn't impress them. As architect Tim Frank, a coordinator for the Palm Beach Landmarks Preservation Commission at the time, said, "Let's face it, everybody that sits on my commission probably—this is just a statement—probably had more money than Trump anyway, so they weren't intimidated by the guy."

The colony largely held disdain for his parties, flashy friends, and the beauty pageants he hosted at Mar-a-Lago. Furthering their ire, he would install his name on a historic coat of arms at the manse.

Even as tensions mounted between him and Palm Beach society during those early days of 1993, he boogied on a Mar-a-Lago dance floor filled with big-haired, blonde cheerleaders for the Miami Dolphins and Buffalo Bills. The semi-professional partiers had worked their way into a frenzy midway into the NFL season.

"Rhythm Is a Dancer" by Snap! pulsated over the sound system. The party host sidled up to billionaire financier Jeffrey Epstein and whispered something so amusing that the Palm Beacher, who would later be convicted of sex trafficking minors, doubled over laughing. After one party, police reported that Anthony Kennedy Shriver tore through the grounds of the famed estate, wheeling his Jeep through shrubbery during the waning hours of intoxication.

Of course, Trump's shenanigans hadn't sullied Palm Beach's reputation nearly as much as the longtime "Palm Beaching" Kennedy clan. William Kennedy Smith's escapades exposed the unseemly side of resort life during his nationally televised trial on rape charges, stemming from picking up a woman at Au Bar.

Islanders' serial infidelities and penchants for drugs also had been publicly paraded during the divorce of Pete and Roxanne "Foxy Roxy" Pulitzer. Bad behavior had been around long before Trump's parties. Wasn't even old Ed Hutton considered somewhat of a playboy? Hadn't the New York gossip columnists written back in the day about him and "the tapping of a pair of pert, French heels belonging to an insouciant minx of 19 or 20"? The Donald's staid neighbors might not like the idea of a new club nearby, but he wasn't really importing anything new to the island—was he?

While indiscretions abounded in the tony town, the barrier island of ten thousand residents had a shortage of something else leading up to the 1990s. The entire social system catered primarily to WASPs [White Anglo-Saxon Protestants] and had no private, social environs for anyone of color or Jewish faith. Trump attorney Paul Rampell later estimated that half of the town was Jewish and yet could not join four of its five exclusive clubs.

For an entrepreneur who had polished a national reputation as a dealmaker, the math was simple.

A club, Trump realized, could also resolve the town's decades-long migraine regarding Mar-a-Lago. He could profit from membership fees and event rentals in much the same way as half a dozen other nearby clubs. Creating a club could save the town from the headaches caused by any future owners who might destroy the estate. Even though it no longer had the potential to serve the public, as it had under federal government ownership, Mar-a-Lago could become a stage for fundraisers and charity events. Admission would be limited to people who could afford tens of thousands of dollars in membership fees or pricey tickets to fundraisers. Only those privileged enough to afford such luxuries, or the waitstaff who served them, might get to study the Thousand-Wing Ceiling or take in the monkey loggia and other wonders created under the watch of Joseph Urban and Marion Sims Wyeth. Wouldn't Post have approved of that kind of select access? Wasn't it simply a way to accomplish what the great lady desired, while still maintaining the exclusivity so critical to the colony?

The idea of a club had undeniable appeal, particularly if Trump agreed to preserve it as part of a historic easement controlled by an outside group. Most important, the easement could unlock a trove of tax breaks for Mar-a-Lago's owner.

Trump bought some time by getting the Boston Safe Deposit and Trust Co. to extend his loan two more years. Then he filed plans to create the club in early 1993. It would have ten guest rooms, a dining room seating as many as six dozen guests, a ballroom with a movie screen, tennis court, swimming pool, nine-hole golf course, and a proposed thirty-five-hundred-square-foot spa. A staff of seventy would run the place. All he needed to do now was convince the power brokers of Palm Beach that a club was the way to go.

As French doors across the island swung open to sunny afternoons, Trump hosted guests affiliated with the Historical Society of Palm Beach County. Another five hundred visitors from the Palm Beach Round Table toured the would-be club.

"I'm doing nothing, absolutely nothing, that is more important than the preservation of Mar-a-Lago," he told guests, later adding that he was likely the "greatest preservationist in Florida."

Dina Merrill, whose parents had built Mar-a-Lago, begged to differ. In a letter to Trump, she implored him to give up an idea that would degrade her mother's long-treasured home into little more than a "bed and breakfast."

For Palm Beach, allowing a real estate celebrity to reinvent the Marjorie Merriweather Post mansion sent the wrong message. Transforming the town's residential hood ornament into a club put out a clear signal: The colony could no longer attract the kind of serious money needed to take on its most prized residence. It looked as though the town could not protect the most significant estate from becoming just another place for rich people to rent. Such a giant party spot would fill the island's constrained streets with an average of more than three hundred cars daily—far more impactful than the handful of shuttle minivans that would have transported visitors under National Park Service plans. Just a decade earlier, town leaders had wrested Mar-a-Lago from the federal government. Now the beleaguered tribe watched as a litigious casino king turned their celebrated manse into a giant social outlet with guest rooms that could be churned almost like hotel suites.

But fresh into his forty-seventh year, Donald John Trump had more moves than even those NFL cheerleaders frolicking on the dance floor of Mar-a-Lago, and he played the town like a DJ with a turntable. The Town Council wouldn't approve the club until he committed to put the estate under a historic easement, which would protect the grounds and parts of the interior for the long term. However, the bank holding his $12 million mortgage blocked that deal. After all, how could bankers go along with an easement when it would sour Mar-a-Lago's market appeal? If the club failed, lenders conjectured, how many buyers would want a costly manse they could not customize to their own needs? Basically, the town wanted Mar-a-Lago frozen in time and the moneymen bankrolling the estate wanted it to be free of all restrictions.

If Trump gave in to the town's demands and lacquered Mar-a-Lago with preservation varnish, his lenders would demand he repay the mortgage. Then he could be stuck with a property that had lost its market appeal. Other than declaring his love for Mar-a-Lago and promising the town he would preserve the landmark, he wasn't budging on signing what amounted to a real estate version of a prenuptial agreement.

"Nobody has ever accused me of being stupid," he told a reporter in early August 1993 regarding his decision to hold off on signing the easement.

Pressures grew like the pregnant belly of his budding actress-girlfriend, Marla Maples, who was expecting their child in mid-October. The Town Council gave him partial approval on the club but kept an ace in their pockets—they would grant the club its mandatory certificate to open only after Trump signed a historic easement protecting Mar-a-Lago from future mutilations.

Further complicating matters, a former Town Council member who previously had worked to remove Mar-a-Lago from the National Park Service now filed a lawsuit against the town for granting any club approvals. Robert Grace's lawsuit aimed to undo Palm Beach's approval of the Mar-a-Lago Club.

"This area is zoned exclusively for highly desirable, single-family residential estates, and is nationally known for its private and exclusive character," the legal complaint read. The club will introduce a "transient" vibe and hurt property values of nearby mansions. Transforming the winter home into a club is illegal "spot zoning," claimed the suit filed by Grace and another neighbor.

A transient vibe, indeed.

In the fall of 1993, the nation chattered about Ruth Bader Ginsburg joining the US Supreme Court. Los Angeles police officers went to jail for beating Rodney King, an African American man who tried to flee police. And the US military shifted to a "don't ask, don't tell" policy for its gay members.

On the last Monday of September, as Americans sipped their Maxwell House and prepped for the week ahead, *CBS This Morning* featured a segment with Marla Maples in her third trimester modeling her new line of maternity clothes. The ever-smiling twenty-nine-year-old actress then left her forty-eight-year-old boyfriend behind in New York and sought the sun and sand of Mar-a-Lago. Just a year earlier, she had played a Ziegfeld chorus girl in the Broadway production of the *Will Rogers Follies*. As it always had, Mar-a-Lago offered an antidote to the stresses of the city. Down on South Ocean Boulevard, motherhood books lay strewn about Maples's quarters. Rather than transform any of Mar-a-Lago's dozens of bedrooms—or its fantastical "Deenie's Room"—Maples repurposed a sunroom as a nursery.

Similar to the way Trump refused to marry the mother of his fourth child until she signed a prenuptial agreement, he would not sign the historic easement for Mar-a-Lago until the town approved his club. By the time newborn Tiffany Ariana Trump had the dexterity and strength to grasp her dad's fingers, her mother agreed to a prenup that was so petite it would have been on the size zero rack down at Bottega Veneta boutique on Worth Avenue. Even Trump would say that the agreement's million-dollar farewell clause, in case of divorce, was modest. He told a reporter for the ABC news program *Primetime Live* that the very concept of a marital exit plan was "lousy" and he hated it, but, alas, it was necessary.

Donald Trump: "And I think $1 million is a lot of money."

Reporter: "No, you don't"

Donald Trump: "No, I don't, actually."

After settling his divorce from Ivana for $14 million, the $1 million he agreed to give to wife number two was equal to about a dozen speaking engagements.

The feat of transforming Marjorie Merriweather Post's winter retreat into a social club carried much more expensive costs and sacrifices than any payout on his recent prenuptial agreement. Not only was he sinking $2 million into renovating the place, but he was also trading off control of the property that had seemingly become his persona. As the long string of Mar-a-Lago window-shoppers knew, the real value was in building as much as possible atop the oceanside acreage. The easement protected everything from the landscaping to the view. By signing over any development rights as part of a historic easement, he would wave goodbye to the prospects of selling it to almost anyone else.

But the sacrifices were worth it. They were so worth it. He would not only gain precious tax breaks, he would tap new streams of income—venue rentals, lodging, and memberships, which initially started at $50,000.

The good townspeople of Palm Beach might be shaking their collective heads over the fate of this onetime national park, but they could not possibly foresee what was to come for their treasured castle on South Ocean Boulevard.

CHAPTER 16

RAIDED AND ARRESTED

W hen the polite society of Palm Beach opened their hometown newspaper on a Sunday morning in early October
1999, there on the editorial page was a cartoon of their
litigious neighbor. At the time, Donald Trump was emerging from
his second divorce and the near-collapse of his casino empire.
His trophy chest held a shifting real estate empire and businesses
including the Miss USA and Miss Universe pageants. And now,
approaching his fifties, he was toying with a run to become president of the United States.

The newspaper cartoon pilloried the notion of him as America's
commander in chief. It depicted him with his signature foppish
combover and a sheepish grin. The caricature held an oversized
pair of binoculars and parodied him saying:

"Because I'm taking my presidential bid seriously, I kept my
distance from the Miss Mar-a-Lago Pageant."

It was 1999 and The Donald had spent much of the decade
railroading Palm Beach locals. He lambasted town leaders, bad-
gered officials, and repeatedly sued the town until it caved on key

demands. Gone were his early promises to limit club traffic to three hundred cars per day. The town's rules about photographers at the social venue were forgotten like poor relatives. The Palm Beach Town Council's earlier requirements that he set aside funds to help maintain Mar-a-Lago? Disappeared. Next to the cartoon blared a headline reading: "Is He Serious? Lawsuit-Happy Trump Lacks Presidential Class." Forget about a "Kennedyesque" Winter White House, editors cautioned:

> He'll flout the law whenever convenient, such as when The Mar-a-Lago Club disregarded its 390-member limit 11 times over the last two years, according to Mar-a-Lago Club attorney Ray Royce. It must also mean he'll sue anyone who stands in his way, such as the time he filed a lawsuit against the town when he failed in his bid three years ago to expand The Mar-a-Lago Club.

Without even the support of his hometown newspaper, the presidential talk faded like old newsprint.

Even as the Palm Beach elite mockingly nudged their wives and mistresses while reading the cartoon, Trump was about to build a supermarket-sized ballroom on the property he had agreed to preserve under the watch of the National Trust for Historic Preservation. What's more, two-thirds of Mar-a-Lago's fifty-eight bedrooms had been reinvented as guest suites for club members. The garage would become a spa where members and guests could exfoliate, luxuriate, and inebriate.

A library was remade as a bar. One wall featured a painting of Trump wearing tennis garb and glowing in the formulaic fashion of a Thomas Kincade landscape. Nearby, a museum-quality portrait of a coiffed and bejeweled Marjorie Merriweather Post suggested a more regal era.

Gone, too, were the library's crafted furnishings. A March 1995 piece in the *Miami Herald* observed: "The dainty antique furniture in the wood-paneled library is being replaced with round wooden tables and chairs befitting a bar lounge."

Mar-a-Lago's most significant adulteration was the dining room, which had been designed as a replica of the one at the sixteenth-century Chigi Palace in Rome. To some, the twenty-nine-foot dining table had been the quintessential piece that defined the very essence of this house. According to the Historic American Buildings Survey, "Perhaps the single most striking piece of furniture in the house is the inlaid marble table in the dining room." Designed by architect Joseph Urban, the thirty-six-seater was built at the School of Medici just as the original one had been. Fifteen artisans birthed it over the course of a year, inlaying precious stones and carving motifs reflective of Florentine galleries.

It was the only marble-top extension table in the world, according to the Historic American Buildings Survey for Mar-a-Lago, compiled in the late 1960s and early 1970s.

Post bequeathed the celebrated, two-ton table, which stretched longer than two midsize sedans, to Hillwood, where it has sometimes been on display in the past.

Years before Palm Beach scoffed at its "presidential" neighbor being lampooned in the local press, at least some of the decorative lanterns that adorned the entry hall and loggia had been auctioned off by Christie's International just before the club opened in early April 1995. Original paintings, $80,000 Persian rugs, an Italian Rococo bureau, and even Louis XIV commodes were similarly sold off. Such interior-design items from America's greatest era of decadence would never be appreciated by the public. That opportunity vanished when Post mistakenly entrusted her home to federal caretakers. Now the treasures would likely be stowed away, as typical, in temperature-controlled vaults as though they were bricks of gold bullion instead of fine art pieces for people to see.

While Christie's estimated the items once belonging to Marjorie Merriweather Post would fetch $450,000 for the March 1995 auction, they instead generated more than triple that amount. The mansion's most important pieces, Trump said, all remained and Mar-a-Lago's vast interiors were little changed.

"The most amazing thing were the items that sold for fifteen and twenty times what the highest estimates were," Trump told a reporter. "What can I tell you about it? I'm very happy with it."

Vows to conserve, preserve, and perpetually protect critical aspects of Mar-a-Lago weren't the only thing to waiver. Trump also quietly agreed to limited visits from the public. He signed an agreement with the National Trust for Historic Preservation to open the estate at least one day a year to people who otherwise wouldn't be allowed inside. The 1995 agreement states that Trump, as owner of Mar-a-Lago, "agrees to hold open the Property (not including the interior of the mansion) to viewing by not more than 100 visitors from the public (who otherwise have no legal ownership or use rights with respect to the Property) one day each year."

And for "not less than one day a year," twenty ordinary people could tour the interior. The key was that they should not be regulars on the Palm Beach social circuit.

Even though it was limited in scope, the general admission idea to allow mere plebeians and scholars into Mar-a-Lago seemed almost a throwback to the National Park Service days when the public might have had a chance to glimpse rare interiors and fine artifacts older than anyone's memory.

Predictably, "Mar-a-Lago Day" never happened.

More than a quarter-century after Trump agreed to crack the door open ever so slightly to the public, there is no report that the requirement was ever met. The National Trust did determine that plenty of guests and people who aren't club members have been able to see it as part of charity events, luncheons, dinners, receptions, and other occasions. In addition to member guests visiting, people could purchase tickets to fundraisers. There was a rescue-dog fundraiser in November 2020 and a gala in May 2021. In addition, members of the National Trust regularly tour it, as called for in the agreement.

"We consider this to be consistent with the public access requirements of the easement," wrote an attorney for the Trust in 2021.

Even if the public could access it, they would experience a Mar-a-Lago Club clearly different from the winter villa created by Marjorie Merriweather Post.

No one suggested that Mar-a-Lago's second owner turned his back on this seaside dwelling resting atop a century of storied history. In fact, many agree that he also lifted it into better shape than when it was owned by the famously meticulous Marjorie Merriweather Post. Of course, it's hard to credit Mar-a-Lago's salvation to an owner who admittedly bought it on the cheap and then attempted to carve it into a subdivision.

On the morning of October 10, 1999, as Palm Beachers sniggered at the cartoon suggesting their "presidential" neighbor was ogling contestants of his beauty pageants, few might have imagined what would unfold in the coming decades—not only his presidential victory but also the throngs of media, protesters, helicopters, gunboats, suited musclemen, and general onlookers who would invade their little South Florida haven. Certainly the town's political machine—the one that fought against even the most benign uses of Mar-a-Lago by the National Park Service—had naïvely hoped for a buyer who would keep this emblem of wealth just as its original owner had.

But any patina-faded memory of the quaint days when Marjorie and Edward Hutton traversed the jungle trail by moonlight with their friends now lay buried under the impenetrable hedges that separate Palm Beach residences and block the public view.

Did Marjorie Merriweather Post's dream—that Mar-a-Lago become a retreat for diplomats and scholars—finally come true? No one can say for certain what the matriarch would have thought about the eventual fate of her residential monument. Rather than selling to any number of suitors, she fought for years to secure it under government oversight. And she died mistakenly thinking she had succeeded.

Years after the *Palm Beach Post*'s cartoon mockery of a Trump presidential bid, the idea would actually gain traction.

In March 2015, it wasn't Trump campaigning at Mar-a-Lago to be the next Republican nominee but New Jersey governor Chris Christie. The feisty governor was the keynote speaker for Palm Beach's Lincoln Day Dinner with about six hundred guests at the mansion on South Ocean Boulevard.

Despite Trump's ongoing fascination with running the country, many still dismissed him. University of North Carolina associate professor Benjamin C. Waterhouse said political insiders and others underestimated him. "Trump faced accusations of being a non-serious candidate, a clown, and a demagogue from the media as well as some Republican leaders," Waterhouse wrote in an article for the nonpartisan Miller Center at the University of Virginia.

This candidate, though, knew how to promote and engage fans. "With his experience in television," Waterhouse continued, "Trump knew how to get attention with outrageous, unconventional, and often untrue statements."

As the election neared, he and his family campaigned around the country. At Mar-a-Lago, camera crews and broadcast personalities helped him use the regal backdrop to offset his image as the host of *The Apprentice* reality television show and a frequent guest of shock-jock Howard Stern.

During a presidential debate with Democratic candidate Hillary Clinton in September 2016, she questioned his family's record of renting to minorities in New York, and he actually cited Mar-a-Lago as evidence that his family's real estate business didn't discriminate.

"In Palm Beach—tough community—brilliant community, a wealthy community, probably the wealthiest community there is in the world, I opened a club," he said. "And really got great credit for it. No discrimination against African Americans, against Muslims, against anybody. And I'm very, very proud of it."

Years later, though, Mar-a-Lago's owner dined at the club with notorious anti-Semites Ye (formerly known as Kanye West) and Nick Fuentes, who claimed there was no Holocaust. The backlash from that dinner would leave the grand master of the house feigning ignorance.

With the chance that Trump might win, the club's ranks grew by dozens and dozens of members during the campaign. The membership roster grew so large that he would joke about raising fees for the newcomers.

On election night—November 8, 2016—the Trumps weren't at Mar-a-Lago, but their winter confines were packed with more than 250 members at a private dinner watch party. Guests and supporters spilled onto the patio and throughout the dining room as bottles of champagne chilled in the ballroom. The corks popped and bubbly poured that night, ushering in a new era not just for Trump but for this historic place.

The nation's new commander in chief wasted no time christening his new Winter White House. Days prior to his January 20, 2017, inauguration, he messaged his millions of Twitter followers a photo of him in a furtive pose at what appears to be the receptionist desk there. He tweeted: "Writing my inaugural address at the Winter White House, Mar-a-Lago, three weeks ago. Looking forward to Friday. #Inauguration."

Sixteen hundred Pennsylvania Avenue in Washington, DC, became the official residence for the forty-fifth president of the United States, but Mar-a-Lago quickly starred as the weekend retreat. A little more than a month into the presidency, the *New York Times* aptly painted the picture: "On any given weekend, you might catch President Trump's son-in-law and top Mideast dealmaker, Jared Kushner, by the beachside soft-serve ice cream machine, or his reclusive chief strategist, Stephen K. Bannon, on the dining patio. If you are lucky, the president himself could stop by your table for a quick chat. But you will have to pay $200,000 for the privilege—and the few available spots are going fast."

Guests who may have made their money in real estate or industry were suddenly thrust into the room with world leaders. One evening, Winter White House dinner guests were treated to the president's discussion of a North Korean missile launch with a foreign head of state while sensitive documents were strewn about the dinner table. Early in Mar-a-Lago's debut as a presidential parlor, photos on social media showed club members posing with the "nuclear football" briefcase known for holding top-secret documents regarding nuclear missiles.

The Secret Service had no record of all the visitors who were there even during Trump's dinners entertaining leaders of China and Japan. He conducted official business at the estate, including ordering Syrian missile strikes. In March of 2019, a thirty-three-year-old Chinese spy, posing as a businesswoman, eluded security by saying she was going to the pool.

What would later aggravate the House Committee on Oversight the most was the Mar-a-Lago Trio. Bolstered by presidential access at the club, the threesome won the president's blessing to "straighten out the VA," which meant outsourcing Veterans Affairs duties and even leveraging the medical records of US vets. As soon as longtime VA administrator David Shulkin was nominated to lead Veteran's Affairs as secretary in 2017, he flew to Mar-a-Lago to meet the three shadow figures—Ike Perlmutter, Marc Sherman, and Bruce Moskowitz—according to an August 2018 *Pro Publica* article citing hundreds of records.

Business boomed, enriching the Trump Organization at this place that once belonged to the public. Nonprofits doing business with Trump's administration reported spending additional millions on events at Mar-a-Lago during the presidency. After doling out more than $150,000 to stage events there, the Christian Broadcasting Network suddenly had exclusives with the leader of the free world, the *New York Times* reported.

Near the end of Trump's administration, the *Times* quoted former national security aide Fernando Cruz: "People know and expect him to be at Mar-a-Lago, so they'll bring a guest or come with a specific idea. With that access, you could pitch your ideas. With this president, he'd actually listen and direct his staff to follow up." Such influence would long outlast Mar-a-Lago's time as a winter White House with the appointment of relatively young federal judges promising a long shelf life. The most powerful would be new Supreme Court justices who grant immunity for the man who nominated them. But even at the district level, Trump's judicial pick for south Florida would play a role in Mar-a-Lago's story.

Popular opinion held that Marjorie Merriweather Post got her wish for her prized palace to host a president. Would she, though, smile at the thought of Donald Trump turning her home into a high-ticket, members-only affair that would become famous for benefiting his business associates and sidestepping Washington channels?

Half a century after former interior secretary Stewart Udall cemented Mar-a-Lago as a National Historic Site and part of the American trust, the monument morphed into a private hangout of the power hungry.

None other than US senator Tom Udall, son of the man who first anointed Mar-a-Lago as a National Historic Site, said the public deserved to have a club roster in order to know the names of everyone who was now privy to matters once reserved for the executive branch.

"This is America's foreign policy, not this week's episode of *Saturday Night Live*," Udall and Senator Sheldon Whitehouse wrote in a letter to President Trump just months into his administration.

But the transparency Udall called for would elude this back-door entrance to the White House.

For Palm Beach, traffic jammed, the Coast Guard patrolled, and parts of South Ocean Boulevard closed when the president was in town. In hopes of reducing access, the town erected barricades and chain-link fencing. When the president was away, hundreds of protesters amassed at intersections, bridges, and areas near the Winter White House. They marched, chanted, held signs, and carried twenty-foot balloons of a diapered "Baby Trump."

Even if Marjorie Merriweather Post had wanted her prized winter possession to serve as a Winter White House to Donald Trump, it ceased being that on January 6, 2021.

The morning was even frostier than the early hours of that cool January day back in 1969 when well-heeled lobbyists and caffeinated congressional staffers traversed the stairs to the Capitol and Secretary Stewart Udall's sun-warmed office over at the Interior Department. In fact, those two January days differed on almost every level. While the earlier one would end in celebration of Mar-a-Lago and its future as a public space, the second one would long haunt the lord of the manor as a day of insurrection and carnage stoked by reelection falsehoods. Thousands of President Trump's followers stampeded—and partly destroyed—the Capitol in hopes of overturning election results.

For Mar-a-Lago, the Capitol riots marked yet another turn, another rotation in its seemingly endless revolution. The grand estate on South Ocean Boulevard was about to retire its role as the Winter White House. The iconic landmark began to shift its identity once again, this time becoming the permanent residence of Mr. Trump and his Slovene American wife, Melania Trump.

For the thirty-plus years he owned Mar-a-Lago, it had always served as a getaway. But when New York prosecutors dogged him for falsely inflating the value of his assets, he severed his ties with his home state and instead claimed this Florida jewel as his permanent address. Not only was Florida run by the political party that he presided over—and would likely never pursue legal actions against him—it was also one of the few states in the country without a state income tax. Before Twitter banned him, Trump used the platform to explain his change of residence:

"I have been treated very badly by the political leaders of both the city and state [of New York]. Few have been treated worse," he said, describing his decision as the "best for all concerned."

Another era now lay before a manse that had been at the center of the world's attention for the last four years. With a centenary looming on the not-so-distant horizon, Mar-a-Lago was still the stage on which the head of the country's Republican Party held court and raised hundreds of millions of dollars. Now it doubled as the headquarters where he strategized his destined comeback.

But had the sheen on this castle almost, perhaps imperceptibly, dulled just a tad now that its chief resident was no longer commander in chief? Without a world leader at the head table, could this stately place still invoke a feeling of stateliness? Perhaps it was time for the tower-topped wonder to surrender what was, candidly, a tiresome spotlight. Imagine that the colony of Palm Beach might once again enjoy the riches of exclusivity without the unflattering glare.

Seasons ticked by, marked more by a springtime exodus and winter influx of luxury vehicles than by a shift in the natural order. The town now fretted over more normal things—like traffic backups during the repainting of the Royal Park Bridge. Encampments of protesters had disappeared like midges in the dead of summer.

Once again, Palm Beach's stalwart full-timers both dreaded the summer's stewing humidity and anticipated its emptied shops and streets.

Such was the scene one morning in early August 2022. As daybreak crested the Atlantic's eastern horizon, a soft glow blanketed the stuccoed walls of Dorian stone that Marjorie Merriweather Post had imported from Genoa, Italy. The estate's loyal summer staffers timed their outdoor tasks for completion before another smoldering afternoon could punish them. That particular morning, as temperatures climbed to the high eighties by 9:00 a.m., salty breezes tempered the heat with the added promise of an afternoon shower. Despite a typical start, this day would be nothing but extraordinary. It had hardly begun when there was a blur by the gate, followed by the commotion of a shiny black vehicle, possibly two, three—no, more—driving onto the property.

FBI agents presented security with something never seen before—a search warrant for the home of a former president. The warrant was not the kind of local paperwork regarding drug stashes from an errant employee or contraband left behind by a forgetful guest. The agents came seeking long-requested documents thought to contain information about US government trade secrets or even nuclear testing.

Throughout its existence, Mar-a-Lago had endured its share of divorce settlements and official plans to subdivide its acreage, but never had it encountered a federal search-and-seizure warrant. The very idea of commandeering a former president's residence in search of documents was unheard of. But Trump's apparent reluctance to return all the documents that actually belonged to the National Archives prompted US attorney general Merrick Garland to authorize a forced return of the records.

Federal officials had worked for more than six months to retrieve from Mar-a-Lago hundreds of documents, despite unsubstantiated claims that Trump had declassified them. During that time, Trump's team at Mar-a-Lago handed over fifteen boxes containing everything from gifts and mementos to papers, including the traditional presidential well-wishes from Trump's predecessor, Barack Obama. The trove also included more than one hundred classified documents, with dozens of top-secret papers touching on intelligence matters, the *Washington Post* reported. But there was more, much more.

Trump attorneys relayed that their boss at one point advised them to turn over anything agents needed. Even though the team indicated they searched further, and despite repeated attempts and a subpoena, they failed to surrender boxes of records.

No guns were drawn when FBI agents, casually wearing khakis, descended on Mar-a-Lago at about 9:00 a.m. on August 8, 2022. As they pulled their black SUVs onto the property, dozens of officers emerged, crossing the grounds with the kind of intent and purpose you don't see from guests and club members. They produced the affidavit that had been signed just three days before by US Magistrate Judge Bruce Reinhart.

The halls of Mar-a-Lago were long accustomed to the footsteps of Secret Service agents, but an invasion of federal agents was new even to a place with more memories than almost anyone alive. Like any self-respecting Palm Beacher, Mr. Trump was far from his home in the tropics that August day. His son Eric Trump later told Fox News that he received a call that morning about the FBI agents searching Mar-a-Lago and immediately notified his father.

Alarms quickly sounded in the Trump Organization, which owns the Mar-a-Lago Club. By about 10:30 a.m., Trump attorney Christina Bobb arrived only to find dozens of FBI agents "rummaging" through the former president's belongings. Bobb had months earlier signed a statement that Mar-a-Lago had been fully searched for any remaining documents.

Now she found herself on the front lines of trying to protect her client from a surprise raid.

Bobb later told hosts for Real America's Voice that she announced herself at Mar-a-Lago that morning as the president's counsel, and requested the warrant.

"Initially they refused and said, you know, 'We don't have to show it to you,'" Bobb, a former Marine and conservative television anchor, told talk-show host Steve Gruber in the days that followed. "There was a little bit of an exchange about whether it's appropriate to withhold the warrant when you're searching the residence of the former president, who is likely to be the Republican nominee in the next election.

"It started out a little heated," Bobb said during her following appearances on conservative news networks. "I mean I was upset, and they were not excited to see me." She said she and the agents "fought" for a few tense minutes.

Finally, the FBI conceded, showing her what she described as a "thin" warrant but not initially giving her a copy. Worse for her, they ejected her from the house.

Palm Beach is a winter haven for a reason—the summers are insufferable. For about eight or nine hours during the midday, Bobb checked her ego in a parking lot outside of the manse. Agents at some point offered her water, but she said she would have really appreciated air-conditioning.

For pretty much the entire day, the team of investigators looked through likely and unlikely places where documents might hide. The search warrant noted boxes of classified materials stowed in a storage area, some sharing space with a coat rack, a few suit coats, and interior-decorating pieces like frames and wall art. The warrant also noted specialized personnel reviewing "Office 45," the home office of the nation's forty-fifth president. Trump, meanwhile, was able to watch the entire search play out remotely from New York using surveillance cameras installed around the property.

In the late afternoon, when agents finished carting dozens of boxes to their vehicles, they gave Bobb an inventory of what they'd taken. It showed eleven sets of documents marked classified but later details confirmed more than one hundred, ranging from confidential to top secret. While most had been in a storage room, others came from Trump's desk, including three passports belonging to Trump. The collection also included more than ten thousand records that appeared unclassified, empty folders marked "Classified," and about twenty gift items or articles of clothing.

As noted by the *New York Times*, much of the top-secret classified information sat proximate to the trimmings and polish needed to keep the club going—cleaning supplies, patio chairs, and umbrellas. For guests and club members, getting access to the often-unlocked storage room could have been as easy as buying a $500 ticket to Mar-a-Lago's Palm Event, an open-air show featuring vintage cars parked around the property.

Born in the 1920s as the residential signature of one of the wealthiest women in the United States, Mar-a-Lago had been in plenty of headlines through the decades—entertaining royalty, becoming part of the National Park Service, landing in the hands of Donald J. Trump, staring at the brink of extinction, transforming into an exclusive club, and then bearing the mantle of Winter White House. Yet all those events combined could not compare with what had just happened.

On the heels of the cavalcade leaving Mar-a-Lago, news began to seep out. At about 6:30 p.m. that Monday evening, Florida politics editor Peter Schorsch tweeted: "Scoop—The Federal Bureau of Investigation @FBI today executed a search warrant at Mar-a-Lago . . . it's real." The longtime political junkie added that he had it confirmed.

Within a half hour, Trump quickly got ahead of the news and began to shape the narrative with his own missive on social platforms: "These are dark times for our Nation, as my beautiful home, Mar-a-Lago in Palm Beach, Florida, is currently under siege, raided, and occupied by a large group of FBI agents.

"They even broke into my safe!" stated the former president, who added that he had cooperated with various government agencies on returning documents.

He would later tell an audience in Pennsylvania: "You saw it when we witnessed one of the most shocking abuses of power by any administration in American history. The shameful raid and break-in of my home, Mar-a-Lago, was a travesty of justice that made a mockery of America's laws, traditions, and principles."

Agents "rifled through" the First Lady's closet drawers, he told his crowd of supporters. He described the FBI's search of his son's room as "ugly and deep" and said they failed to restore it to order.

"The entire world was watching and they're shocked," he said. "They're shocked."

As the sun set behind Mar-a-Lago that day, the flashing blue lights of a police car parked in front of Mar-a-Lago illuminated its façade. A helicopter hovered overhead. Death threats surfaced against Reinhart, Garland, and others behind the search. Pickup trucks again started cruising past with US flags planted in the truck beds. Police had to establish an around-the-clock presence as this once-regal home had become an unparalleled crime scene.

Now caught in the middle of warring factions, Mar-a-Lago was cast by one side as a hideaway for dangerous documents capable of undermining national security. Others saw it as an attack by an arm of the government against a former president who might run against US president Joe Biden. But the federal government's move to reclaim classified documents would come undone at the hands of U.S. District Judge Aileen Cannon, a 43-year-old Trump appointee. Amidst Trump's election bid, she ruled in July 2024 that Special Counsel Jack Smith had no authority.

Just as quickly as the FBI descended on Mar-a-Lago, the case lost its legal footing.

Trump's reported violations of the Presidential Records Act were hardly the sole looming threat. The US Justice Department was investigating his role in the January 6, 2021 riot at the US Capitol. And Manhattan district attorney Alvin Bragg pushed to indict him for doctoring business records so he could hide an affair with former porn star Stormy Daniels. Throughout the investigations, Trump railed against what he saw as injustices aimed at undoing his political comeback.

In Palm Beach, the impending legal storms mounted just as the winter season of 2023 neared an end. Every March, the town's winter revelry gives way to humid afternoons and a piercing sun. Private jets fuel at Palm Beach International to head back north again. Crews prep yachts to navigate the channels leading back to New York. As Palm Beach society readied for its next migration that spring, reports began to swirl of an impending New York indictment.

An arrest, it appeared, was imminent.

The very idea of a former president being arrested was unheard of in a country where fewer than four dozen people had ever held the nation's top office. For ardent fans impatiently awaiting Trump's return to power, these impending challenges only stoked their indignation. Leveraging social media, they swore allegiances, pledged their loyalties, and conspired to stand by him. Some promised to descend on the streets of Palm Beach if an arrest became apparent. They could form a human barricade around the house that Marjorie Post built to keep law enforcement at bay.

Even as threats of mayhem spread, the Secret Service sought to further reinvent Mar-a-Lago by building a one-story guardhouse of concrete and impact glass. Despite growing concerns, the Town Council deferred the idea due to worsening traffic, the *Palm Beach Daily News* reported.

The idea of a showdown between Trump's base and the police must have sped up the packing process for Palm Beach's winter set. And as attractive as the idea of an insurrection might have been to Trump, he did not want to share the spotlight with his chief rival for the 2024 Republican nomination—Florida governor Ron DeSantis, who could gain attention by blocking an extradition.

And so, instead of a civil war at Mar-a-Lago, it would be a surrender to the Manhattan district attorney in New York.

The day before his April 4 arrest, Trump joined Secret Service agents and key members of his inner circle as they loaded themselves into black sport utility vehicles outside Mar-a-Lago. After they crossed the bridge leading to the mainland, the back window of one SUV slid down and Trump gave a thumbs up to fans along the announced route, reported the *Palm Beach Post*. Government-edition vehicles tooted their horns at a group of supporters waving Trump 2024 signs in front of the Publix grocery store, which was their rallying point. Even though the grocery conglomerate had denounced the Capitol riots, an heiress of the supermarket family had plowed millions of dollars into efforts to overturn the results of Trump's failed election, newspaper accounts of her deposition reported.

By mid-afternoon the next day, a Manhattan judge would read thirty-four felony counts, and this MAGA chieftain would plead "not guilty" to every one of them.

Even as he proclaimed his innocence in Manhattan, a few stalwart fans in Palm Beach claimed spots in front of Publix. They would not miss the return of their persecuted hero. Their ranks gradually swelled over the afternoon. By the time the gleaming Trump Force One 757 airliner landed a few miles away at the airport, about two hundred people had gathered in front of the Publix shopping center.

Suntanned and sporting sunglasses under red baseball caps emblazoned with white "Make America Great Again" lettering, they wielded handheld loudspeakers and chanted: "U-S-A! U-S-A!" They hoisted Trump 2024 flags. The number "45" marked tee shirts, banners, and moist face paintings. (Wasn't the idea now to become the 47th president?) A monster truck professionally wrapped in a salute to Trump did, however, boast #47. But could the events of this day diminish the chances that their leader would claim presidential spot number 47? Not if they could help it.

Commuters on Southern Boulevard tooted horns and did a slow roll as they passed the self-described patriots that afternoon. Then, in the hint of evening, headlights of the long-awaited motorcade neared. Sitting in the backseat of one of the onyx-colored vehicles, Trump popped up a thumb and gave an occasional wave from behind darkly tinted window glass.

Trump's son, Eric, later told Fox News that they saw "tens and tens of thousands of people" lining the roads from Palm Beach International to Mar-a-Lago.

"The love is incredible," he said. "No one's ever seen that kind of love."

Waving fans stood along the bridge leading to the famous estate on South Ocean Boulevard. The bridge connected the mainland to a barrier reef that was home. One by one, the SUVs rolled through the arched entry of Mar-a-Lago while sunset-colored clouds buffeted the estate's iconic tower. The entourage rolled up a driveway bordered by palm trees that appeared to lean in toward this small parade. This was only the opening act.

Instead of laying low following a humiliation of historic proportions, the day called instead for a celebration. Soon, in the same way that the crowd in front of the Palm Beach Publix had swelled, Mar-a-Lago's ivory and cream-walled ballroom started to stir.

Rather than the elite of the Republican Party, the personalities emerging for the post-arrest event included political consultant Roger Stone, who had been convicted for obstructing justice before Trump pardoned him at the end of his presidency. Failed Arizona gubernatorial candidate Kari Lake spoke to the media about how much people in the airport appreciated her Trump 2024 hat. Georgia congresswoman and far-right conspiracy theorist Marjorie Taylor Greene was also on hand. Trump campaign aide Jason Miller tweeted out a photo of the fanfare, showing the media platform and more than a hundred guests mingling under the crystal chandeliers that dangled from the ballroom's richly coffered ceiling. Like some other guests, Miller had his distinctions. He became notable in 2019 for losing a defamation case regarding an abortion pill he allegedly gave to a stripper he impregnated, according to court documents. Also, there was Matt Gaetz, the Florida congressman who recently beat sex-trafficking charges. Gaetz later lingered for an interview until the place had virtually emptied and the lights dimmed. He joked that it wasn't the first time he had outlasted the lights there. Not everyone could make it. Embattled congressman George Santos, known for fabricating pretty much his entire background, showed his support for Trump earlier in the day outside the courthouse in Manhattan.

Over the ballroom's audio system, a patriotic song set the scene. Then, somewhat oddly, the stereo gave way to David Bowie's "Rebel Rebel," which is a tribute to a makeup-wearing boy. A few Trump family members walked past the room's marble Corinthian columns. They beamed, roused the crowd, and led the way for the guest of honor.

"Ladies and gentlemen. . . . Mister President," an announcer boomed.

For the next three minutes, Trump edged his way up through a crowd that flashed smiles, shouted support, and held up cell-phone cameras to commemorate what might be the event of a lifetime. Some wept. The unbridled adoration was far different than the reception he had just gotten hours earlier in New York, where law enforcement didn't even bother to hold the door open as the former leader of the free world entered a courtroom corridor. In stark contrast to the gushing fans in Palm Beach, crowds outside the Manhattan courthouse had parodied and pilloried #45 as he headed for a highly choreographed version of a perp walk.

Now, after suffering those indignations, Trump made his way to a ballroom stage bathed in brightness from spotlights bolted into Mar-a-Lago's otherwise elegant ceiling. As he made his way up the few stairs leading to the stage, the seventy-six-year-old leaned onto the handrail. He was no longer the strapping young man who had bought Mar-a-Lago almost forty years earlier. In fact, he was now the same age Joe Biden had been when Trump suggested his opponent seemed too old to run for president. His still-stunning wife might have lent him an air of virility, had she been there.

Chants of "U-S-A! U-S-A! U-S-A!" emanated from a crowd that was on its feet as their host made his way to the podium. Mar-a-Lago had never looked so resplendent with swags of ivory and beige fabric tufted and draping down walls trimmed in a gold-chord pattern that was echoed on the podium. The fine details, though, were a bit lost under a blue podium sign that entreated viewers to "Text TRUMP to 88022" so they could help make America great again.

With campaign spigots fully open, Donald John Trump approached center stage. His blue suit, white shirt, and red tie melded into a backdrop of larger-than-life flags bordered with gold fringe and resting on flagpoles topped by eagle emblems. With angled teleprompters flanking him, he spoke publicly for the first time of his arrest just hours earlier.

"I never thought anything like this could happen in America," he said. "Never thought it could happen." His only crime, he reminded the crowd, had been to "fearlessly defend our country against those who seek to destroy it."

Boos rose suddenly from the audience as he spoke about the August raid of the very property on which they stood. He had been within his rights, he told them, to negotiate the return of federal documents. The fact that the Presidential Records Act doesn't mention negotiations was a mere technicality.

If Mar-a-Lago had earlier served as a backdoor to the White House and private parlor for public business, it was now preened, polished, and presented as an American castle crafted to inspire political patronage for a man who was now a criminal suspect.

Quickly joining Mar-a-Lago as a spectacle of unprecedented controversy would be its one-time sister estate—Topridge in the Adirondacks. Post died thinking she'd left it safely in the hands of New York state but, in 1985, Governor Mario Cuomo disapproved of annual upkeep mounting upwards of $250,000 and ordered most of it auctioned off. Instead of the public enjoying the history of this legendary estate, it gained notoriety as the exclusive and undisclosed get-away for Supreme Court Justice Clarence Thomas and his wife, as guests of Texas billionaire Harlan Crow.

The American public not only lost both of Post's properties, but Mar-a-Lago and Topridge went on to become conduits where billionaires could access the country's highest-ranking officials— all out of the public eye.

For Mar-a-Lago, the venerable winter home designed long ago by opposing architects has withstood hurricanes, serial divorces, financial collapses, apathetic heirs, National Park Service abandonment, subdivision plans, blanket commercialization, and now the harsh limelight of federal investigations. Its future as a club— built atop the popularity of one man—is anything but certain.

Just as they did when Post first scouted the grounds a century ago, waves from the Atlantic still chase gulls and sandpipers hunting the shoreline. Tides rise a little higher now, although not as high as they will. Salt-infused breezes still buffet the house Marjorie built with Edward Hutton. Guests still crane their necks as they take in an homage to the Thousand-Wing Ceiling of the Accademia in Venice. And on certain evenings, for those of privilege, the famous monkey loggia still glows with riverine sunsets the color of orange sherbet.

ACKNOWLEDGMENTS

This story would not be possible without the tireless work of journalists and authors who have, for decades, chronicled the lives, events, and personalities related to Mar-a-Lago. Most importantly, I would not have undertaken this project if not for a National Park Service forum that mentioned the late NPS administrator Dwight F. Rettie, his book *Our National Park System*, and his insights into the park service's abandonment of Mar-a-Lago.

The Historical Society of Palm Beach County's research director, Rose Guerrero, deserves recognition for her assistance. Archivists and librarians for the following institutions also helped inform this work: Bentley Historical Library at the University of Michigan, Dumbarton Oaks Library and Archives, George A. Smathers Libraries of the University of Florida, John C. Hitt Library of the University of Central Florida, the Library of Congress, and the Smithsonian Institution Archives.

The presidential libraries for Lyndon B. Johnson, Richard M. Nixon, Gerald R. Ford, and Jimmy Carter all aided in overall research. Thanks also go to Joy Perry for referencing Lady Bird Johnson's journal entries regarding the First Lady's tour of Mar-a-Lago.

I am indebted to the attorneys, authors, architects, and others who voiced their own stories related to Mar-a-Lago, including Boca Raton attorney Robert I. Maclaren, II and *Hillwood: The Long Island Estate of Marjorie Merriweather Post* coauthor

Kenneth Mensing. Former congressman Daniel Andrew Mica deserves special recognition for relaying his pivotal role in the fate of the estate.

Early on, Laureen Crowley provided me with trusted copy-editing guidance. I owe deep appreciation to my agent, Murray Weiss, for his belief in my manuscript and suggestions to help shape it. I also appreciate Keith Wallman and his staff at Diversion Books for all their meaningful edits, photo acquisition help, and general publishing polish.

Lastly, thank you to Randa Marder and Beth Ruchlin for their support and to all my other friends and family who encouraged me throughout this four-year process.

NOTES

CHAPTER 1. A CAPITOL DAY

2. Udall. *Washington Post*. March 21, 2010. 5. Post lobbies Florida. *Miami Herald*. December 11, 1983, 367. 5. "plan to acquire." *Tallahassee Democrat*. June 22, 1965, 6. 5. Acquisition team. Rettie (Parks), 96. 6. "Negotiations fell through." *Tallahassee Democrat*. June 22, 1965, 9. 6. Udall, *PB Post*. April 29, 1979. 74. 6. Lady Bird Johnson trip. April 3, 1968, 2. 6. Lady Bird Johnson. Sweig, Julia. *In Plain Sight*, Episode 7. 7. Lady Bird tour, LBJ Library. Lady Bird diary collection. April 4, 1968. https://www.discoverlbj. org/item/ctjd-19680404. 7. Hickel. Cook Inlet Historical Society. https:// www.alaskahistory.org/biographies/hickel-walter-j-wally/.

CHAPTER 2. DEATH'S DOOR

9. Spanish flu. "Spanish Flu and the First Amendment." First Amendment Museum. https://firstamendmentmuseum.org/learn/spanish-flu-and-th e-first-amendment/. 9–10. Winter in New York. *New York Times*. February 20, 1977, 348. 10. Soldier gifts. *New York Times*. December 9, 1917, 7. 10. Cillis letter. New York Historical Society. December 6, 1927. 10. Blanche Hutton. Find a Grave. https://www.findagrave.com/memorial/61930092 /blanche-conant-hutton. 10–11. Blanche Hutton. An Open Book. http:// brookspeters.blogspot.com/2012/07/. 11. Blanche Hutton obituary. *San Francisco Chronicle*, December 19, 1917, 4. 11. Spanish flu. Centers for Disease Control. https://www.cdc.gov/flu/pandemic-resources /1918-commemoration/1918-pandemic-history.htm. 12. Edna Hutton death. History Collection. https://historycollection.com/a-tragic-countdown-throug h-the-life-of-americas-poor-little-rich-girl-barbara-hutton/12/. 12. Blanche Hutton. An Open Book. http://brookspeters.blogspot.com/2012/07/. 12. Blanche Hutton estate. *New York Herald*. March 3, 1918, 9. 13. Hutton houseboat. *PB Post*. February 18, 1920, 8. 14. Florida Association of

Native Nurseries. **15.** Post divorce from Close. *Meriden Daily Journal*. November 7, 1919, 1. **15.** Edward Close marriage. Rubin (Empress). Kindle. **16.** "She became so independent." History Chicks. June 11, 2021. http://thehistorychicks.com/episode-178-marjorie-merriweather-post-par t-one/. **17.** "Taj Mahal." Palm Beach Historical Survey 9. **17.** Florida land boom. "Flagler Era Through Boom-to-Bust." https://pbchistory.org/ flagler-era-through-boom-to-bust/. **18.** Huttons' honeymoon. *NY Tribune*. July 18, 1920, 37. **17–19.** Wall Street bombing. Manning (Crime). http:// www.crimemagazine.com/916-terrorists-bomb-wall-street. **19–20.** Wall Street bombing description. FBI Media. https://multimedia.fbi.gov/?q=&perp-age=50&page=1&searchType=image **19–20.** Wall Street Bombing. Manning, 2. **20.** Lodge. *Philadelphia Inquirer*. July 10, 1920, 5. **20–21.** Halcourt Hutton. *Brooklyn Daily Eagle*. July 18, 1915, 4. **21.** Harkness Tower. Yale Guide. https://guides.library.yale.edu/yalehistory. **21–22.** Halcourt Hutton death. *NY Tribune*. September 27, 1920, 1.

CHAPTER 3. BORN ON A BED OF CORAL

23–24. Ponzi. *PB Post*. October 5, 1920, 6. **24.** Resale of Florida land. *Journal of Land*, 113–131. **24.** Resale of Florida land. *Journal of Land*, 113–132. **25.** Land values quintupled. Palm Beach County History. "The Boom." http://www.pbchistoryonline.org/page/the-boom. **25.** Land Boom. http://floridahistory.org/landboom.htm. **25–26.** Florida income tax. IRS Guide. 1993, 27. **26.** Everglades Club. Florida Memory. https://www. floridamemory.com/items/show/40091. **26.** Hogarcito. NY Social Diary. https://www.newyorksocialdiary.com/mrs-posts-mar-a-lago/. **26.** Huttons at Everglades Club. *NY Herald*. January 7, 1921, 11. **26.** Hutton chairman at Post. *NY Times*. July 12, 1962, 29. **26–27.** Hutton takes Post Cereal public. *NY Times*. July 12, 1962, 29 **27** El Mirasol. Urban's Palm Beach, 436–457. **27–28.** Post land search. Bently Historical Library recordings, Part 1. **28.** Post selected land atop coral reef. Bently Historical Library recordings, Part 1. **29.** Huttons buy property. *PB Post*. May 2, 1925, 10. **29–30.** Post interview. University of Michigan. https://deepblue.lib.umich.edu /handle/2027.42/122150. **31.** Burden Mansion, *NY Times*. November 19, 1924, 21. **31.** 6sqft. "New York's First-Ever Penthouse." https://www.6sqft. com/new-yorks-first-ever-penthouse-a-54-room-upper-east-side-mansion-buil t-for-a-cereal-heiress/. **31.** Burden mansion description. http://landmarkbrand-ing.com/1107-fifth-avenue/. **31–32.** Hutridge elevator. NY Social Diary. https://www.newyorksocialdiary.com/mrs-posts-mar-a-lago/. **32.** Hutridge details. *NY Times*. August 19, 1984, 49. **32.** Hutridge embellishments. US Department of the Interior. https://npgallery.nps.gov/NRHP/GetAsset/ NRHP/64000555_text. **32.** Hutridge scope. Camp Topridge Historic Details. https://localwiki.org/hsl/Camp_Topridge. **32.** Udall frequented Topridge. *PB Post*. April 29, 1979, 74. **32.** Hutridge self-sustaining. Rubin (Empress). Kindle. **33.** Breakers Hotel fire. PBC History Online. "1925 Hotel Fires." http://www.pbchistoryonline.org/page/hotel-fires. **34.** Hutton introduction to Joseph Urban. "Mrs. Post's Mar-a-Lago." https://www.newyorksocialdiary. com/mrs-posts-mar-a-lago/.

CHAPTER 4. THE TRUTH ABOUT FLORIDA

35. Florida IRS office. IRS Guide. 1993, 109. **35.** Martin at Waldorf. CJR. "Florida Candidates Short-Sighted." https://www.cjr.org/special_report/ midterms-2018-florida-algae-hurricane-michael.php. **36.** Weather Service warnings. NWS. "Great Miami Hurricane." https://www.weather.gov/mfl/ miami_hurricane. **36.** "barely an hour." Jones (Tempest), 384. **36.** "suddenly trapped." Ferguson, 24. **37.** Miami radio. PBS (Hurricane of 1926). https:// www.pbs.org/wgbh/americanexperience/features/miami-hurricane-1926/. **37.** Mayor is contractor. *PB Post*. April 17, 1925, 8. **37.** Conscripted. Jones (Tempest), 402. **37.** Lightbrown. HABS. 6. **38.** "The stones looked." Lady Bird Johnson audio collection. April 2, 1968. https://discoverlbj.org/ item/ctjd-19680402. 6. **38.** Craftsmanship. HABS. 7. **38–39.** "America's Treasures." National Register (Mar-a-Lago), 5. https://npgallery.nps.gov/ NRHP/GetAsset/NHLS/80000961_text. **39.** Urban's design styles. Arnold (Theatrical Vision). 4. **39.** Description of Mar-a-Lago. "Lady Bird Johnson audio collection. April 2–3, 1963. https://discoverlbj.org/item/ctjd-19680402. **40.** Amenities. HABS. 7. **40.** "most pretentious." *PB Post*. January 14, 1926, 1. **40.** Club delayed. "Mrs. Post's Mar-a-Lago." https://www.newyo-rksocialdiary.com/mrs-posts-mar-a-lago/. **40.** Resort life before Depression. HABS. 1. **40–41.** Garish interiors. *Miami Herald* (Hard Sell). December 11, 1983, 369. **41.** Wyeth disavowal of Mar-a-Lago. *PB Post*. March 16, 1981, 5. **41.** Mar-a-Lago architect Wyeth disavowed. Curl, Donald (Urban's), 442. **41.** Best dinner party. *Philadelphia Inquirer*. March 2, 1927, 2. **41.** Tea. *Brooklyn Life and Activities of Long Island Society*. March 2, 1929, 14. **41.** Animal rescue benefit. *PB Post*. March 11, 1928, 14. **42.** Consumerism. Page (History of Conspicuous Consumerism). https://www.acrwebsite.org/ volumes/12197/volumes/sv08/SV. **43.** Florida oil boom. *PB Post* (Florida Oil

Boom). February15, 1929, 8. **43.** Banks closing. PB History Online. "The Bust." **43.** "Signs of Life." *PB Post*. December 4, 1927, 11. **43.** Recessions. "Palm Beach is the Big Stadium." *NY Times*. March 21, 1971, 79. **44.** Hurricane conditions. Mitchell. "Weather Review." September 1928, 338. **45.** Hurricane to bypass Florida. Gerstel (Hurricane of 1928). **45.** Saturday night warnings. Mitchell. "Weather Review." September 1928, 338. **45.** Residents secure belongings. Gerstel (Hurricane of 1928). **45.** Sounded like NY Subway. Mitchell. "Weather Review." September 1928, 348. **47.** "There's no place." *NY Daily News*. September 19, 1928, 6. **47.** "The writer cast." *NY Daily News*. September 19, 1928, 6. **47.** Hurricane damage. University of Florida. Digital Collection. http://purl.flvc.org/fcla/tc/fhp/UF00001306. pdf. **48.** "The very first year." University of Michigan. https://deepblue.lib. umich.edu/handle/2027.42/122150. **48–49.** Two mules. "Post family." Griffin interview. University of Michigan. **49.** "One of the noteworthy." Mitchell. "Weather Review." September 1928, 349. **49.** "Nowhere for nobody." Williams. https://youtu.be/Op__faFyIZU. **50.** Burials. University of Florida. Digital Collection. http://purl.flvc.org/fcla/tc/fhp/UF00001306.pdf. **50.** "Well I remember." Herron. https://youtu.be/Op__faFyIZU.

CHAPTER 5. THE CIRCUS

52. North of Mar-a-Lago. "Ghost Mansions." F10. **52.** Hutton family members. "Palm Beach Society" *PB Post*. December 16, 1928, 10. **52.** "My dears." *NY Daily News* (Randolph). January 31, 1929, 9. **52.** "A society publication." *Brooklyn Life and Activities of Long Island Society*. March 2, 1929, 14. **52.** "At two benefits." *PB Post*. "Huttons present circus." March 12, 1929, 6. **53.** "After taking Postum public." *New York Times*. Post obituary. September 13, 1973, 50. **53.** Mar-a-Lago golf course. Donald Ross Directory, 5. **53.** Dow growth. History.com. "Stock Market Crash." https://www. history.com/topics/great-depression/1929-stock-market-crash. **54.** Florida's economy. Florida Department of State (Great Depression). https://dos.myflor-ida.com/florida-facts/florida-history/a-brief-history/the-great-depression-in-florida/. **54.** "We do not think." *Times Herald* (Stock Letter). October 3, 1929, 8. **54.** Critical. *Times Herald* (Stock Letter). October 3, 1929, 8. **55.** Equilibrium. *Buffalo News*. October 25, 1929, 3. **55.** "Our belief." *Brooklyn Daily Eagle*. October 25, 1929, 46. **55.** Gerald Loeb. *New York Times*. April 16, 1974, 42. **56.** Palm Beach banks. PB History Online. "The Bust." http:// www.pbchistoryonline.org/page/the-bust. **56.** Families. University of South Florida. "Exploring Florida." 2002. **56.** Bankrupt railways. PB History

Online. "The Bust." 56. Post stowed jewels. *Victorian Antique Jewelry Blog*. 56. Hell's Kitchen. Rubin (Empress). Kindle. 56. Lady Bird. Lady Bird diary collection. Audio diary. April 2, 1968. https://www.discoverlbj.org/item/ctjd-19680404. 56–57. "What they did do." "Post family." Griffin interview. University of Michigan. 57. Post profits. Rubin (Empress). Kindle. 57. Recessions. *New York Times*. "Palm Beach is the Big Stadium." March 21, 1971, 79. 58. Stotesbury party. University of South Carolina. Moving Research Image Collection. 58. Stotesbury improvements. *PB Post* (Extensive Development). October 18, 1931, 14. 59. "With interiors described as." Sea History (Burgman), 16–20. 59. Huttons sail instead of winter in Palm Beach. *NY Daily News*. December 3, 1932, 227. 59. *Hussar V* amenities. Sea History (Burgman), 16–20. 59. *Hussar V* amenities. Sea History (Burgman), 16–20. 59. *Hussar* size. Travel Lady. (Lopez-Fabrega). August 22, 2000. 59. Post absence from Palm Beach. *NY Daily News* (Rudolph column). December 3, 1931, 227 59–60. Post absence from Palm Beach. *NY Daily News* (Rudolph column). January 14, 1932, 162. 60. Ban on "depression." *Burlington Daily News*. February 16, 1933, 6. 61. Bradley. *PB Post*. April 9, 1933, 8. 61. Hutton cruise. *Brooklyn Daily Eagle*. August 20, 1933, 16. 62. Mar-a-Lago closed. *Star Tribune*. August 12, 1934, 45. 62. "It's no secret." *NY Daily News*. February 4, 1935, 105.

CHAPTER 6. "AN INSOUCIANT MINX"

64. Knott, James to Lester Waterbury. January 11, 1969. Knott Collection. Palm Beach Historical Society. Box 19. Folder 4. 64. Women's property rights. Florida Women's Hall of Fame (Baker). https://flwomenshalloffame.org/bio/mary-lou-baker/ 64. Post a guest in Palm Beach. *NY Daily News*. February 11, 1935, 331. 64. Davies. Rubin (Empress). Kindle. 65. Hutton and American Liberty League. *Dayton Daily News*. August 24, 1934, 34. 65. Extramarital affair. *Times Union*. September 7, 1935, 1. 65–66. Divorce settlement. Rubin (Empress). Kindle. 66. Newspaper image of Hutton. *Philadelphia Inquirer*. September 10, 1935, 14. 66. Visitation. Rubin (Empress). Kindle. 66. Davies. Rubin (Empress). Kindle. 66. Engagement. *NY Daily News*. October 21, 1935, 31. 66. New beau. Battle Creek Enquirer. September 29, 1935, 14. 66. Metzger divorce. *NY Daily News*. January 26, 1936, 332. 67. Metzger ex-husband. *Philadelphia Inquirer*. October 19, 1935, 2. 67. "gang up." *Honolulu Star-Bulletin*. December 11, 1935, 6. 67. Apology. *Pittsburgh Press*. November 22, 1935, 6. 67. General Foods Board. *NY Times*. April 9, 1936, 25. 68. Hutton's *Hussar* farewell.

NY Daily News. November 15, 1935, 28. **68**. Davies wedding. *NY Daily News*. November 15, 1935, 28. **68–69**. Post stepdaughter. *Washington Post*. Tregaron's Dynasty: January 24, 1978. https://www.washington-post.com/archive/politics/1978/01/24/tregarons-dynasty-the-davies-fam-ily/e08395ca-f23c-43b0-9062-caf400755522/ **69**. Architectural designs. "Mar-a-Lago." https://www.historic-details.com/places/fl/mar-a-lago-estat e-palm-beach-fl/ **70**. Depression. Florida Center for Instructional Technology. "Great Depression and the New Deal." https://fcit.usf.edu/florida/lessons/ depress/depress1.htm. **71**. "With the Great Depression." *New York Times*. August 1, 2008. https://www.nytimes.com/2008/08/01/greathomesanddesti-nations/01mark.html. **71**. Cielito Lindo. *PB Post*. November 10, 1935, 2. **71**. Playa Riente. PB History Online (Mizner). http://www.pbchistoryonline.org/ page/mizner-in-palm-beach. **71–72**. Davies received in society. *Philadelphia Inquirer*. April 12, 1936, 56. **72**. Huttons' reception. *NY Daily News*. February 28, 1936, 622. **72**. Huttons' new house. *Tampa Tribune*. September 12, 1937, 10. **73**. Consuelo Vanderbilt. *NY Daily News*. November 7, 1936, 44. **73**. Stotesbury birthday party. *NY Daily News*. February 27, 1939, 336. **73–74**. Stotesbury financial affairs. *Philadelphia Business Journal*. January 10, 1920. https://www.bizjournals.com/philadelphia/stories/2000/01/10/story6. html. **74**. Stotesbury death. *PB Post*. May 17, 1983, 5. **74**. Pulitzer purchase. *PB Post*. January 10, 1940, 1. **74**. El Mirasol subdivide. *PB Post*. March 28, 1940, 1. **75**. Darkened mansions (Blackout). https://www.floridamemory. com/items/show/339333. **75**. Mar-a-Lago opened. *PB Post*. February 14, 1940, 7. **76**. Tregaron. Tregaron Conservancy. https://tregaron.org/history/. **76**. "more time here." *PB Post*. February 14, 1940, 1. **77**. Rations. Palm Beach County History Online (Military). http://www.pbchistoryonline.org/ page/us-military-in-west-palm-beach. **77**. Soldiers at El Mirasol. Palm Beach Historical Survey. 17. https://www.townofpalmbeach.com/DocumentCenter/ View/167/Historic-Sites-Survey. **77**. Hospital at The Breakers. NY Social Diary (Mrs. Post's). https://www.newyorksocialdiary.com/mrs-posts-mar-a-lago/. **78**. Mar-a-Lago offered in service. *Capital Times of Madison*. April 9, 1944, 6. **78**. Soldier convalescence at Mar-a-Lago. *St. Louis Star and Times*. April 4, 1944, 15. **78**. Bus tours of Mar-a-Lago. *Miami News*. February 24, 1941, 10.

CHAPTER 7. MONUMENTAL ALBATROSSES

79. Eva Stotesbury illness. *PB Post*. May 13, 1945, 11. **80**. El Mirasol as san-atorium. *PB Post*. June 29, 1945, 6. **80**. Palm Beach officials buy at Stotesbury

Park. *PB Post*. September 28, 1946, 6. 80. Stotesbury rezoning. *PB Post*. July 6, 1945, 14. 80. Stotesbury death. *Baltimore Evening Sun*. May 23, 1946, 2. 80. El Mirasol value. *PB Post*. October 8, 1946, 12. 80. El Mirasol price. *PB Post*. November 24, 1945, 9. 81. El Mirasol auction sign. Florida Memory. http://www.floridamemory.com/items/show/65571. 81. El Mirasol auction items. *PB Post*. February 6, 1947, 4. 81. El Mirasol auction crowds. *PB Post*. February 22, 1947, 4. 81. "Half empty." *PB Post*. March 4, 1947, 6. 81. "Shiver of sadness." *Minneapolis Star Tribune* (Greenman letter). March 16, 1947, 59. 82. Stotesbury heirs. *Honolulu Advertiser* (Cholly Knickerbocker). April 13, 1947, 51. 82. "bon bons." *Chicago Tribune* (Smith).December 29, 1946, 140. 82–83. "24 carat." *NY Daily News*. January 1947, 50. 83. Cielito Lindo's swan song. Preservation Foundation of PB. https://preservation-foundationofpalmbeach.omeka.net/items/show/190. 84. Rezoning meeting. *Brooklyn Daily Eagle*. July 11, 1947, 1 84. Hillwood description. Old Long Island website. http://www.oldlongisland.com/2008/08/hillwood.html. 85. Hillwood wedding. *NY Daily News* March 24, 1964, 232. 86. Mackay mansion. *Newsday* (Demolition crew). April 15, 1947. 86. Mackay entertaining. Mackay History (Harbor Hill). http://www.mackayhistory.com/HarborHill. html. 88. Merrill's life. *WAPO* (obituary). May 22, 2017. 88–89. "Life being what it is." *Sun Sentinel* (Party Time at Mar-a-Lago). June 18, 1985. 89. "She should have been." Trump, Donald (Art of Comeback). 89. Mar-a-Lago demolition. *Miami News*. November 18, 1951, 37. 90. "orders to raze." *San Francisco Examiner* (Cholly Knickerbocker). November 23, 1951, 12. 90. Davies divorce. *PB Post* (Cholly Knickerbocker). September 11, 1952, 21. 90. Children don't want. *Pittsburgh Press*. May 27, 1962, 27. 90. Davies divorce. Rubin (Empress). Kindle. 90. Divorce property split. *Madisonville Messenger* (Washington Daybook). April 18, 1955, 6. 90–91. Divorce and DC property purchase. *NY Daily News*. March 10, 1995, 66. 90–91. Abremont purchase. *LA Times*. February 11, 1955, 35. 91. Hillwood collections. *WAPO*. February 2, 2014. 91. "In this charming little room." "Notes on Hillwood" (Breakfast Room), 43 92. "Post essentially ignored." Inge. "Culture and Diplomacy." 92. "This art was available." Dumbarton Oaks.

CHAPTER 8. "LUSTER'S LAST STAND"

95. "attractive blonde." *PB Post* (Council). May 27, 1961, 8. 95. Membership. Council of 100. (Progress Report). November 3, 1964, 4. 95. Post wealth. *Baltimore Evening Sun*. May 12, 1958, 4. 96. Herb May. *Baltimore Evening Sun*. May 12, 1958, 4. 96. "Wife, Marjorie." Council of 100. (Progress

Report). November 3, 1964, 4. **96.** Council luncheon at Mar-a-Lago. *PB Post.* May 7, 1961, 1. **96.** Mar-a-Lago auction. *Oakland Tribune.* January 12, 1958, 110. **96.** Restauranter purchase. *Philadelphia Inquirer.* March 10, 1958, 11. **96.** Syracuse U. considered buying. *Oakland Tribune.* January 12, 1958, 110. **97.** Saudi king. *NY Daily News.* February 9, 1962, 39. **97.** Saudi king. Bentley Historical Library recordings, Part 1. **97.** Donate Mar-a-Lago to church. *NY Daily News.* February 1, 1961, 6. **97–98.** Post donation to Smithsonian. Bradley oral interviews. Smithsonian Institution Archives, 305. **98.** Post endowment for Hillwood. Bradley oral interviews. Smithsonian Institution Archives, 307. **98.** "There are flowers." *PB Post.* April 6, 1963, 47. **98.** Twist banned. *Philadelphia Inquirer.* April 1, 1962, 145. **98.** Post looked exquisite. *Tampa Bay Times* (photo). April 6, 1963, 7. **98.** Post donation to cultural center. *New York Times* (obituary). Accessed February 17, 2023. **100.** "The Mediterranean architecture." *Tampa Bay Times* (photo). April 6, 1963, 7. **100.** Possible uses. *PB Post.* April 6, 1962, 1. *Miami Herald.* **100.** Select scholars. "Center for Advanced Scholars." Yonge Library. University of Florida. **100–01.** Center for studies. *Miami Herald.* February 1, 1964, 53. **101.** State fund to support. *PB Post.* October 9, 1963, 3. **102.** Slow transition. *Miami Herald* (Parker). February 1, 1964, 53. **102.** "Dealmakers called for." **102.** Lost tax revenue. *PB Post.* October 9, 1963, 3. **103.** Center revenues. (Summary of Support). PBCHS. **103.** Zoning. *PB Post.* October 9, 1963, 3. **103.** Mounting costs. *PB Post.* October 4, 1964, 45. **103.** Reduce servants. *New York Times.* October 22, 1972. https://www.nytimes.com/1972/10/22/archives/a-palm-beach-guest-house-for-presidents-and-kings.html?searchResultPosition=1. **103.** Detailed costs. *Miami Herald.* May 25, 1963, 51. **104.** Ford sponsorship. *PB Post.* October 4, 1964, 45. **104.** Post endowment prioritized Hillwood. *PB Post.* October 4, 1964, 45. **104.** Palm Beach opposed. *PB Post.* October 4, 1964, 45. **105.** Keep PB exclusive. *PB Post.* October 4, 1964, 45. **105.** Losing Sanson ally. *New York Times.* December 22, 1964. **106.** Real gaff. *Oakland Tribune.* July 11, 1965, 132. **106.** Rollins College. Fearing, Gwen. November 8, 1965. **106.** Bath & Tennis Club. Norris. April, 26, 1967. **106.** Town of PB. Town correspondence. February 22, 1967. **106.** Honorary citizen. *Tallahassee Democrat.* June 29, 1965, 2. **107.** Florida State plans. Fleming. March 29, 1967. **107.** Florida State plans. McKay. April 12, 1967. **107.** Blast of publicity. Knott. May 23, 1967.

CHAPTER 9. LADY BIRD LANDS

109. White House billed. *Tallahassee Record*, April 4, 1968, 2. 109. Small gifts, LBJ Library. Lady Bird diary collection. Audio diary. April 4, 1968. https://www.discoverlbj.org/item/ctjd-19680404. 109. Hartzogs. LBJ Library. Lady Bird diary collection. Audio diary. April 4, 1968. https://www.discoverlbj .org/item/ctjd-19680404. 109–110. Plane's interior. *Battle Creek Enquirer.* February 25, 1960, 12. 110. Purchase of the plane. *Pittsburgh Post-Gazette.* February 26, 1959, 8. 111. Henry Flagler estate. https://www.westpalm-beach.com/attractions/flagler/. 111. Henry Flagler estate. HABS. FLA-224. 111. Flagler Museum. *PB Post.* February 8, 1960, 6. 112. Johnson arrival. LBJ Library. Lady Bird diary collection. Audio diary. April 4, 1968. https:// www.discoverlbj.org/item/ctjd-19680404. 112. "There was." LBJ Library. Lady Bird diary collection. Audio diary. April 4, 1968. https://www.discov-erlbj.org/item/ctjd-19680404. 112. "When I stood." LBJ Library. Lady Bird diary collection. Audio diary. April 4, 1968. https://www.discoverlbj.org/ item/ctjd-19680405. 113. Johnson donned. LBJ Library. Lady Bird diary collection. Audio diary. April 4, 1968. https://www.discoverlbj.org/item/ ctjd-19680406. 113. Appetizers floated past. *PB Post* (Knott). February 8, 1981, 47. 113. Glasses were filled. *PB Post* (Knott). February 8, 1981, 47. 114. A spokesperson. *Lansing State Journal.* April 14, 1968, 43. 114. "Quite true." *Lansing State Journal.* April 14, 1968, 43. 115. A month after. *PB Post.* May 4, 1968, 2. 115. Alaska preservation efforts. *Fairbanks Daily News.* January 31, 1969, 4. 115. Before administration ends. Johnson, LB. UVA. 116. Kennedy purchase offer. *LA Times.* April 4, 1961, 2. 116. Hartzog visit. *Rockland Journal.* April 12, 1968, 3. 116. Kennedy's Palm Beach experiences. *PB Post* online. May 29, 2017. https://www.palmbeachpost.com/story/ lifestyle/2017/05/26/jfk-s-100th-birthday-100/6922394007/. 116. Kennedy interest. *Call-Leader.* January 25, 1961, 12. 116. PB officials urge purchase. *LA Times.* October 16, 1968, 80. 116–17. Kennedy at Palm Beach. TCPALM. https://www.tcpalm.com/story/opinion/contributors/2017/05/28/guest-colum n-his-100th-birthday-recalling-jfks-winter-white-house/349113001/ 117. Kennedy airport. *Elmira Advertiser.* November 12, 1960, 1. 117. Tourist attraction. *PB Post.* November 4, 1962, 44. 117. Joint chiefs. *Pittsburgh Post-Gazette.* December 28, 1962, 10. 118. Bomb shelter, pavilion. *PB Post.* December 12, 1962, 9. 118. Kennedy assassination attempt. US Secret Service. https://www.secretservice.gov/sites/default/files/reports/2020-05/ Pavlick_FOIA.pdf. 118. Kennedy's Udall appointment. JFK, Udall. (Smith). 118. Kennedy stadium. *Boston Globe.* July 5, 1968, 25. 118. "A few hours

later." *Boston Globe*. January 26, 1969, 66. **119.** Nixon inauguration. *Deseret News*, January 20, 1969, 11. **119.** Wally Findlay Gallery. *Hartford Courant*. January 22, 1969, 22. **119.** "Still beautiful." *Hartford Courant*. January 22, 1969, 23. **120.** Garden club tours. *Miami Herald*. March 14, 1965, 172 **120.** Last of the great. *PB Post*. February 26 1961, 32. **120.** Princess Astrid. *Tennessean*. March 18, 1956, 50. **120.** Duke of Windsor. *PB Post*. April 23, 1968, 8. **120–21.** Sea Cloud buyers. *Messenger-Inquirer*. March 9, 1961, 8. **121.** Sea Cloud sale. *Fort Lauderdale News*. October 7, 1955, 13. **121.** Trujillo purchase. "*Sea Cloud*." https://www.history.navy.mil/content/history/nhhc/research/histories/ship-histories/danfs/s/sea-cloud.html.

CHAPTER 10. THE PRESIDENT AND BEBE

123. Helicopters violate. *PB Daily News* (Nixon tour). February 18, 2019. **123.** Rebozo. *New York Times*. July 7, 1974. **123.** Nixon tour *Sun Sentinel*. April 23, 1994. https://www.sun-sentinel.com/news/fl-xpm-1994-04-23-9404230039-story.html. **124.** Passengers. *PB Post*. July 8, 1974, 4. **124.** Private tour. *New York Times*. July 8, 1974. **124.** Conger visit. *Miami Herald*. April 14, 1970, 49. **124.** "Whoopee." *Miami Herald*. April 14, 1970, 49. **124.** Nixon diary. Nixon Library. July 17, 1974. **124.** "Men in suits." *PB Post*. July 8, 1974, 4. **125.** "I have visited Mar-a-Lago." Congressional Record (Aspinall). **125.** "a gift to the people." Deed (Post). HSPBC. **125.** "Unlike any other." National Park System (Rettie), 88. **126.** Nixon signed. National Park System (Rettie), 87. **126.** Griffin on Nixon visit. *PB Post*. December 8, 2004, 354. **126.** Rogers withdraws support. *PB Post*. May 10, 1972, 30. **127.** Died in Hillwood. *New York Times*. September 13, 1973. **127.** Topridge gift to NY. *Adirondack Alamack*. https://www.adirondackalmanack.com/2016/02/a-visit-to-camp-topridge.html. **127.** Robert Grace. *PB Post*. May 2, 1972, 21. **127.** Town seeks control. *PB Post*. May 2, 1972, 21. **128.** Smith background. "Smith Papers." Hoover Institution. https://oac.cdlib.org/findaid/ark:/13030/kt8t1nf6nx/entire_text/. **128.** Pulitzer lunch. "Top Lunch." Getty Images. April 1972. **128.** Committee background. Oehlert. https://www.fordlibrarymuseum.gov/library/document/0019/4520826.pdf. **128.** Dudley defense. *PB Post*. September 13, 1972, 105. **129.** "My sadness." *Sun Sentinel* (Party Time at Mar-a-Lago). June 18, 1985. **129.** Nixon will never use. *PB Post*. July 8, 1974, 1.

CHAPTER 11. SMITHSONIAN SWAY

131. Panda visitation. Zoogoer, Smithsonian. 3–4/1992. 16. 132. Hillwood to Smithsonian. *New York Times,* January 18, 1969. 132. Post jewels. *Indianapolis Star.* September 8, 1974, 104. 132. Hillwood featured. *New York Times.* September 26, 1972. 133. "When I first saw." "Notes on Hillwood." 19. 133. "We have stepped up." *Indianapolis Star.* September 8, 1974, 104. 133. Post jewels. *Gazette.* September 8, 1974, 53. 134. Operating costs climbed. Bradley interview. Smithsonian Archives, 320. 134. Trust liquidity issues. Bradley interview. Smithsonian Archives, 318. 134. "uneasy feelings." Bradley interview. Smithsonian Archives, 319. 134. Security guards. Bradley interview. Smithsonian Archives, 319. 134–35. Smithsonian shortfalls. "Unexpected Bequests." Damerville. 135. Hillwood returned. *New York Times.* April 30, 1976. https://www.nytimes.com/1976/04/30/archives/saddened-smithsonian-returns-gift-of-estate.html. 135. Gift horse. *New York Times.* April 30, 1976. https://www.nytimes.com/1976/04/30/archives/saddened-smithsonian-returns-gift-of-estate.html. 136. "There were some." Bradley interview. Smithsonian Archives, 311. 136. Problematic donations. Smithsonian (Gift Horse). https://www.si.edu/Content/Governance/pdf/Archives_06-24-2013.pdf. 137. "We in this town." Phillips, JG. Knott Collection. Historical Society of Palm Beach County. Box 19. Folder 4. 137. Very special institution. Phillips, JG. Knott Collection. Historical Society of Palm Beach County. Box 19, Folder 4.

CHAPTER 12. MAR-A-LAGO NATIONAL PARK

147. Admission prices. Rettie (Parks), 94. 147. Vans. Rettie (Parks), 91. 147–48. Minimal NPS effort. Rettie (Parks), 89. 148. Service "held disdain." Rettie (Parks), 89. 149. Cost for mothbaling. *PB Post.* April 29, 1979, 74. 149. "in any case." Rettie (Parks), 100. 150. Wrong location. "Oh Ranger!" https://www.nps.gov/parkhistory/online_books/albright3/chap12.htm. 150. Commission. Rettie (Parks), 100. 151. national treasure. Congressional Record (Aspinall). October 10, 1972, 34655. 152. Grace complaints. *PB Post.* May 28, 1972, 77. 152. Admissions elsewhere. Rettie (Parks), 102. 153. "Sufficient" funds. *PB Post.* December 1974, 18. 153. Foundation will sell. Rettie (Parks) May 18, 1975, 87. 153. Mar-a-Lago sale needed for Hillwood. Dumbarton Oaks. 154. Griffin view. Rettie (Parks), 103. 154. Hoffstot. *PB Post.* December 22, 1980, 20. 155. "What's [the] story." Dick Cheney correspondence. February 25, 1975. 155. Varnum correspondence. Gerald Ford Library (Box 50 - Buchen) 9.

CHAPTER 13. PARK BARREL POLITICS

157. Vodka straight. Burton. http://digitalcommons.law.ggu.edu/ggulrev/vol13/iss2/1. 157. Vodka straight. Burton, 2. 157. "the most abrasive." Tutorow, 411. 157. "But they did it." Burton, 395. 157. Imposing political figure. Litton. 2 minutes 45 seconds. 158. Rogers repeatedly. *PB Post.* February 4, 1978, 55. 158. "You don't solve." *PB Post.* April 29, 1979, 74. 158. "I had announced." Mica interview. 158. "incendiary tactics." *Orlando Sentinel.* March 21 1988, 9. 159. Blaze. *Orlando Sentinel.* March 1988, 31. 159. "We were elated." Mica interview. 159. Burton requests. Mica interview. 159. A few weeks before. Mica interview. 160. Joining Burton. *PB Post.* February 19, 1979, 22. 160. "We get all set up." Mica interview. 160. "Columbo style." Mica interview. 160. "We're just maintaining." *Miami Herald.* February 25, 1980, 121. 161. With cloth coverings. *New York Times.* July 8, 1981. https://www.nytimes.com/1981/07/16/garden/post-home-for-sale-for-20.html. 161. Mar-a-Lago details. https://www.historic-details.com/places/fl/mar-a-lago-estate-palm-beach-fl/mar-a-lago-structure-and-materials/. 161. Congressman Murphy. *PB Post.* February 19, 1979, 22. 161. Burton undecided. *PB Post.* February 19, 1979, 22. 162. Racing through a Rembrandt. *Miami Herald.* February 19, 1979, 55. 162. "It just wouldn't be the same." Watt (HSPBC). 162. Bauman. Jacobs, 360. 162. Editorial board questioned. *Miami Herald.* February 25, 1979, 196. 163. Bull in China shop. Mica interview. 163. Bill of the century. Jacobs, 370. 163. Burton ran full throttle. Jacobs, 377. 163. Senator Byrd. Jacobs, 378. 163. Senator Nelson. Jacobs. Opening pages. 163. "Irreversible act." *Miami Herald.* February 25, 1980, 123. 164. Even worse for Mica. *Miami Herald.* February 25, 1980, 123. 164. Chairman Sydney Yates. Rettie (Parks), 97. 164. "down the drain." *Miami Herald.* February 25, 1980, 123. 164. "tidiest thing." *Miami Herald.* February 25, 1980, 123. 164–65. On the floor. Mica interview. 165. "I wasn't even aware." Mica 165. The Arkansas senator. Mica interview. 165. Congressman John Rousselot. Mica interview. 166. "I'm sitting here." Mica interview. 166. "deplored." Sebelius. Congressional Record. 32611. 166. "the best interests." Sebelius. Congressional Record. 32611. 166. Once President Carter. Rettie (Parks), 98. 166. "All they seem to have." Hogenauer. 167. National treasure. Congressional Record (Aspinall). October 10, 1972. 34655. 167. Not the costliest. Rettie (Parks), 99. 167. With the exception. Mackintosh. 168. Chattanooga. Mackintosh. 168. New Echota Marker. Mackintosh. 170. Beautiful white elephant. *NY Daily News.* December 23, 1980, 180. 170. Stalemate broken. *Miami Herald.* December 28, 1980, 424.

170. Stalemate broken. *Miami Herald*. December 15, 1980, Mon, 119. 171. Editors warned. *PB Post*. December 8, 1980, 14.

CHAPTER 14. THE SINKING OF THE OUTRAGEOUS
173. Tammy Wynette. *Miami Herald*. February 18, 1984, 172. 174. "One of those." *Miami Herald*. February 18, 1984, 172. 174. "The Outrageous" *Miami Herald*. February 18, 1984, 172. 175. "Bill was very beguiling." MacLaren. 176. Marriott. *Miami Herald*. December 11, 1983, 370. 176. No takers. *Miami Herald*. December 11, 1983, 370. 176. One real estate agent. *Miami Herald*. December 11, 1983, 370. 176. "How are we going to." MacLaren. 177. "Hot to trot." MacLaren. 177. Sunrise Savings. *Sun-Sentinel*. https://www.sun-sentinel.com/news/fl-xpm-1988-11-30-8803090697-story. html. 177. Without the blessing. *Miami Herald*. May 5, 1984, 216. 177. Without the blessing. *Sun-Sentinel*. https://www.sun-sentinel.com/news/ fl-xpm-1988-11-30-8803090697-story.html. 178. Sunrise folded. *New York Times*. https://www.nytimes.com/1987/02/21/business/indictments-issue d-in-thrift-unit-case.html. 178. Cerf Stanford Ross. *PB Post*. January 28, 1983, 98. 178. Paramount Theatre. *PB Post*. January 28, 1983, 98. 179. Paramount plans. *Miami Herald*. April 22, 1983, 8. 179. Plans abandoned. *PB Post*. July 17, 1983, 390. 179. Mar-a-Lago development. *PB Post*. August 23, 1984, 128. 179. Selling Mar-a-Lago lots. *PB Post*. January 23, 1985, 128. 179. Town supported. *Miami Herald*. March 14, 1985. 179. Town has backup. *PB Daily News*. December 13, 1984, 4. 179. Standing suntanned. *PB Post*. August 26, 1984, 449. 179. Extension. *Miami Herald*. September 11, 1985, 169.

CHAPTER 15. TRUMP'S HOUSE OF CARDS
181. Estee Lauder. *PB Post*. March 9, 1986, 27. 181. Iaccoca *PB Post*. March 9 1986, 27. 181. Peggy Iacocca. *Daily Press*. https://www.dailypress.com/ news/dp-xpm-20000302-2000-03-02-0003020120-story.html, 181. Rogers. *PB Post*. March 9, 1986, 27. 181. Ivana. *PB Post*. March 9, 1986, 27. 181. Designer gown. *NY Daily News*, March 11, 1985, 307. 182. Returned tickets. *NY Daily News*. March 11, 1985, 307. 182. Guest list. *NY Daily News*. March 11, 1985, 307. 182. Lifestyles of the Rich. *NY Daily News*. March 11 1986, 26. 182. Rather than guests. *NY Daily News*. March 11 1986, 26. 182–83. "By taking on." *NY Daily News*. March 11, 1986, 26. 183. Ross forfeited. *PB Daily News*. October 9, 1985, 1. 183. Flamboyant. *Miami Herald*. October 11, 1985, 257. 183. Crooned. *Miami Herald*. October 11,

1985, 257. 183. Smith. *PB Post.* March 9, 1986, 27. 183. Only private owner. Hogenauer. "Update." 183. Smith and wife. *New York Times,* March 9, 1968. https://timesmachine.nytimes.com/timesmachine/1968/03/09/77175838. html?pageNumber=20. 183–84. "Mind-boggling." *Miami Herald.* October 11, 1985, 257. 184. "Pipe dream." *Sun Sentinel.* October 11, 1985, 7. 184. Landmarks Commission. *Miami Herald.* March 14, 1985, 631. 184. Menu. *Fort Lauderdale News.* March 16, 1986, 77. 184. "Great deal." Trump (Art of Deal). Kindle. 184–85. Moneymaker. *PB Post.* June 18, 1989, 10. 185. Temporary residence. Congressional Record (Aspinall). 185. The book stated. Walker v. Trump. 185. The book stated. *PB Post.* February 22, 1972, 19. 185. As he described. *PB Post.* February 22, 1972, 19. 185. Chase Manhattan. *Miami Herald.* September 25, 2016, 2. 185. Rabbit-warren condo. *PB Post.* June 18, 1989, 10. 186. Jack Massey. *PB Post.* June 18, 1989, 10. 186. Doyle Rogers. *PB Post.* June 18, 1989, 10. 186. No matter how. Walker v. Trump. 186. Jimmy Carter. *Columbian.* December 13, 1987, 17. 186. Boston Safe. *Miami Herald.* November 10, 1988, 795. 187. Navratilova. *New York Times.* March 9, 1986. https://www.nytimes.com/1986/03/09/sports/navratilova-takes-us-indoor-title.html. 187. Driver test. *PB Post.* March 6, 1986, 1. 187. Annenberg Hooker. *NY Daily News.* March 11, 1986, 307. 187. Duchin. Preservation Society newsletter. 188. Trump benefactors. *New York Times.* June 26, 1990. https://www.nytimes.com/1990/06/26/business/quick-who-d-have-trouble-living-on-450000-a-month.html?-searchResultPosition=1. 188. WNJO Trump pledge. *PB Daily News.* June 7, 1990, 4. 188. Trump allowance. *New York Times.* June 26, 1990. https://www.nytimes.com/1990/06/26/business/quick-who-d-have-trouble-livin g-on-450000-a-month.html?searchResultPosition=1. 188. Loan terms. *PB Post.* September 6, 1990, 50. 188. Damage from fire. *PB Post.* June 10, 1990, 2. 188. "One wonders." *PB Post.* September 6, 1990, 50. 189. Incorporated his brand. Hirschman. 189. Preservationists' retribution. *PB Daily News.* August 11, 1991, 1. 189–90. Furniture line. *Miami Herald.* June 2, 1991, 883. 190. "I seriously doubt." Watt letter. PBCHS. 190. Buying Mar-a-Lago. Trump "Art of Deal." 190. "No, no, no." *Town and Country.* March 1986. 190. $2 billion. *PB Daily News.* June 7, 1990, 1. 191. *Forbes* list. October 9, 1990. https://apnews.com/article/64a97ffd61c3c807b7bedf53d992d7d5. 191. *Forbes* list. October 9, 1989. https://apnews.com/article/78e27c5e1e-03b1a91f23d64735a6c65c. 191. Subdivide. *New York Times.* February 21, 1991. https://timesmachine.nytimes.com/timesmachine/1991/02/21/742491. html?pageNumber=42. 192. Out of love. *PB Daily News.* February 19,

1991, 1. 191–92. "Almost from the time." *PB Daily News*. February 19, 1991, 1. 192. "What Donald Trump." *PB Daily News*. February 16, 1991, 4. 192–93. Trump staked. *WAPO*. August 6, 1991, 3. 193. "Barring any," *PB Daily News*. May 14, 1991, 1. 193. "Mr. Trump." *PB Daily News*. May 18, 1991, 1. 193. Vanderbilt dean. *PB Daily News*. May 18, 1991, 1. 194. Landscape society. *Miami Herald*. June 16, 1991, 124. 194. "Any subdivision." *PB Daily News*. May 18, 1991, 4. 194. Greed. *Miami Herald*. June 16, 1991, 124. 194. Debt payment. *WSJ*. May 31, 1991. https://www.proquest.com/newspapers/trump-may-have-borrow-funds-his-father/docview/398290293/se-2?accountid=10003. 194. Moonies. *PB Daily News*. May 23, 1991, 1. 194. "If the town." *PB Daily News*. May 23, 1991, 1. 195. Party at Mar-a-Lago. *Sun-Sentinel*. June 18, 1995. https://www.sun-sentinel.com/news/fl-xpm-1995-06-18-9506220187-story.html. 195. "It shows" *Sun-Sentinel*. June 18, 1995. https://www.sun-sentinel.com/news/fl-xpm-1995-06-18-9506220187-story.html. 196. Lawsuit. *Miami Herald*. November 10, 1992, 86. 196. "If anyone else." *PB Daily News*. August 11, 1991, 1. 196. Boston Safe execs. *Boston Globe*. April 1991, 15. 197. $12 million payment. *PB Daily News*. October 10, 1993, 1. 197. Foreclosure prospects. *Boston Globe*. 1. October 5, 2016. 197. "Let's face it." *Business Insider*. July 4, 2021. 197. Coat of arms. *New York Times*. May 28, 2017. https://www.nytimes.com/2017/05/28/business/trump-coat-of-arms.html?-searchResultPosition=1. 198. Epstein. *The Today Show*. https://youtu.be/AUDr_c2PalI. 198. Kennedy Shriver. *Montgomery Advertiser*. February 3, 1993, 2. 198–99. Paul Rampell. Leamer. *Politico*. https://www.politico.com/magazine/story/2019/02/01/donald-trump-mar-a-lago-anti-semitism-town-council-palm-beach-politics-224537/. 199. Boston Safe extension. *PB Post*. November 5, 1992, 33. 199. Club plans. *PB Daily News*. May 9, 1993, 1. 200. Hosts Society. *PB Daily News*. February 19, 1993, 1. 200. "I'm doing nothing." *Sun Sentinel*. February 20, 1993, 42. 200. "Bed and breakfast." *PB Daily News*. November 9, 1997, 2. 200. Added traffic. *PB Daily News*. May 9, 1993, 6. 201. Boston Safe approvals. *PB Daily News*. September 23, 1993, 1. 201. "Nobody has ever." *PB Daily News*. August 1, 1993, 1. 201. Town council. *PB Daily News*. May 14, 1993, 1. 201. Lawsuit. *PB Post*. October 9, 1993, 121. 201. "This area is zoned." *PB Post*. October 9, 1993, 121. 202. "Just a year earlier." Marla Maples. https://www.ibdb.com/broadway-cast-staff/marla-maples-84176. 202. As it always had. *PB Daily News*. October 4, 1993, 1. 202. Nursery. *PB Daily News*. October 4, 1993, 3. 202. Prenuptial. *Star-Telegram*. July 16, 1991, 15. 202–03. He told a reporter.

Trump interview. Primetime. https://www.youtube.com/watch?v=zfMqg-dOA5PM 203. Speaking engagement. *WAPO*. https://www.proquest.com/newspapers/reliable-source/docview/307991099/se-2?accountid=10003. 203. The feat. *PB Post*. March 30, 1995, 159. 203. Club revenue. *PB Daily News*. June 22, 1995, 1.

CHAPTER 16. RAIDED AND ARRESTED

205. Miss Mar-a-Lago Contest. *PB Daily News*. October 10, 1999, 10. 206. "He'll flout." *PB Daily News*. October 10, 1999, 11. 206. Ballroom and bedrooms. *LA Times*, April 9, 1995. https://www.latimes.com/archives/la-xpm-1995-04-09-re-52667-story.html. 207. The dainty. *Miami Herald*. March 24, 1995, 159. 207. Mar-a-Lago site. HABS. 207. Post bequeathed. Hillwood Museum. https://hillwoodmuseum.org/collection/item/33.50. 207. Auctioned off. *Miami Herald*. July 9, 1995, 84. 207. Rugs, bureau. Christie's. https://www.christies.com/en/auction/property-fro m-mar-a-lago-sold-by-donald-j-trump-5922/?filters=&page=1&search-phrase=&sortby=realisedprice_desc&themes=. 207–08. Furnishings. *Miami Herald*. February 18, 1995, 112. 208. "The most amazing." *PB Daily News*. March 31, 1995. 1. 208. He signed. Easement. National Trust. 208. "And for." Easement. National Trust. 208–09. National Trust. NTHP Deputy General Counsel Ross M. Bradford personal communication to Mary Shanklin. November 15, 2021. 209. "We consider this." Ross M. Bradford personal communication to Mary Shanklin. November 15, 2021. 210. Chris Christie. *Sun Sentinel*. March 4, 2015, A10. 210. Trump faced. Waterhouse. UVA. 210. The candidate, though. Waterhouse. UVA. 211. Presidential debate. *Politico* transcript. https://www.politico.com/story/2016/09/full-transcript-first-2016-presidential-debate-228761 211. Kanye West, Nick Fuentes. *New York Times*. https://www.nytimes.com/2022/11/25/us/politics/trump-nick-fuentes-dinner.html 211. Club roster. *New York Times*. https://www.nytimes.com/interactive/2020/10/10/us/trump-properties-swamp.html?smid=tw-nytimes&smtyp=cur. 211. On election night. *PB Daily News*. November 9, 2016, A1. 211. "Writing my inaugural." Trump. Twitter. January 18, 2017. 212. "On any given weekend." *New York Times*. February 19, 2017. https://www.nytimes.com/2017/02/18/us/mar-a-lago-trump-ethics-winter-white-house.html. 212. Guests who may have. *New York Times*. https://www.nytimes.com/2017/02/13/us/politics/mar-a-lago-north-korea-trump.htm. 212. Secret Service access. *Politico*. October 10, 2017. https://www.politico.com/story/2017/10/05/

mar-a-lago-visitor-logs-secret-service-trump-243478 212. Mar-a-Lago trio. *ProPublica*. August 7, 2018. https://www.propublica.org/article/ ike-perlmutter-bruce-moskowitz-marc-sherman-shadow-rulers-of-the-va 213. Udall, Whitehouse. Whitehouse press release. February 3, 2017. 02.03.17 https://www.whitehouse.senate.gov/news/release/senators-to-trump-show -us-who-is-buying-access-to-the-winter-white-house 213–14. "Saturday Night Live." Whitehouse press release. February 13, 2017. https://www. whitehouse.senate.gov/news/release/whitehouse-and-udall-call-on-republic ans-to-end-trumps-rash-behavior-at-mar-a-lago. 215. Change residency. *WAPO*. December 17, 2020. https://www.proquest.com/newspapers/mar-lag o-neighbors-deliver-not-so-warm-welcome/docview/2470501671/se-2. 215."I have been treated." Trump. Twitter. October 31, 2019. 216. Stored documents. *WAPO*. August 30, 2022. https://www.proquest.com/docview/2708091737# 216. Federal officials. *WAPO*. August 30, 2022. https://www.proquest. com/docview/2708091737#. 217. FBI agents. *WAPO*. December 23, 2022. https://www.proquest.com/usmajordailies/docview/2756874212/citation/ AA81EF58672840C8PQ/1?accountid=10003. 217. Eric Trump. *NY Post*. https://nypost.com/2022/08/09/eric-trump-alerted-his-dad-to-the-mar-a-lago- raid/. 217. Christina Bobb. *The Hill*. August 10, 2022. https://thehill.com/ regulation/court-battles/3595946-who-is-trump-attorney-christina-bobb-w ho-met-fbi-at-mar-a-lago/. 217–18. Christina Bobb. *New York Times*. https:// www.nytimes.com/2022/10/11/us/politics/christina-bobb-trump-lawyer-in- vestigation.html. 218. "Initially they refused." Bobb. America's Voice Network. August 8, 2022. https://grabien.com/file.php?id=1616740. 218. "Started out a little bit heated." Raid. Grabien. August 12, 2022. https://news.grabien.com/story-trump-lawyer-says-they-have-inventory- list-boxes-taken-ingra. 218. Finally, the FBI conceded. Bobb. America's Voice Network. August 8, 2022. https://grabien.com/file.php?id=1616740. 218. Waited in heat. Raid. Grabien. August 12, 2022. https://news.grabien. com/story-trump-lawyer-says-they-have-inventory-list-boxes-taken-ingra. 218. Stored documents. *WAPO*. August 30, 2022. https://www.proquest. com/docview/2708091737# 218. Document storage spaces. *NY Times*. December 15, 2022. https://www.nytimes.com/interactive/2022/12/15/ us/mar-a-lago-trump-documents.html. 218. Warrant. US District Court. August 5, 2022. https://www.flsd.uscourts.gov/sites/flsd/files/22mj8332_ DE17UnsealedNotice.pdf. 218. Office 45. US District Court. August 5, 2022. https://www.flsd.uscourts.gov/sites/flsd/files/22mj8332_DE17UnsealedNotice. pdf. 218. Trump watched remotely. *Newsweek*. August 10, 2022. https://

www.newsweek.com/eric-trump-says-mar-lago-security-cameras-captured
-fbi-acting-improperly-during-raid-1732672. 218–19. Bobb signed inventory. US District Court. August 5, 2022. https://www.flsd.uscourts.gov/
sites/flsd/files/22mj8332_DE17UnsealedNotice.pdf. 219. Document storage spaces. *New York Times,* December 15, 2022. https://www.nytimes.
com/interactive/2022/12/15/us/mar-a-lago-trump-documents.html. 219.
Schorsh broke story. *WAPO.* August 9, 2022. https://www.proquest.com/
docview/2700164171/citation/2B852955oD304271PQ/1?accountid=10003.
219. Dark times (Trump). CBS. August 8, 2022. https://www.cbsnews.com/
miami/news/trump-says-mar-a-lago-home-under-siege-raided-by-fbi/. 220.
Broke into. (Trump). CBS. August 8, 2022. https://www.cbsnews.com/miami/
news/trump-says-mar-a-lago-home-under-siege-raided-by-fbi/. 220. "You saw
it." Trump Pennsylvania rally. September 2, 2022. https://www.c-span.org/
video/?522469-1/president-trump-holds-rally-wilkes-barre-pennsylvania.
220. "Rifled through." Trump Pennsylvania rally. September 2, 2022. https://
www.c-span.org/video/?522469-1/president-trump-holds-rally-wilkes-barre-
pennsylvania 220. "The entire world." Trump Pennsylvania rally. September
2 2022. https://www.c-span.org/video/?522469-1/president-trump-holds-rall
y-wilkes-barre-pennsylvania. 220. Death threats. "Trump Supporters" PBS.
August 17, 2022. https://www.pbs.org/newshour/politics/donald-trum
p-supporters-send-death-threats-to-judge-who-approved-mar-a-lago-search.
220–21. Raid reaction. "Trump Supporters" *Washington Examiner*. August
9, 2022. https://www.washingtonexaminer.com/news/trump-supporter
s-descend-mar-a-lago-resort.

BIBLIOGRAPHY

ACADEMIC JOURNALS, PAPERS

Barnett, Cynthia. "Florida Candidates Shortsighted on Climate Changes Long-Term Impacts." *Columbia Journalism Review*, October 24, 2018. https://www.cjr.org/special_report/midterms-2018-florida-algae-hurricane-michael.php.

Burgman, Todd. "*Sea Cloud*'s Nine Lives." *Sea History,* Summer 2010. National Maritime Historical Society.

Burton, John. "A Tribute to Phil Burton." 13 *Golden Gate University Law Review*, 1983. http://digitalcommons.law.ggu.edu/ggulrev/vol13/iss2/1.

Curl, Donald W. "Joseph Urban's Palm Beach Architecture." *Florida Historical Quarterly* 71, no. 4 (1993): 436–57. http://www.jstor.org/stable/30150391.

Damerville, Laura, George D. Karibjanian, and Stephen K. Urice. "Surprise! Managing Unexpected Bequests." American Law Institute Continuing Legal Education. March 2020.

Ferguson, Robert. "Hurricane Threat to Florida." Science and Public Policy Institute, October 2007. Revised March 2008.

Hogenauer, Alan K. "Gone, but Not Forgotten: The Delisted Units of the U.S. National Park System." *George Wright Forum* 7, no. 4 (1991): 2–19. http://www.jstor.org/stable/43597156.

Hogenauer, Alan K. "An Update to 'Gone, but Not Forgotten: The Delisted Units of the U.S. National Park System.'" *George Wright Forum* 8, No. 3 (1991): 26–28. http://www.jstor.org/stable/43597194.

Inge, Lindsay T. "Culture and Diplomacy: Marjorie Merriweather Post and Soviet-American Relations, 1933–1939." Thesis, University of Maryland, 2016.

Jones, Marian Moser. "Tempest in the Forbidden City: Racism, Violence, and Vulnerability in the 1926 Miami Hurricane." *Journal of Policy History* 26, No. 3 (2014): 384–405. muse.jhu.edu/article/547677.

Mitchell, Charles. "North Atlantic Ocean." *Monthly Weather Review* 56, No. 9 (August 1928). US Department of Commerce. Atlantic Oceanographic & Meteorological Laboratory.

Smith, Thomas G. "John Kennedy, Stewart Udall, and New Frontier Conservation." *Pacific Historical Review* 64, No. 3 (1995): 329–62. https://doi.org/10.2307/3641005.

Vanderblue, Homer. "The Florida Land Boom." *Journal of Land & Public Utility Economics* 3, No. 2, May 1927. University of Wisconsin Press.

BOOKS, BOOKLETS

Aronson, Arnold, Derek E. Ostergard, and Matthew Wilson Smith. *Architect of Dreams: The Theatrical Vision of Joseph Urban.* New York: Miriam and Ira D. Wallach Art Gallery, Columbia University, 2000.

Jacobs, John. *A Rage for Justice: The Passion and Politics of Phillip Burton.* Berkeley and Los Angeles: University of California Press, 1995.

Post, Marjorie Merriweather. *Notes on Hillwood.* Washington, DC: Corporate Press. 1979.

Rettie, Dwight. *Our National Park System: Caring for America's Greatest Natural and Historic Treasures.* Urbana, and Chicago: University of Illinois Press, 1995.

Rubin, Nancy. *American Empress: The Life and Times of Marjorie Merriweather Post.* Lincoln, Nebraska: iUniverse Star Inc. 1995, 2004. Kindle.

Trump, Donald J., and Kate Bohner. *Trump: Art of the Comeback.* New York: Times Books, 1997.

Trump, Donald J., and Tony Schwartz. *Trump: The Art of the Deal.* New York: Random House Publishing Group, 1987. Kindle.

US Department of the Treasury. *IRS Historical Fact Book: A Chronology, 1646–1992.* 1993

GOVERNMENT DOCUMENTS, PRESIDENTIAL RECORDS, LEGAL FILINGS

Aspinall, Wayne. Congressional Record. US House of Representatives. October 10, 1972. 34655.

Bradley, James C. Smithsonian Institution Archives. Oral History. Interview by Pamela M. Henson. February 3, 1977. Interview 17. 304–21.

City of Pahokee. "Storm of 1928." Interview with Lucille Salvatore Herron and with Ethel Williams. Accessed February 13, 2023. https://youtu.be/Op_faFyIZU.

Donald Ross Society and the Tufts Archives. "Directory of Golf Courses Designed by Donald Ross," 1986 with revisions through 2018.

Florida Council of 100. "Progress Report." November 3, 1964.

French, Jay T. to Philip W. Buchen. "President - Personal Home - Mara-Lago[sic] Estate," Oehlert correspondence, December 11, 1974.

Gerald R. Ford Presidential Library and Museum, Box 50. https://www.fordlibrarymuseum.gov/library/document/0019/4520826.pdf.

Gerald R. Ford Presidential Library and Museum. "Presidential Handwriting, 2/25/1975 (2)," Box C14. https://www.fordlibrarymuseum.gov/library/document/0047/phw19750225-07.pdf.

Griffin, James. "Post family. Interview of Mr. Griffin." Bentley Historical Library, University of Michigan. Item 10. Part 1.

Historic American Buildings Survey, Archeology and Historic Preservation, National Park Service, Department of the Interior, HABS FL NO. 195.

Historic American Buildings Survey, Heritage Conservation and Recreation Service. Department of the Interior, "Henry M. Flagler Mansion." HABS No. FLA-224.

Historic American Buildings Survey, Heritage Conservation and Recreation Service. Department of the Interior. "Mar-a-Lago," Spring 1967. HABS No. FLA-195.

Historical Society of Palm Beach County. "Summary of Anticipated Support" for Marjorie Merriweather Post Institute. James R. Knott Collection. Box 19, Folder 4.

Johnson, Claudia "Lady Bird" Alta. Lady Bird Johnson's White House Diary Collection. Lyndon Baines Johnson Library and Museum. Audio diary and annotated transcript. April 4, 1968. https://www.discoverlbj.org/item/ctjd-19680404.

Johnson, Lyndon B. "January 14, 1969: State of the Union Address." University of Virginia, Miller Center. Lyndon Baines Johnson Library and Museum. https://millercenter.org/the-presidency/presidential-speeches/january-14-1969-state-union-address.

Knott, James R. to Lester E. Waterbury. January 11, 1969. Knott Collection, Historical Society of Palm Beach County, Box 19, Folder 4.

Litton, Jerry. "Dialogue with Litton." Jerry L. Litton Papers. State Historical Society of Missouri. November 24, 1975. https://youtu.be/-E24-aXLPiQ.

National Trust for Historic Preservation. Deed of Conservation and Preservation Easement from Donald J. Trump to National Trust for Historic Preservation. March 21, 1995.

New York Historical Society Digital Collections. Salvator Cillis correspondence. Letter to Mr. Van Veen. December 6, 1917. https://digitalcollections.nyhistory.org/islandora/object/islandora%3A114954.

Palm Beach, Town of. "2010 Historical Sites Survey." Research Atlantica Inc. December 2010.

Post, Marjorie M. Recorded deed. Historical Society of Palm Beach County. James R. Knott Collection. Box 19, Folder 4.

Post, Marjorie Merriweather, interview. Part 1, Bentley Historical Library. University of Michigan. February 19, 1962.

Richard Nixon Presidential Library and Museum. President Richard Nixon Diary, July 7, 1974. https://www.nixonlibrary.gov/sites/default/files/virtuallibrary/documents/PDD/1974/127%20July%201974.pdf.

Sebelius, Keith (congressman). "Providing for the Orderly Disposal of Certain Federal Lands." Congressional Record. December 5, 1980.

Smithsonian Institution Archives. Zoogoer, 3–4/1992, pp. 23–25. Annual Report of the Smithsonian Institution for the year 1972, p. 16.

Taylor, Paul. Congressional Record. US House of Representatives. October 10, 1972. 34655.

US Department of Interior, National Register of Historic Places Inventory, McKithan, Cecil. "Mar-a-Lago." https://npgallery.nps.gov/NRHP/GetAsset/NHLS/80000961_text.

US District Court Southern District of Florida. Reinhart, Bruce (Magistrate). Search and Seizure Warrant. August 5, 2022. https://www.flsd.uscourts.gov/sites/flsd/files/22mj8332_DE17UnsealedNotice.pdf.

US Secret Service. Richard Paul Pavlick report. Accessed February 18, 2023. https://www.secretservice.gov/sites/default/files/reports/2020-05/Pavlick_FOIA.pdf.

University of Florida. "PALM BEACH HURRICANE, SEPT. 16, 1928." George A. Smathers Libraries. Florida Heritage Collection. http://purl.flvc.org/fcla/tc/fhp/UF00001306.pdf. Digital Collection.

University of South Carolina. "Stotesbury Party." Moving Research Image Collection. Accessed February 25, 2023. https://digital.library.sc.edu/departments/mirc/.

Walker v. Trump, 549 So. 2d 1098 (Fla. Dist. Ct. App. 1989). Accessed February 22, 2023. https://casetext.com/case/walker-v-trump.

Watt, Jim (Florida Representative) to Phillip Burton. Correspondence. James R. Knott Collection. Historical Society of Palm Beach County. Box 19, Folder 4. February 20, 1979.

NEWS MEDIA, MAGAZINES, PODCASTS, TELEVISION
ABC News, *Primetime Live.*
Associated Press
Baltimore Evening Sun (Maryland)
Battle Creek Enquirer (Michigan)
Boston Globe (Massachusetts)
Brooklyn Daily Eagle (New York)
Brooklyn Life and Activities of Long Island Society (New York)
Burlington Daily News (Vermont)
Business Insider
Call Leader (Elwood, Indiana)
Capital Times (Madison, Wisconsin)
Carlisle Evening Herald (Pennsylvania)
CBS News
Chicago Tribune (Illinois)
Commercial Appeal (Memphis, Tennessee)
C-Span
Daily Press (Virginia)
Dayton Daily News (Ohio)
Deseret News (Salt Lake City, Utah)
Elmira Advertiser (New York)
Fairbanks Daily News (Alaska)
Fort Lauderdale News (Florida)
Grabien News
Hartford Courant (Connecticut)
Honolulu Advertiser (Hawaii)
Honolulu Star-Bulletin (Hawaii)
Indianapolis Star (Indiana)
Lansing State Journal (Michigan)
Los Angeles Times (California)
Madisonville Messenger (Kentucky)
Meriden Daily Journal (Connecticut)
Messenger-Inquirer (Kentucky)
Miami Herald (Florida)

Miami News (Florida)
Minneapolis Star Tribune (Minnesota)
Montgomery Advertiser (Alabama)
NBC News, *Today Show*
New York Daily News (New York)
New York Herald (New York)
New York Post (New York)
New York Times (New York)
New York Tribune (New York)
Newsday
Newsweek
Oakland Tribune (California)
Orlando Sentinel (Florida)
Palm Beach Daily News (Florida)
Palm Beach Post (Florida)
PBS
Philadelphia Business Journal (Pennsylvania)
Philadelphia Inquirer (Pennsylvania)
Pittsburgh Post-Gazette (Pennsylvania)
Pittsburgh Press (Pennsylvania)
Politico
ProPublica
Rockland County Journal News (New York)
Sacramento Bee (California)
San Francisco Chronicle (California)
San Francisco Examiner (California)
South Florida Sun Sentinel (Florida)
St. Louis Star and Times (Missouri)
St. Petersburg Times (Florida)
Star Tribune (Minnesota)
Star-Telegram (Texas)
Tallahassee Democrat (Florida)
Tallahassee Record (Florida)
Tampa Bay Times (Florida)
Tampa Tribune (Florida)
Tennessean (Nashville)
The Columbian (Washington)
The Gazette (Iowa)

The Hill
Times Herald (Michigan)
Times Union
Town and Country
Travel Lady
Treasure Coast Palm News (Florida)
Wall Street Journal
Washington Examiner
Washington Post
WXELTV, Heritage Thursdays

WEBSITES, SOCIAL MEDIA

A&E Television Networks. History.com. "Stock Market Crash of 1929," May 10, 2010. https://www.history.com/topics/great-depression/1929 -stock-market-crash.

Blanche Conant Horton Hutton. Find a Grave. Accessed February 11, 2023. https://www.findagrave.com/memorial/61930092/blanche-conant-hutton.

Centers for Disease Control. "History of 1918 Flu Pandemic." Accessed February 11, 2023. https://www.cdc.gov/flu/pandemic-resources/1918 -commemoration/1918-pandemic-history.htm.

Christie's. "Property from Mar-a-Lago Sold by Donald J. Trump." March 30, 1995. https://www.christies.com/en/auction/property-from-mar-a-lago -sold-by-donald-j-trump-5922/?filters=&page=1&searchphrase=&sortby =realisedprice_desc&themes=.

Cook Inlet Historical Society. Walter J. "Wally" Hickel biography. Accessed February 11, 2023. https://www.alaskahistory.org/biographies /hickel-walter-j-wally/.

Dumbarton Oaks Archives. "Hillwood Estate, Museum & Gardens." Mapping Cultural Philanthropy. Accessed February 17, 2023. https://www.doaks .org/resources/cultural-philanthropy/hillwood-estate-museum-gardens.

Duvall, Lorraine. "A Visit to Camp Topridge on Upper St. Regis Lake." February 14, 2016, *Adirondack Almanack*. https://www.adirondackalmanack .com/2016/02/a-visit-to-camp-topridge.html.

FBI Media. "Wall Street bombings." https://www.fbi.gov/history /famous-cases/wall-street-bombing-1920.

First Amendment Museum. "Spanish Flu and the First Amendment." Accessed February 22, 2023. https://firstamendmentmuseum.org/learn/spanish-flu -and-the-first-amendment/. Video and transcript.

Florida Association of Native Nurseries. Accessed February 11, 2023. https://www.fann.org/county/palm-beach.

Florida Center for Instructional Technology. "Great Depression and The New Deal." Accessed February 16, 2023. https://fcit.usf.edu/florida/lessons/depress/depress1.htm.

Florida Department of State. "The Great Depression in Florida." Accessed February 13, 2023. https://dos.myflorida.com/florida-facts/florida-history/a-brief-history/the-great-depression-in-florida/.

Florida History Internet Center. "Florida in the 1920s: The Great Florida Land Boom." Accessed February 13, 2023. http://floridahistory.org/landboom.htm.

Florida Memory, State Library and Archives of Florida. "Blackout and Air Raid Precautions, ca. 1943." Accessed February 17, 2023. https://www.floridamemory.com/items/show/339333. Photograph.

Florida Memory, State Library and Archives of Florida. "The Everglades Club—Palm Beach, Florida." Accessed February 11, 2023. https://www.floridamemory.com/items/show/40091. Photograph.

Florida Memory, State Library and Archives of Florida. "Sign with Information for the Auction at the Stotesbury Estate, El Mirasol—Palm Beach, Florida." Accessed February 17, 2023. http://www.floridamemory.com/items/show/65571. Photograph.

Florida Women's Hall of Fame. "Mary Lou Baker." Accessed February 16, 2023. https://flwomenshalloffame.org/bio/mary-lou-baker/.

Hillwood Estate, Museum and Gardens. "Table." Bequest of Marjorie Merriweather Post, 1973. Accessed February 23, 2023. https://hillwoodmuseum.org/collection/item/33.50.

Historic Details. "Mar-a-Lago." Accessed February 16, 2023. https://www.historic-details.com/places/fl/mar-a-lago-estate-palm-beach-fl/.

Historic Saranac Lake Wiki. "Camp Topridge." Accessed February 12, 2023. https://localwiki.org/hsl/Camp_Topridge.

Historical Society of Palm Beach County. "Flagler Era Through Boom-to-Bust." Accessed February 11, 2023. https://pbchistory.org/flagler-era-through-boom-to-bust/.

Internet Broadway Database. "Marla Maples." Accessed February 23, 2023. https://www.ibdb.com/broadway-cast-staff/marla-maples-84176.

Landmark Branding. "1107 Fifth Avenue." Accessed February 12, 2023. http://landmarkbranding.com/1107-fifth-avenue/.

Leamer, Laurence. "How Mar-a-Lago Taught Trump to Play Politics."
February 1, 2019. *Politico.* https://www.politico.com/magazine
/story/2019/02/01/donald-trump-mar-a-lago-anti-semitism-town
-council-palm-beach-politics-224537/.

Mackay History. "Harbor Hill." Accessed February 17, 2023.

Mackintosh, Barry. "Former National Park System Units: An Analysis."
National Park Service: History eLibrary. 1995. Accessed February 21,
2013. http://npshistory.com/publications/former-nps-units/index.htm.

Mayhew, Augustus. "Mrs. Post's Mar-a-Lago." August 28, 2019. New
York Social Diary: Palm Beach. https://www.newyorksocialdiary.com
/mrs-posts-mar-a-lago/.

McCombs, Phil. "Tregaron's Dynasty: The Davies Family." January
24, 1978. *Washington Post.* https://www.washingtonpost.com
/archive/politics/1978/01/24/tregarons-dynasty-the-davies-family
/e08395ca-f23c-43b0-9062-caf400755522/.

National Weather Service. "Great Miami Hurricane of 1926." Accessed
February 12, 2023. https://www.weather.gov/mfl/miami_hurricane.

Naval History and Heritage Command. "*Sea Cloud.*" Accessed February
18, 2023. https://www.history.navy.mil/content/history/nhhc/research
/histories/ship-histories/danfs/s/sea-cloud.html.

Old Long Island. "Hillwood." August 20, 2008. http://www.oldlongisland
.com/2008/08/hillwood.html.

Palm Beach County History Online. "Architects: Mizner in Palm Beach."
Accessed February 17, 2023. http://www.pbchistoryonline.org/page
/mizner-in-palm-beach (page discontinued).

Palm Beach County History Online. "The Boom." Accessed February 24,
2023. http://www.pbchistoryonline.org/page/the-boom (page discontinued).

Palm Beach County History Online. "The Bust." Accessed February 13, 2023.
http://www.pbchistoryonline.org/page/the-bust (page discontinued).

Palm Beach County History Online. "1925 Hotel Fires." Accessed February 12,
2023. http://www.pbchistoryonline.org/page/hotel-fires (page discontinued).

Palm Beach County History Online. "U.S. Military in Palm Beach."
Accessed February 17, 2023. http://www.pbchistoryonline.org/page
/us-military-in-west-palm-beach (page discontinued).

PBS. "The Hurricane of 1926." *American Experience.* Accessed February
2023. https://www.pbs.org/wgbh/americanexperience/features/miami
-hurricane-1926/.

Peters, Brooks. An Open Book. "Death of a Flapper: Part Two." July 25, 2012. http://brookspeters.blogspot.com/2012/07/.

Politico. "First 2016 Presidential Debate." September 27, 2016. https://www.politico.com/story/2016/09/full-transcript-first-2016 -presidential-debate-228761. Transcript.

Price, Lauren. "New York's First-Ever Penthouse." July 13, 2015, 6sqft. https://www.6sqft.com/new-yorks-first-ever-penthouse-a-54-room -upper-east-side-mansion-built-for-a-cereal-heiress/.

Smithsonian Institution. From the Archives. "Don't Look a Gift Horse in the Mouth: Problematic Donations to the Smithsonian." August 24, 2013. https://www.si.edu/Content/Governance/pdf/Archives_06-24-2013.pdf.

Tregaron Conservancy. "History of the Tregaron Estate." Accessed February 17, 2023. https://tregaron.org/history/.

Trista. "A Tragic Countdown Through the Life of America's Poor Little Rich Girl, Barbara Hutton." December 4, 2018. History Collection. https://historycollection.com/a-tragic-countdown-through-the-life -of-americas-poor-little-rich-girl-barbara-hutton/12/.

Trump, Donald J. @realdonaldtrump. Twitter. January 18, 2017, 12:33 p.m. https://twitter.com/realDonaldTrump/status/821772494864580614.

US Department of Interior, National Register of Historic Places Inventory, "Great Camps of the Adirondacks." September 24, 1986. https://npgallery .nps.gov/NRHP/GetAsset/NRHP/64000555_text.

Victorian Antique & Fine Jewelry Blog. "Marjorie Merriweather Post." Accessed June 5, 2021. http://www.victorianajewelry.com/blog/2017/ (site discontinued).

Vloet, Katie. "Polite Society?" *Michigan Today*. University of Michigan. May 17, 2018. https://michigantoday.umich.edu/2018/05/17/polite -society/.

Waterhouse, Benjamin C. "Donald J. Trump: Campaigns and Elections." Miller Center. University of Virginia. Accessed February 24, 2023. https:// millercenter.org/president/trump/campaigns-and-elections.

Whitehouse, Sheldon (US Senator). "Senators to Trump: Show Us Who Is Buying Access to the 'Winter White House.'" February 13, 2017. https:// www.whitehouse.senate.gov/news/release/senators-to-trump-show-us -who-is-buying-access-to-the-winter-white-house.

Whitehouse, Sheldon (US Senator). "Whitehouse and Udall Call on Republicans to End Trump's 'Rash' Behavior at Mar-a-Lago." February 13, 2017. https://www.whitehouse.senate.gov/news/release/whitehouse -and-udall-call-on-republicans-to-end-trumps-rash-behavior-at -mar-a-lago. Press release.

The Yale Guide. "Resources on Yale History: A Brief History of Yale." Accessed February 11, 2023. Resources on Yale History: A Brief History of Yale

INDEX

ABOUT THE AUTHOR

Journalist MARY C. SHANKLIN has written for decades about real estate schemes, housing busts, hurricanes, and government misdeeds. Her stories have appeared in the *Chicago Tribune, Los Angeles Times, Orlando Sentinel, USA Today, Architectural Record*, and elsewhere. Mary was a Pulitzer Prize co-finalist for a series on the Pulse nightclub shootings and has won journalism awards from the Society of Professional Journalists, Investigative Reporters and Editors, the Education Writers Association, the National Association of Real Estate Editors, and the Gerald Loeb Award for Distinguished Business and Financial Journalism. Her work on *American Castle* has been highlighted in *Newsday, Newsweek*, WKMG, the *Palm Beach Daily News*, the *Deseret News*, and more. She also teaches journalism at the University of Central Florida. When she's not researching or teaching, she can often be found riding her bike near her home in Winter Garden, Florida.